DEAD COWS
FOR PIRANHAS

DEAD COWS FOR PIRANHAS

A perilous journey inside the
South African Drug Trade

Hazel Friedman

Jonathan Ball Publishers

Johannesburg & Cape Town

First published in 2014 by
JONATHAN BALL PUBLISHERS
A division of Media24 Limited
PO Box 33977
Jeppestown
2043

ISBN 978-1-86842-533-4
Also available as an ebook
ebook ISBN 978-1-86842-534-1

*Every effort has been made to trace copyright holders and
obtain their permission for the use of copyright material.
The publishers apologise for any errors or omissions and
would be grateful to be notified of any corrections that
should be incorporated in future editions of this book.*

Cover design by publicide
Typeset by Triple M Design
Set in 10/15 pt Lucida Std
Printed and bound by Paarl Media, Paarl

Twitter: www.twitter.com/JonathanBallPub
Facebook: www.facebook.com/JonathanBallPublishers
Blog: http://jonathanball.bookslive.co.za/

CONTENTS

PREFACE

It began in 2008 with an anguished phone call from the sister of a convicted South African drug mule incarcerated in Thailand, who asked me to travel to Bangkok to interview him. That was how this book was spawned: that interview shoved me into an investigation that will continue years beyond the final punctuation mark of the last page.

The origins of this book, however, are really rooted in 1994, the year of South Africa's first non-racial democratic elections, the apogee in our national quest for a more just society, free from an oppressive past. That also happened to be the year in which several South Africans were arrested in Thailand for drug trafficking. Their imprisonment coincided with the growing pains of post-apartheid South Africa. By May 2014, 20 years into our democracy, all of the South African citizens arrested in 1994, except for one, who had died in prison, had been released. For their families, their return home imbued a tumultuous era of triumph and trauma with an almost poetic sense of circuitry.

But by 2014, the vacated cells once inhabited by the mules of 1994 had been filled by another batch of convicted South African drug mules, and then another. They were imprisoned not only in Thailand, but in countries as far afield as Brazil, India, China, Nepal, Mauritius and Mozambique. Today, it is estimated that there are over a thousand convicted South African drug mules incarcerated abroad – and this is regarded as a conservative figure. Almost every month, the media report yet another busted South African desperate, greedy, naive or stupid enough to get sucked into the global narco-lair.

So, why should we care? 'Do the crime, do the time' is the dominant refrain of nations, communities, families and individuals debilitated by the unrelenting epidemic of narcotics on our streets, in our schools, in our homes. This was pretty much my attitude too when I embarked on what I mistakenly believed would be a fairly straightforward investigation for SABC's *Special Assignment* programme: to interview South African drug mules incarcerated in Thailand and speak to their families back home. I began this assignment without imposing my own judgement on the inmates. They had already been judged and, some might argue, the severity of their punishment had far exceeded their crimes. But I wasn't particularly sympathetic towards their plight either. After all, they knew what they were doing, so they would have to bear the consequences, no matter how abominable, of their crimes ...

Until I met 23-year-old Nontando Pendu (Thando), who had been arrested at Bangkok's Suvarnabhumi Airport in October 2008 with 48 bags of heroin strapped to her chest. She was sentenced to 25 years' imprisonment.

Thando had been lured to Thailand with the promise of a job, only to discover that the payback for a passport and accommodation entailed smuggling drugs. But Thando was not meant to deliver her illicit cargo: she had been set up as a decoy, which means that her sole purpose was to enable professional drug mules to slip past customs undetected.

Thando's horrifying ordeal dispelled every preconception I had harboured about the individuals convicted of committing this crime. Although the prima facie evidence appeared incontrovertibly to weigh against her, I realised that Thando was not guilty of drug trafficking but, instead, she was a victim of human trafficking. If this could happen to her, I thought, there must be other South African citizens who have been wrongfully convicted and who are suffering terrible human-rights violations abroad. Such people should be assisted by the South African Government. Their convictions should be overturned and they should be set free as soon as possible. That's what our democratic Constitution, laws and policies are there for, right?

Not quite.

South Africa cannot be accused of doing things in half measures. We don't believe in half-baked celebrations or crises. Like the nursery rhyme about the little girl with the curl on her forehead, when we're good, we're very, very good and capable of spectacular acts of generosity and heroism. But when we're bad, we can be spectacularly cruel. Such were the bipolarities that dogged this investigation. Contrary to my expectation, my efforts to prove the link between drug trafficking and human trafficking were met with indifference, even hostility, by government and the law-enforcement authorities. Despite our progressive Constitution and policies that uphold human rights, the prevailing approach is punitive towards both the victims of this crime and their families. It is a case of 'out of sight, out of mind'.

At the time of writing this book, South Africa was one of three countries worldwide that has refused to enter into a prisoner transfer treaty with other countries – Ghana and Nepal are the other two. Such a treaty would at least enable citizens convicted for crimes committed abroad to serve a portion of their sentences in their home countries, close to their loved ones. For those guilty of wittingly smuggling drugs, this treaty would not signify condonement. It would simply constitute a humanitarian gesture by our government, whose leaders and cadres had been oppressed, criminalised, imprisoned and exiled for decades themselves – a government that, after defeating apartheid, had extended the hand of forgiveness and reconciliation to its foes.

For drug mules, a prisoner transfer treaty would offer the possibility of a second chance. For genuine victims of human trafficking, such an agreement would provide them with, if not some form of restitution, then at least the sense that South Africa had not abandoned them to decades behind bars for a crime they insisted they had no intent to commit.

The purpose in writing this book, therefore, was not predicated on the desire for subject matter. I did not want to appropriate the stories of others, but rather to weave aspects of their narratives into my investigations. I believed that this could only be narrated effectively within the broader context of the global war on drugs and the influence of global narcotics syndicates on what seems like every sphere of society. I came perilously close to attempting to cover a history of nearly everything. Were it not for the tactful interventions of my long-suffering publisher, I would have ended up writing very little about anything at all.

Like corruption, organised crime involves an omnibus of activities – I call them CEOs, or cross-enterprise operations – that include protection services, prostitution, poaching, smuggling of minerals and weapons, not to mention modern-day slavery in the form of human trafficking. Narcotics still remain its most lucrative, contested currency, though. The reality is that the global business of drug trafficking benefits enormously from the arrest of decoys, like Thando, by creating the perception of a supply shortage, thereby increasing demand, securing higher profits and augmenting violent competition for this lucrative global market.

Much more systematic research needs to be conducted on the magnitude of the transnational drug-trafficking industry and its relationship to human trafficking. I hope this book will facilitate greater recognition of this link and, at the same time, serve as a warning to impressionable South Africans that there is no such thing as a free ride. I also hope it will encourage the establishment of a coherent and comprehensive government strategy to tackle the narcotics industry from source of supply through to the point of consumption. Clearly, the drugs trade is fuelled as much by demand as supply. The inconvenient truth is that anyone who has ever used narcotics, even for recreational purposes, forms an inextricable link in the drug-trafficking industry.

For every South African imprisoned abroad for drug trafficking, there is a drug syndicate operating with impunity at home. A prisoner transfer treaty could facilitate investigations into the organised-crime hierarchies that recruit the mules or coerce the decoys into becoming drug couriers. Syndicate members have only partial comprehension of their role in the chain of command. As is the case with a conventional army, the basic building block of all syndicates is the individual 'soldier'. As the elements of the syndicate's organisational structure become larger and more complex, they include more and more subordinate elements. It makes sense, therefore, to tackle each component up through the chain of command – from the mules, to the recruiters, until one reaches the apex. But many of the sultans of sin reigning over the transnational criminal economy have succeeded in consolidating seemingly impregnable fiefdoms in South Africa. As the detours in my investigations would reveal, there still exists a disturbingly ambivalent relationship between South Africa's past and its present, and in its competing histories of truth. The fault lines between criminal power and political corruption have become increasingly opaque.

The world of global drug trafficking and its connection to political machinations would not be out of place in an Orwellian nightmare, with its doublespeak spouted by power mongers who degrade and dehumanise their minions – the mules and decoys – to the status of 'unpersons'. For the drug lords and their lieutenants, there is only the crude binary of asset or liability. There is nothing in between these dualities – for them, a human being has value as either a drug mule (courier) or a dead cow (decoy); they are either a beast of burden or bait.

Dead Cows for Piranhas – the title of this book – emanates from the moniker customs officials and drug syndicates give to the decoys who are used to divert attention from the professional mules slipping through with larger quantities of drugs. The image of dead carcasses being ripped apart by predators possibly provides a hint of the pernicious trajectory I have followed into a psychotropic wilderness so bewilderingly dense that I sometimes feared I would not make it to the clearing. But, thanks to some of the unlikeliest of heroes, an unexpected alchemy began to occur ...

ACKNOWLEDGEMENTS

I wish to thank the following people for propelling me into dark places, illuminating the path or helping me to load-shed when I needed it most:

Shani Krebs, for asking me to visit him in the Bangkwang maximum-security prison. Joan Sacks, Shani's selfless sister, for persuading me to go. *Special Assignment*, for getting me there and bringing me back (albeit in pieces). SABC cameramen Byron Taylor and Sibusiso (Sbu) Mncedane, for trusting my direction even when I lost all sense of it. Thando Pendu, for trusting me enough to publicise her personal pain. Nozukile Pendu, for hoping, as only a mother can. Jabulani Khubune, for his devotion to Thando's family. Patricia Gerber, an unlikely heroine, for her courage, pit-bull tenacity and determination to bring home all of our citizens who are locked up abroad. Sabelo Sibanda, for his commitment to justice, and his passion, vision and intellectual acuity. Henk van Staen – for his compassion, courage, dedication, friendship and ingenuity. Louise Roth Fischer, for caring about the women in Klong Prem Prison and for supporting all South Africans incarcerated abroad. Johanna 'Hannetjie' Strauss, for caring so profoundly for the women in Klong Prem Prison. Jeremy Boraine of Jonathan Ball Publishers, for firmly but gently prodding me to finish the bloody book that seemed at times an excruciating rite. Ceri Prenter, for her creative book design. Mark Ronan, for priming, trimming, truncating, varnishing and, in short, performing his own meticulous alchemy on some pretty rough-hewn prose. The legless sluts and fellow slurchers who kept my glass filled while I wrote. My family and friends, who continue to cheer me on, often in the absence of reason. A kindred spirit in the wetlands who reminded me to laugh at the moon, embrace absurdity, forgive failure and exploit the lunacy that lurks within. Rob Piper, for always lightening the load and for lovingly keeping me together, even when I was clearly falling apart.

This book is dedicated to the memory of my mother, Rita, who died shortly before this odyssey began.

1

IN THE BELLY OF THE BEAST

July 2008

Airbus A319; flight 2443, departing from Jorge Chávez International Airport, Peru; destination: São Paulo; distance: 3 423.5 kilometres.

Three more hours remain of the four-and-a-half-hour flight. There are 130 passengers on board, of whom 24 are in business class. For the rest, in the bulging economy section of the plane, there are only two toilets in the rear.

She is in seat 12F. Can her bowels behave or will they rebel before she makes it? More turbulence: her gut murmurs indignantly while the spasms become sharper and the intervals between them shorter. She tries to focus on the in-flight magazine, but the words float in front of her eyes. She stares out of the window as the aeroplane seems to bounce from cotton-wool cloud to cotton-wool cloud ...

'Beef or fish?'

Skin or scales? She stares blankly at the flight attendant before shaking her head. She feels nauseated, but simultaneously starving. Despite the increasingly audible whine emanating from her innards, she dare not eat, lest the food activates her acidic digestive juices. She can taste the sourness of the bile on her breath, courtesy of a liver sluggish from stress and the Imodium tablets she ingested an hour before the flight was due to take off.

Damn that six-hour delay. By now she should have already landed, checked into her hotel room and started to divest herself of her illicit cargo. Instead, she feels as though her intestines are about to rupture. At best, if she makes it to the bathroom in time, she will have to fish the *bolitas* (the Spanish term for cocaine capsules smuggled inside the body) out of the toilet bowl, clean them of all remnants of shit and swallow all 80 of them again, torturously, one at a time.

At worst, one or more of the *bolitas* – already compromised by her digestive juices eating into the latex packaging – will tear, spilling its lethal contents into her gut. She will either have a seizure, stroke, brain haemorrhage or heart attack. She had heard of someone whose blood vessels overheated and who literally boiled to death. Her name would then be added to the 56 per cent of packers, swallowers or stuffers who die when their cargo leaks.

* * *

This description is based on a factual account given to me by a professional body packer. I have named her Stella, for no particular reason. She is just one of several conduits to a trajectory of horror that, in many ways, defies exegesis. In the parlance popularised by the media, Stella is a drug mule – the term given to individuals who smuggle parcels of narcotics concealed in an anatomical cavity or among legitimate possessions – from one destination to another.

She detests the moniker because it denotes a beast of burden, forced to lumber along, back buckling under an enormous load. Stella doesn't care much for the zoomorphic terminology sometimes used by both her handlers and the customs officials to describe the decoys: 'donkeys' or 'dead cows for piranhas'. They are the stupid ones, the dead meat thrown to the authorities to distract their attention from the professionals who, like Stella, carry much larger quantities of drugs. Although they are

2

completely unaware of it, decoys serve a crucial purpose for the drug trade. Stella winces at the thought of demotion from her status of mule to that of dead cow, as much as from the cramps she is now experiencing.

It's not that Stella was held at gunpoint or her life threatened. She was simply desperate for the money – the elixir to a life free from the drudgery and debt that she had inherited from an abusive father and a submissive mother. She simply wanted more, but without a higher education, spectacular looks or charm – she just had a *straatwys* sense of self – her options were limited.

She also did it for the rush of the risk – as addictive as the drugs packed into her gut. However, this is definitely her last run, she vows. The first was in 1994. She was 19 years old, a runaway who had fled the small-town claustrophobia of a township near Witbank, eMalahleni, for the bright lights of the big city. She had landed up at Ponte, in Hillbrow – Little Lagos, as it was then called. By the time Stella had been initiated into the building's criminal economy of prostitution and drug dealing, Ponte had become emblematic of the inner city's decline into decay and crime. The hollow core of Africa's first cylindrical skyscraper was filled five storeys high with rubble, litter and the detritus of its then thriving third economy.

Her first run entailed a trip to Lima, Peru, all expenses paid, with the promise of a substantial reward upon returning with 80 *bolitas* (also termed 'bananas' or 'pieces') to South Africa. Each *bolita* contained 10 grams of pure cocaine. Her bodily cargo amounted to a total street value of almost $1 000. (The average street price for a gram of cut cocaine was R350 back then.)

She was told it would be like swallowing large grapes. They felt more like grapes of lead. At first she had puked, her spittle flecked with blood, her throat inflamed and raw, as though scraped with gravel. She had to practise by swallowing baby carrots, peeled and halved, about the size of her thumb. Gradually, she learnt the technique of deep-throating – tipping back her neck like a circus sword-eater and relaxing her neck muscles to facilitate the unobstructed passage of the pieces. From the carrots, she graduated to plastic capsules, approximately the size of the real thing. They were empty, so if she failed to expel them it was no financial loss to her handlers. In those days, the latex capsules in which the drugs were sealed were fashioned from condoms, the fingers of rubber gloves or party balloons. Even with a double layer of foil or sticky tape, the crudely hand-wrapped pellets were prone to bursting. To help her swallow the capsules, she would be administered an anaesthetising cocktail of cocaine and Coca-Cola.

These days, the really jacked-up handlers have mastered the art of machine-wrapping the capsules, which are reinforced to avoid spillage using a combination of paraffin, duct tape or candle wax to construct a beetle-like shell. Aluminium foil, plastic food wrap and carbon paper are also incorporated, in an attempt to limit the risk of detection. The body packers are also put on a diet of oily soup before the run as a lubricant to facilitate the smooth passage of the capsules.

For her first run, Stella had swallowed four separate batches four hours apart, which filled her entire gastrointestinal tract. For her (literal) pains, she was paid R5 000 – not much more than the value of one *bolita*. Her last trip earned her a neat 35 grand. Not bad for an eight-hour working day. She also got R5 000 to R7 000 for every new recruit. Her net worth had certainly increased incrementally.

She did many more runs, carrying anything between 10 and 20 kilograms of cargo, and became an expert in the art of body packaging. After ingesting the capsules, she would insert metallic embellishments in her clothing to confound detection of the contraband by X-ray machines. The only time she had nearly been busted was in 1998, at Schiphol Airport, Amsterdam, as she was about to board the plane back to South Africa. Maybe there was something about her gait – she had Ecstasy tablets stuffed up her rectum and vagina. Customs wanted to X-ray her. It was only the fact she was six months pregnant that prevented her from being subjected to the radiographical eye. Pregnant suspects are usually sent directly for a stool assessment without radiography, but, for some inexplicable reason, customs officials had let her through. Again, she had won another round in this game of Russian roulette.

Had she been examined, she would probably have been deported back to South Africa because the Dutch tend to go easy on first-time offenders. Unlike in Asia: she had heard about the dozen or so South Africans who had been caught in 1994 in Thailand, and would serve sentences of anywhere between 20 and 100 years. Sentencing was less stiff in South America, but prison conditions in countries like Peru and Venezuela, she had been told, were horrendous, particularly for women.

*   *   *

Her forehead feels clammy, her heartbeat erratic and her stomach bloated. But the spasms have subsided. 'Nerves, nerves, nerves,' she chides herself. 'Why the hell am I so nervous this time?'

She eases herself towards the rear of the plane, past a young woman sitting in seat 23C. Her table, like Stella's, is still folded, unused, in the seat in front of her. She, too, has not eaten. Good! Her eyes had bulged and widened at Stella's graphic lecture on the perils of in-flight food consumption. 'You'll be okay,' Stella had cooed when the woman began to cry. 'Just do as you are told and you'll be fine.' For a second, their eyes meet, two pairs of dilated pupils interlocked in an unspoken pact – the seal of the body packers.

Plucked by Stella off a street corner, somewhere along Mew Way, in Khayelitsha, Cape Town, she was in her early 20s, a single parent, homeless, jobless. Stella had been instructed by her handlers to 'recruit' a potential traveller. (The linguistic protocol of drug-syndicate recruitment requires the avoidance of any terminology associated with narcotics, in favour of more generic terms such as 'travelling'.) The carrot is an all-expenses-paid trip to South America, Asia or Mauritius. That was how the young woman had been reeled in. She was standing there like an abandoned dog, with a desperate message scrawled across a piece of cardboard, which she clutched against her chest. She might as well have been advertising her candidacy as a courier.

Stella had befriended her, and initially provided her with food and clothing, then some casual chores in her apartment. The grooming process took about two weeks, including shopping sprees and a makeover sponsored by Stella's Nigerian bosses. Then came the offer of a lifetime: a trip to Brazil, the finer details of which were brushed over quickly. By the time the young woman had realised there is no such thing as a free ride, it was too late. Stella had been paid six grand as a finder's or recruiter's fee and would receive an additional R25 000 for accompanying the young woman on the plane and stuffing a couple of kilos down her own throat.

Stella had always rationalised her own role in the narcotics chain of command. She was expendable, she realised: if she didn't do the job, someone equally or more desperate would, motivated by the desire to do anything to improve their material circumstance, driven by a global economic system that allows exploitation of the poor to satisfy the pleasures of the privileged. This is a crime, she reasoned, driven as much by the demands of the rich and idle as it is by supply.

But although she could justify her own complicity in the hierarchy of kingpins and pawns, she was not comfortable with the coercion of an innocent. Yet she had said nothing of her disquiet to Peter, her Nigerian ('Nigie') contact in Cape Town, who would connect her and the newest recruit to Hilda and Tony in São Paulo. She had flinched when the poor girl, unable to swallow the *bolitas*, had been force-fed an oily, drug-laced concoction to simultaneously lubricate and numb her throat, but which had made her heave and retch. Her fragile frame could only accommodate 20 *bolitas*.

6

The young woman turns a paler shade of grey. She is a decoy, a piece of dead meat about to be thrown to the piranhas, not a drug mule, more like a sacrificial lamb.

'We are about to begin our descent. Please return to your seats.'

Stella can't afford compassion. She needs to pass through customs, get to the hotel, take laxatives and rid herself of the rapidly digesting *bolitas* before they obstruct her intestine or rupture. All she can think of is removing them or the prospect of death.

São Paulo's Guarulhos International is Brazil's busiest airport, with flight connections to 53 countries. It is also the main exit point for drug mules carrying cocaine from South America to the rest of the world. It is all a blur as Stella makes her way to passport control, rectum straining, glazed eyes focused on the official who skims her passport and waves her through.

As she passes through customs, Stella briefly turns around. The homeless woman she had befriended in Khayelitsha has been surrounded by a sea of uniforms.

2

THE RETURN

April 2012

They converged on the arrivals gate at OR Tambo International Airport, black T-shirts emblazoned with the words 'Shani, we love you!', waving welcoming balloons and banners. A small but noticeable security contingent was positioned nearby, edgily communicating through wireless earpieces and microphones, neck muscles bulging, eyes darting through the swelling crowd, alerted to any sudden potential threat.

I peered through a gap in the frosted glass, straining to spot him, with SABC cameraman Roy Freeman ready to shoot his first steps through the sliding airport doors. I had been deployed from Cape Town to cover Krebs's release and arrival home because I was the journalist who had visited and interviewed him in Bangkok's Bangkwang Prison, in January 2009. His story had subsequently been broadcast on the SABC's *Special Assignment* programme. Although I had negotiated an exclusive interview with Krebs at his home, the airport arrival was an event for all the local media. His return was big news.

On Facebook, where a large global support group had been established in 2008, Shani Krebs's friends had been devotedly posting messages of support and marking the countdown to his release. 'Shani, only 56 days to go ... every day gets brighter,' wrote Sue. 'Support our friend in the last steps to victory,' said

Erwin. There were pictures and photoshopped collages of Krebs on an aeroplane, giving the thumbs up and reunited with his family in Johannesburg. All these artworks had been transformed into a massive banner, a patchwork display of support held aloft at the airport by his family and friends.

Then we glimpsed him weaving his way through passport control. As the arrivals doors slid open, he walked past the crowd, hesitated, and for a second appeared intent on bolting back through customs or out a side entrance in an effort to evade the welcoming throng. Then he seemed to shrug. He turned around and stepped across the threshold. His 85-year-old Hungarian mother, Katarina Link, was the first to reach him. Holding a bunch of flowers in one hand, she tiptoed to embrace him, her frail attenuated neck straining upwards. Then, his younger sister, Joan Sacks, visibly exhausted, her cheeks tear-smudged, lurched towards him, wailing, 'Shani, you look so beautiful, so beautiful ...' The crowd waved and cheered. Despite being clearly overwhelmed by the rapturous welcome, Krebs smiled and waved back.

Fifty-two-year-old Alexander 'Shani' Krebs had returned home, almost 18 years to the day that he had been arrested in Thailand for drug trafficking. Until that moment, he had not spent a second in post-apartheid South Africa, as he had been arrested on 26 April 1994 – a day before South Africa's first democratic elections.

'Yesterday was Freedom Day. Today is Shani's Freedom Day!' shouted his elated mother in broken English, whose only wish for the past 18 years had been to see her son again before she dies.

Joan nodded, too emotional to speak. Years of campaigning tirelessly for his early release, a transfer to a South African prison or a royal pardon from the Thai monarch had taken their toll. She appeared about to collapse; a friend stepped in to support her sagging frame.

At the time of his arrest for heroin trafficking, Shani was 34. He had been initially condemned to death, but his sentence was commuted to 100 years' imprisonment, and later it was reduced to 40 years. He was the only South African in Bangkwang, Thailand's notorious maximum-security prison, where he had earned the tragic reputation of being the longest-serving 'farang', or foreigner. There, his fate had been determined by the vagaries of Thailand's criminal-justice system and by will or whim – a royal birthday here, a public holiday there. The stroke of the Thai monarch's pen would determine who should live, die or be released. On 5 December 2011, Thailand's King Bhumibol Adulyadej issued an amnesty of sorts, courtesy of his birthday, to all farangs convicted of drug offences. In Thailand the seventh cycle, or 84th birthday, of the monarch is a significant milestone and special celebrations are organised for the entire year. For the farang inmates, this meant that their sentences had been reduced by one-sixth. For prisoners incarcerated since 1994, like Shani, it signalled an early release.

Surrounded by his family, childhood friends and Facebook fans at the airport, Shani posed for photographs. Then, poised and confident – and surprisingly media-savvy – he held an impromptu press conference at the airport, before being ushered towards the exit by the bouncer types assigned to provide protection. It was like a celebrity's welcome – for a convicted drug mule.

'We have to arrange security,' Joan had explained to me the day before. 'His release has provoked a very emotional response, both in support of and against it. We don't know what to expect.' Eyes brimming, she had added: 'Who would have thought when I contacted you in 2008 that four years later he would be home?'

April 2008

It began with a phone call: 'This is Joan Sacks. My brother would like you to write about his art.'

'Who is your brother?' I enquired.

'His name is Shani Krebs and he is serving a life sentence in Thailand.'

Entirely self-taught, Krebs's artistic prowess had flowered in prison. His delicately rendered paintings ranged from carbon portraits of Nelson Mandela, Thabo Mbeki, Louis Armstrong and James Dean to abstract compositions, rendered with a psyche-delic palette, and sensual nudes, bordering on the erotic. His art had served both as his creative panacea and the key to his salvation. It was the myrrh for his wounded spirit and the buffer between sanity and madness. And it was the principal compo-nent – alongside his spiritual faith – of his inmate survival kit, which he needed when the creeping despair that all he might ever do in his life was time threatened to derail his hope of an early release.

Shani clearly wasn't wasting any more time. And he wasn't going to let himself be buried in the waste of it either. He'd read an *FHM* interview with me after the publication of a 'faction' (fact-fiction) novel I had written on carjacking syndicates. After checking out my bona fides – I am also an arts writer – he had appointed me to be his critic of choice. The fact that he had delegated to his sister the task of contacting me from the confines of his cell in Bangkwang rendered his request all the more enticing.

I was intrigued by the fact that he had not sought my assis-tance to publicise his plight or expose the horrific conditions of his prison – the kind of stories that a seasoned drain sniffer like me would embrace – but rather to critically review his art. That request underscored an innate self-belief and confidence in his work. Sixteen years into his incarceration, and divested of any right to exercise the most basic of choices, such as when to eat and sleep, or even what to wear, Shani had managed to construct an uncanny semblance of power despite his imprisonment.

But the most overt measure of control he exerted was over his loved ones in South Africa, whose lives were circumscribed entirely around his. This power was cemented by a cellphone that Joan had smuggled to him hidden inside a radio.

Shortly after my exchange with Joan, Shani called me. I was enjoying a sundowner at a local watering hole in Cape Town; in

Bangkwang Prison it was well after midnight, a five-hour time difference. I was initially overwhelmed by how unreal it felt to be conversing surreptitiously with a convicted drug mule thousands of kilometres away. I tried mouthing a couple of homespun aphorisms and homilies, conveyed with an air of earnest but detached professionalism. 'I am the journo here,' I said to myself – I get to control the tempo of our first exchange. But I was instantly disarmed by his self-assuredness and the intimacy of his tone. His voice was measured, soft, soothing, reassuring – as if through practice in persuading coy, reluctant subjects to sit for his portraits. He enquired how my day had been and asked my opinion of the artworks on the Shani Krebs Captivated Artist page that Joan had created for him on Facebook. Within minutes, Shani spoke as though he were a lifelong friend.

In fact, Shani and I were not complete strangers to one another. I had been vaguely aware of his arrest in 1994, through the desperate, albeit short-lived, media campaign launched by Joan after he had been arrested. We both grew up in the insular Jewish community of Johannesburg, so our paths had been interwoven during our youth. Although we didn't personally know each other, we mixed in similar social circles, primarily on the 'wrong' side of Louis Botha Avenue, in the white, middle- to lower-class suburbs populated by the European diaspora of second-generation Jewish, Greek, Italian, Lebanese and Portuguese immigrants. We had jolled at the same teenage parties and, as adults, trawled the clubs and bars of Hillbrow and Joburg's northern suburbs. After Joan had mentioned his name to me, the opaque memory surfaced of an intense young man with curling, long blond hair, who had walked on the wild side with too much gusto. Together with Joan, he had been raised in the Arcadia Jewish Orphanage in Johannesburg. His was a troubled childhood and adolescence, with the fumes of his latent anger doused only partially by his charm and compelling personality. He was also highly creative, excelling in poetry and art. Yet it was only in prison that the latter truly began to flourish.

At the time of his arrest, Shani had protested his innocence, and his family had doggedly insisted that he had been the victim of a cruel set-up, choreographed by a Nigerian syndicate. His story carried a familiar refrain: in Thailand on vacation, he was holed up in a backpackers, where his traveller's cheques had been stolen. He was stranded and desperate. A member of Bangkok's Nigerian community had then offered him a way of making a quick, relatively low-risk buck.

'There's no way he knew that the suitcase he was carrying contained heroin. He thought it was dollars,' Joan had insisted, throughout his incarceration. Of course he knew. Sure, he had been used as a decoy, but he was no unwitting victim. In fact, Shani had been sailing a bit too close to the wind for many years and had notched up quite a reputation for hard living. And hard drugs. After his release, he publicly admitted having lied. Privately, he had confessed to me during one of our telephone chats that he had been a cocaine addict. Becoming a mule was a choice he made to subsidise his habit. So, ironically, his incarceration had probably saved his life.

* * *

Joan's phone call to me in 2008 and my subsequent long-distance contact with Shani inspired me to get the 'inside' story on South African drug mules incarcerated in Thailand. Although I was interested in reviewing Shani's art, the human-interest angle of the story beckoned with greater vigour. Problem was, I had never been to Bangkok, had no contacts there and scant idea of how I was going to document the story of a South African drug mule from his first drug run to his arrest and incarceration. What made the story more compelling was that Shani was not the only South African imprisoned in Thailand for drug smuggling. I discovered there were about a dozen of my compatriots behind bars in Bangkok, most of them women, who had been languishing there for over a decade. While Shani would be a powerful, principal 'case study', I was also particularly curious to meet former South African beauty-queen finalist Vanessa Goosen, who, like Shani, had been busted in 1994. She was pregnant at the time and had given birth in prison, only to have her daughter wrenched from her at the age of four. That was all my cursory research of media reports from 1994 to 1997 could unearth of her. Thereafter, the articles had tapered off. The South African mules had been relegated to the furthermost recesses of the media's fickle memory.

The plan was to interview both Shani and Vanessa on the dire consequences of drug trafficking. I did not intend to judge them: I understood that supply and demand were co-dependent, albeit volatile, partners in the narcotics industry, and that drug mules were at the bottom of the food chain, while the drug lords were the apex predators. But my spoonful of sympathy was laced, admittedly, with flecks of contempt. How stupid for anyone, no matter how desperate, to allow themselves to be used as a mule, the lowest link in the narcotics chain of command. Hadn't they watched movies like *Midnight Express* and *Brokedown Palace*, both of which had hammered home in no uncertain terms their anti-trafficking messages?

I wanted to get inside their heads, though. I wanted to locate the exact moment when otherwise law-abiding individuals change lanes into criminality. Vanessa, the beautiful celebrity turned centrefold for South African drug mules, and Shani, the charismatic, talented, troubled artist behind bars; she in Lard Yao Prison, the women's section of Bangkok's sprawling Klong Prem high-security Correctional Facility; he in Bangkwang, the hardest-core prison in Thailand. But my innocuously worded email requests for permission to conduct on-camera interviews with them had been ignored by the Thai prison authorities, so I had to devise another angle that would evoke the trauma of incarceration in a foreign country.

I had heard a remarkable story of suffering and redemption, narrated by William Bosch and Sean Allan, two South Africans who in 1996 had been sentenced to 15 years for possession of 50 grams of speed stashed in a cigarette pack. They had served nine years when they were granted a royal pardon by the Thai monarch in April 2005 – a gesture that instantly expunged their crime. I contacted the Randburg-born William, now living in China. Together with the Eikenhof-raised Sean, he agreed to join me in Bangkok for a revisitation of sorts.

Although the SABC had given the assignment the go-ahead, consent was based on the assumption that before my departure I would be able to secure a one-on-one with either Shani or Vanessa, and preferably both. The Thai authorities would not prevent me from visiting Shani in prison, but I couldn't exactly saunter in, camera in hand, to shoot an interview without the consent of Bangkok's Department of Corrections. Yet they hadn't even acknowledged receipt of my request to conduct an interview. Now, as the date of my flight drew nearer, I still hadn't closed the deal. Khadija Bradlow, the *Special Assignment* story editor, had raised a cynical eyebrow when I had tried to pitch my story angle without the guarantee of on-camera interviews.

In addition to recreating the dramatic build-up to the arrest, conviction and royal pardon of William and Sean, I planned to report on my visits to Krebs and Goosen, and include quotes from dated press reports, correspondence they had exchanged with members of a faith-based support group in Bangkok who visited them in prison and, of course, Krebs's evocative paintings. William and Sean would be my security blankets. I rationalised that they would be the voices of those incarcerated and that the authenticity of their experience behind bars would help evoke the emotional presence of their compatriots. Although the circumstances surrounding each arrest were vastly different, they all carried a poignant recurring refrain: an error of judgement made in a nanosecond that would have devastating consequences, not only for them, but also for their loved ones back home.

William and Sean's narrative begins in 1993 when the former, a dancer and choreographer, was leading a troupe of exotic dancers, including Sean and another South African, on a tour of Asia. For three years, they performed and lived it up with libertine abandon in the cabaret circuit across South East Asia. On 11 May 1996, in Qingyuan, China, they were rounded up and arrested as part of the Chinese Government's Strike Hard campaign against social deviance. They were detained for not being in possession of their papers, but were released three days later after their agent had paid the Chinese authorities $20 000 and each had paid a $1 000 fine. They suddenly found themselves broke and stranded. 'We desperately tried to get home and consulted the South African Embassy, but the officials said they couldn't assist us with funds. We lived in a ... hovel, and we soon ran out of things to sell,' recalls William, in his book, *Royal Pardon*,[1] which he penned shortly after their release.

'We were almost reduced to beggars,' Sean explained during an interview in 2008 at his smallholding on the outskirts of Johannesburg, where he still lives with his wife and child. (They had been childhood sweethearts who had reunited a couple of years after his release.) He had greeted me warmly, his small, wiry frame still taut from years of intensive martial-arts training. His vocal intonation, although audible, was slightly thickened due to a hearing impairment. Struggling to communicate as a disabled farang must have augmented the anguish of incarceration. But, surely, begging would have constituted a more honourable choice than small-time drug smuggling? 'We were too proud to beg,' reflected Sean. 'We thought, just this once or twice.'

Sean and William are now both committed Christians, but at the time of their arrest, crime had seemed a preferable alternative to destitution. A 'contact' had suggested to William that he should strap 2 kilograms of dagga to his body and fly to China, where drug smuggling – even involving small quantities – carries the death penalty. 'I did it. It was either that or life on the streets. It was as simple as that. I was never a drug dealer – I was an entertainer. I did it because I was forced by circumstances. It's easy to point a finger and say, "You are bad", but don't judge me until you've been there.'

For his dagga run, William was paid HK$6 000 (about R5 000) – just enough to settle their accommodation debt and buy food for a few days. A week later, Sean approached the contact: 'I went to China and met someone who gave me 3 kilograms of ice [amphetamine]. I remember shaking from fear.'

He travelled by taxi to the border, passing through customs without a hitch. Once in Hong Kong, he flew to South Korea, where he handed over the drugs and received HK$12 000. After skimming off some of the consignment for personal consumption – about 50 grams – Sean then returned to Hong Kong.

Meanwhile, William had succeeded in securing a contract for a series of cabarets at the Hard Rock Cafe in Hong Kong for September 1996. They just needed to survive through August. They decided to take the small quantity of speed that Sean had taken from the consignment and sell it in Thailand.

After flying to Bangkok, they arranged to meet a contact at McDonalds, who offered to pay $40 per gram. 'I could sense there was something wrong when we arrived,' recalled Sean. 'People were looking at us strangely. We wanted to leave. The contact suggested we rather meet at an ice-cream shop.'

While the contact was chatting to William, Sean got up to get rid of the stash. Suddenly 15 police officers had surrounded the pair, punching and kicking them.

After awaiting trial for three years, they were sentenced in 1999 to 15 years, reduced by five years because they pleaded guilty. Shackled to each other by leg irons, they were sent to Klong Prem, which has up to 20 000 inmates and which, as mentioned, also houses Lard Yao Prison, where the South African women were being held.

For almost nine years, William and Sean slept on a cement floor sardine-style with scores of other prisoners, without hot water or bedding and merely a trough for a toilet. Prison fare included rotten sweet potatoes and cabbage stems garnished with the occasional scrawny chicken claw or neck. Inside Klong Prem, physical and sexual violence are rife.

'We realised we had to face up to the wrongs we had done and make the most of this, however horrible it was,' acknowledged Sean. 'There were two choices we could make: either join the gangs or separate ourselves from them and seek God's grace. So we sought God daily, year in and year out. God used us mightily. We went into the rough area and helped our fellow inmates to come out of their drug dependency and violent ways. And our prayers to God continuously opened our eyes to the suffering of the people around us.'

Although the conditions in Thai prisons are horrific, if farang inmates have the contacts and means they are entitled to study by correspondence. Since 1994 the South African Embassy in Bangkok has been mandated to facilitate the provision of educational material and a suitable area for the prisoners to write exams, usually in a space allocated for contact visits, called the Embassy Room. It is impossible to even imagine the challenges of attempting assignments in such a cramped, fetid environment, let alone studying for, and passing, exams. But such is the resilience of the human spirit. William and Sean excelled in theology, which they studied through Unisa. They also established a church mission in Klong Prem, where they counselled prisoners, taught English and raised funds for inmates who couldn't afford to purchase even the most rudimentary of supplies.

In 1998 a South African, Coreen Laurens, heard of their plight on a community-based Christian radio station, Radio Pulpit. She corresponded with them and went to visit them in Bangkok. While she was there, she went to the royal palace and submitted a request for the king to release the pair. In 2005 they became the first South Africans imprisoned in Thailand to be granted a royal pardon.

* * *

As my departure date for Bangkok approached, the pace of emails between William, Sean and me increased. The plan was that they would both land in Bangkok the night before me and SABC cameraman Byron Taylor, who was accompanying me to Bangkok to shoot the story. We would meet at the apartment of Anke van Niekerk, a South African who belonged to a Christian prisoner-support group and whose husband was based in Bangkok. I had briefed Shani on my approach to the story and he seemed satisfied. I had also upgraded my covert 'arsenal' in the form of a Tom Thumb spy camera the size of a chewing-gum wrapper, in case the opportunity should arise to use it inside Bangkwang Prison. It was an ingeniously designed, albeit operationally erratic, device, with a retractable memory card for recording and playing back the data. Shani's sister, Joan, and his mother had lovingly prepared a box of essentials for him – clothing, books and his precious paintbrushes – which I would deliver to him.

Six hours before Byron and I were due to fly to Bangkok to meet them, I received a frantic call from Anke: 'William and Sean have been arrested at Bangkok Airport. The South African Embassy has been notified. They are being detained in Bangkok's Immigration Detention Centre and will be deported – William back to China and Sean to South Africa – on the next available flights.'

It seems that, although the royal pardon had cleared William and Sean's criminal record, it had not erased their 'undesirable persons' status. Although only briefly detained in the dank, over-crowded detention centre before their deportation, both must have suffered a return of the trauma and humiliation they had endured during their first years of incarceration.

So, hours before my take-off, a substantial chunk of my story had already crumbled.

3

SHANI

January 2009

We had booked into the Atlanta Hotel, in Bangkok's Sukhumvit district. During its halcyon era in the 1950s, this once grand edifice had accommodated statesmen, soldiers, seditionists and civilians alike. Now, despite being somewhat moth-eaten, or, more precisely, mosquito-eaten, it still boasted the oldest authentic art-deco foyer in Thailand. The hotel had a strictly non-negotiable policy of zero tolerance towards sex and drugs tourism. This was reinforced by a notice outside: 'No sex or drugs tourism,' a protocol that is somewhat anachronistic in a city whose tourism trade stereotypically thrives on both.

In certain parts of Bangkok, sex flaunts itself facetiously in your face. In others, it peers out coquettishly from adverts offering the G.F.E. – 'girlfriend experience'. Translated, that means a Thai or Vietnamese hooker who will cater to the Western male fantasy of an Asian erotic experience: a 'girlfriend' with the perineum of a prepubescent virgin, the coital agility of an acrobat and the submissiveness of a slave.

I had done some dilettante-style research on the city that was established in 1767 as an obscure Chinese trading port and which, today, is home to 12 million. In many respects, the paradoxical identity of Bangkok encapsulates the complex history of Thailand. The etymology of the name Bangkok is layered in the mists of lore. 'Bang' is a Thai word meaning 'a village situated on a stream'. It is likely that Bangkok was a colloquial name, one widely adopted by farangs, and the unintended sexual pun of the name is echoed in the similarly suggestive names of suburbs like Patpong, the epicentre of Bangkok's knock-off trade.

In Sanskrit and Pali, Bangkok is described as a 'city of treasures gracing the ocean' or a city of angels. But that depends on the angle one adopts. And there is always an angle to be taken or tried in a city that, for farangs anyway, represents a veritable fairyland of fornication and forbidden fruits – the latter in the form of narcotics.

The city has also embarked upon a thriving source of income generation from foreigners in search of more sobering kicks: prison tourism. Tourists, usually backpackers, visit other foreigners incarcerated in some of the world's most fearsome correctional centres for drug possession or smuggling. Notices in low-budget hotels and newspapers encourage this activity, perhaps as a deterrent to partaking of the island's illicit bounty, or just as a source of morbid entertainment. During one of our nocturnal conversations, Shani had mentioned how a group of prison tourists had come and stared at him. After struggling to answer a series of puerile questions, he had jumped up, grunting and beating his chest, mutating from inmate to primate, much to the bemusement of his curious visitors. 'They made me feel like a monkey in a cage,' he laughed, while I giggled uncontrollably at the zoomorphic scene he described.

* * *

My main mission: to interview Shani Krebs, a South African drug mule, arrested the day before South Africa's first democratic elections. He had been incarcerated for 16 years in Bangkwang, sarcastically named the Bangkok Hilton, or the Big Tiger because it was notorious for eating men alive.

I was feeling increasingly desperate, with my finger hovering precariously on the 'abort mission' button. This was due, partly, to the ignominious deportation of William Bosch and Sean Allen – my erstwhile portals to securing the story. I would have physical access to Shani, and probably Vanessa, but until I secured credible visual material, I had nothing. There was also the logistical nightmare of navigating an unfamiliar city, with its vast, confusing latticework of neighbourhoods, and I did not even have the luxury of an assignment 'recce'.

The fact that the Thai Department of Corrections had still not responded to my repeated requests for on-camera interviews with either Shani or Vanessa had escalated the normal frustration and self-doubt experienced by journalists when an investigation doesn't seem to be panning out into hand-wringing, nail-chomping angst.

My feeling of desperation was only marginally mitigated by the hour-long ferry ride along the Chao Phraya, Bangkok's main river, to the prison. As the boat bobbed along, different histories seemed to emerge and converge. The ferry would stop to load barefoot Buddhist monks with their trademark shaven heads and flowing orange tunics, melding with the throngs of backpackers and businesspeople. Eyes diffidently lowered, ears seemingly impervious to the babble of voices surrounding them, the monks appeared serenely out of place on a boat en route to a maximum-security facility. After disembarking, they appeared to glide, ghost-like between the contours of edifices ancient and new, faith-filled and secular.

This was the other Bangkok, detached from the fast foods of sex and drugs that are legally prohibited in Thailand but, paradoxically, available on every street corner, with one proviso: don't get caught! This side of the city of angels was entrancing: temples, like that of the Emerald Buddha, the Thai monarch's Grand Palace, barges, floating shanties and shoreline shacks sagging lopsidedly into the weeds, opulent hotels and gargantuan skyscrapers, the engineering marvel of the majestic Rama III

Bridge, as well as other architectural-engineering monuments to modernity that reflect Bangkok's status as a global hub.

I had already edited and scripted the opening sequence of my story: evocative tracking shots, multiple dissolves, plaintive soundtrack – the epic journey to Bangkwang, the Alcatraz of Asia, looming ominously from an ethereal mist. Except that, from the outside, Bangkwang turned out to be nothing like the monolithic, foreboding fortress of its US counterpart. In fact, apart from the garish yellow of the main prison entrance, even its threshold appeared nondescript, hinting at nothing of the anguish inside.

Built in the 1930s to hold 3 500, the prison at the time of my visit housed around 8 000 inmates sentenced to more than 25 years, as well as hundreds awaiting pending appeals, or death. Although executions had rarely taken place since 2004, for Bangkwang lifers, time signified a living death.

Visiting Shani in prison will go down in the annals of my investigative journalism as a harrowing ordeal. This was due, not least of all, to the sombre guard who scanned my identity papers with suspicion – at least it appeared that way from my increasingly paranoid perspective – before pointing me to a set of metal detectors and past a corroding gate of iron bars to the visitors' area. It was also partly due to the burly female warder who body-searched me with a tad too much alacrity before whisking away the box of supplies I had brought for Shani from his family. Should the box never reach him, Shani would have no recourse to articulate his objection. Although there was a formal complaints structure on paper, in reality it was so overridingly biased in favour of the prison authority's chain of command that written complaints addressed directly to the Department of Corrections were often intercepted in the mail room and never reached their intended recipients. And those that did might result in further victimisation of the prisoner and even his visitors.

Aggravating the harrowing component of this assignment was

the presence of my cunningly camouflaged spycam, smuggled inside a metal clip holding my hair in a demure chignon. This would constitute plan B, a backup contingency to allow me to document my prison dispatches. The pressure to deliver the goods was immense. Apart from some great shots of Bangkok, diligently filmed by Byron from every conceivable angle, without compelling prison footage the entire story would be swept into the Chao Phraya and drown among the debris of despondency. My overextended imagination had conjured up a category at the annual Sleaze 'n Cheese Journo Awards – the most reckless and ineptly conducted investigation. I would be a shoe-in for the prize. I would be forced to return home empty-handed and the SABC would dismiss my excuses and refuse all my future requests to conduct overseas investigations.

Therefore, after William and Sean had been deported from Bangkok, the possibility of failure had become a probability, unless I took the risk of smuggling my spy camera into Bangkwang. The previous day I had purchased this state-of-the-art covert device. If the prison metal detector went off as I passed through, I would remove the hair clip in which the tiny camera was hidden and whisk it inside my cardigan sleeve (female visitors are instructed to cover up, despite the often overwhelming heat). I would then deftly deposit them both in my handbag, which I was obviously not allowed to take inside.

It was a simple but, in retrospect, hare-brained strategy. Despite several practice runs in front of the hotel mirror, should my nerves have caused me to drop to my covert armoury, I would have faced the unforgiving might of Thailand's penal policy, which forbids taking pictures in prison. Fortunately, though, the metal detector was faulty, so, like a drug mule carrying my own illicit cargo snugly concealed in my hair clip, I smuggled through my Tom Thumb camera undetected.

* * *

A few months before my visit to meet Shani, global media attention had focused on the fate of an award-winning author, Harry Nicolaides, from Melbourne, Australia, who had penned a book on the Thai monarchy. The 41-year-old English teacher had been a regular visitor to Thailand and had lived there from 2003 to 2005. He worked as a lecturer in social psychology at the Prince of Songkla University in Phuket and travelled extensively countrywide to gather material for his book. Published in 2005, Nicolaides's novel, *Verisimilitude*, provided a 'factional' narrative about an Asian monarch. One critic apparently described the book as an exploration of 'the development of Thailand as an emerging Third World country grappling with corruption, nepotism and a sycophantic adoration of Western affluence and materialism'.[1]

On 31 August 2008, three years after *Verisimilitude* had been published, during a stopover in Bangkok en route to Melbourne, Nicolaides was arrested under lese-majesty – an antiquated Thai law prohibiting the royal family from being criticised.

The offending paragraph that brought the full weight of the monarchical ruling on Nicolaides's hapless head read as follows:

> From King Rama to the Crown Prince, the nobility was renowned for their romantic entanglements and intrigues. The Crown Prince had many wives 'major and minor' with a coterie of concubines for entertainment. One of his recent wives was exiled with her entire family, including a son they conceived together, for an undisclosed indiscretion. He subsequently remarried with another woman and fathered another child. It was rumoured that if the prince fell in love with one of his minor wives and she betrayed him, she and her family would disappear with their name, familial lineage and all vestiges of their existence expunged forever.[2]

This was hardly a major blow to the monarchy. On the Richter scale of subversive content, the paragraph in question wouldn't have registered a tremor. This was not the sort of literature attracting the publicity accorded Salman Rushdie's opus on Islam, *Satanic Verses*, which incurred the wrath of the Muslim world and resulted in a fatwa being issued on the Nobel Literature Prize winner. In fact, if Nicolaides's self-published book sold ten copies, it was a lot.

However, it did not deter the Thai authorities from pouncing. Nicolaides was dumped into the Bangkok Remand Prison, where he lay for weeks, delirious with influenza and malnutrition, among scores of half-naked inmates. Although Australia had signed a prisoner transfer treaty with the monarchy, the Aussie authorities appeared powerless to intervene.

On 19 January 2009, several months after his arrest, his case went to trial. His court date coincided with my arrival in Bangkok, enabling me to witness Thai justice first-hand. It was a horrifying spectacle. Hollow-eyed and emaciated, Nicolaides was shackled and locked in a cage with an assortment of Thailand's most notorious criminals and some unfortunate individuals who, like him, had been in the wrong place at the wrong time. He was utterly distraught, alternating between hysterical sobbing and glazed disorientation. A gaggle of Thai and international media people were jostling for position. Nicolaides tried to cover his face with one hand while with the other he attempted to hold his shackles off the ground. Unable to maintain his balance, he tottered and stumbled against the bars of the cage, before slumping into a squat of despair.

At Nicolaides's trial, the judge concluded that he had 'written a book that slandered the king, the crown prince and Thailand and the monarchy'.

For his sins, he was sentenced to six years, which was reduced to three due to his 'confession' to transgressing a law he didn't even understand. But Nicolaides should never have been jailed in the first place. The lese-majesty law – the crime of insulting a monarch – violates article 19 of the International Covenant on Civil and Political Rights, which guarantees freedom of expression. Thailand is a signatory to the covenant.

Six months later, Nicolaides was pardoned, released and repatriated to Australia. But his arrest and conviction had served to reinforce the disquieting subtext of a legal system that is patently designed to discourage those accused of crimes from defending charges. If defendants plead guilty, they automatically receive a commuted sentence of half the declared term of imprisonment. Those who choose to fight must contend with duplicitous witnesses, missing or incomplete evidence, translation difficulties, court-assigned interpreters and a complicit Thai legal system that submits to judicial corruption.

* * *

Having witnessed Nicolaides's court treatment, I harboured no illusions as to what my fate would be at the hands of Thailand's criminal-justice system if I were apprehended breaking prison-authority rules by smuggling in a covert camera. And having read his account that even cats vomit after being fed Thai prison food, I knew my delicate constitution would not survive a diet of incarceration. Byron, the *Special Assignment* cameraman, had been understandably infuriated by my irresponsibility in trying to get the story at all costs. Even performing a standard drive-by tracking shot of Bangkwang Prison was risky. A strapping man, Byron had somehow succeeded in contorting himself, Houdini-style, in the rear seat of a taxi, so that the camera would be invisible to pedestrians, prison officials and our cab driver. While I tried to distract the driver with standard tourist prattle, he furtively aimed the camera lens like the periscope of a submarine and filmed the massive military-style compound encircling the maximum-security prison.

Walking towards the Bangkwang visitors' centre felt like the stomach-churning build-up to a first date. Since his first call, Shani and I had communicated frequently, by text and telephone, during the early hours of the Bangkok dawn. The phone conversations were always conducted with a mixture of levity, almost flirtatiousness, and furtive intensity – as though (to my imagination anyway) our surreptitious interaction might at any moment be cut short by the thud of a warder's boot. It all felt seductively illicit. But while I might have been his long-distance art critic of choice, I certainly wasn't the only beneficiary of his persuasive charm. In fact, thanks to Facebook and other products of the techno age, Shani had built up an extensive fan base. Unlike many of the other South Africans incarcerated in Bangkok, he was not short of support, either in the form of childhood friends who had been raised with him in the orphanage or from King David School, where he was educated. There were also long-distance benefactors whom Joan had tenaciously lobbied for assistance. These included sympathetic members of the Jewish community not only in South Africa, but also worldwide. And a disproportionately large number of his friends were women who wanted to adopt him, marry him and/or bear his children.

I definitely wasn't a prospect for joining a cult of convict celebrity. Playing the groupie to his jail-star image would have been contrary to my personal and professional credo. But I had fantasised about our first meeting: me, the hard-core drain sniffer bristling with missionary zeal; he, the hard-core rebel/mule/painter/poet, trapped within the citadel of broken dreams. How would he perceive me? As a creative conduit? An emissary of hope? Would our meeting constitute the crossing of a Rubicon of sorts, for both of us? Thus far, I wasn't particularly upbeat about my prospects of a successful mission. As my meeting with Shani approached, I felt an anxiety-induced migraine throbbing in my ears. Streams of sweat started to feel like a deluge down my face and arms, staining my dress, even soaking the nylon cardigan I was wearing on one of Bangkok's muggier mornings.

As I crossed the courtyard separating the visitors' section from the cavernous entrance to the jail, I noticed a prisoner in brown prison garb being led by a warder with what looked like a leash attached to his wrists. He wasn't walking so much as waddling, like a duck with oversized feet. Shackles, I was to learn, are a fixture of Thai prison life. They are compulsory when inmates leave their cells for court appearances in the morning and are removed when they return; they are also a 24/7 accoutrement for certain inmates. They provide a means of status identification: new prisoners wear theirs for the first three months of their incarceration, while those on death row have their shackles permanently welded on.

Joan had recounted to me in detail how she had felt when she saw those medieval restraints clamped around her brother's ankles in 1994. She had contacted the newly established South African Embassy in Bangkok and, mercifully, the shackles had been removed.

But, in the main, Thailand's Department of Corrections is not beholden to any ruling. That's the way it works in 'Die-land'. The leg irons are mandatory for court appearances. Depending on where inmates are contained in the sprawling fortress of Bangkwang, the shackling ritual normally begins at 6.30 am at the premises of a blacksmith, akin to a medieval torture chamber, replete with giant clamps and anvils bolted to the concrete floor, a club hammer and chains of various thickness weighing up to 10 kilograms. The prisoner's feet are slipped through a steel bar shaped like an incomplete figure of eight. The top end of the bar is hammered over the prisoner's feet, forming a loop that sometimes traps the skin in its nutcracker grip. The prisoners are then herded to the prison bus, the soles of their feet scalded by the blistering tar.

They stand in the courtroom, stifling from the humidity, heat and smog of an average Bangkok day, their chafed ankles oozing from the friction of metal on skin. The chains remain on until they return at 8 pm, in the standing-room-only van, to the prison and its hordes of prisoners pressed up against metal fences with spikes and razor wire, behind the gargantuan, solid-steel gates.

Located near the main prison entrance, the visitors' section was starting to teem with the families and friends of inmates. Fumbling my way through the narrow passage, I paused before each semi-partitioned cubicle, as though searching for Shani. I had successfully retrieved the spy camera from my hair and was now clutching it in my fist, the minuscule lens recording the poignant exchanges between the prisoners and their visitors.

Then Shani appeared through a door. He was wearing immaculately pressed blue pants and a crisp, white T-shirt. Looking tanned and relaxed, he waved, located an empty cubicle, sat down and beckoned me to lift the tele-receiver. I indicated the spycam in my hand, which I had informed him I would be smuggling into Bangkwang. Waving again, he gave me the thumbs up, this time for the benefit of Tom Thumb.

For several seconds, I thought I was facing an animated portrait of Dorian Gray, or a formaldehyde-injected, but still very much alive, installation by conceptual artist Damien Hirst. During his 16 years of incarceration, most of those spent in Bangkwang when he was not awaiting trial or in solitary confinement, Shani Krebs appeared not to have aged. His long curly hair was still blond, his tattooed body lean and sculpted from years of pumping iron, playing soccer and a disciplined eating regimen. The conventional markings of time, the ravages of hard-learnt lessons and the general wear and tear of age that add creases, folds and furrows to the rest of us, seemed not to have become permanent engravings in his case.

But distance, both physical and mental, is an effective mediating device, particularly through the prism of the double layer of glass and bars through which I saw Shani. Although time inside might have insulated Shani from some of life's ageing processes, it had subjected him to unspeakable torture. Not that he revealed anything of the latter, mind. He firmly refused to divulge details of his incarceration: the agonising months in solitary confinement, forced to remain horizontal in the darkness because of the lack of space between ceiling and floor; the pain and despair he must have felt at being separated from his family; the self-rage and regret of a decision that could cost him the rest of his adult life; and, of course, the maddening mundaneness of prison life, the sheer waste of time.

He made no mention of 16 years of sleeping on a concrete floor, the memory of a hot shower relegated to the realm of delusion; or of the sweat-soaked bodies crammed into cells measuring 6 metres by 4, forced to sleep cheek by jowl; or of the pungency of the open sewerage system – a hole in the ground serving both as toilet and tap, one bucket for scores of prisoners in which to piss, shit and shower; or the cesspool of disease that is Bangkwang.

Instead, he was as endearingly optimistic as he had been since the start of our long-distance communication. He'd been up most of the night, copiously preparing notes for our first interview, he said, pulling a pair of reading glasses from his pocket together with a diligently prepared list of issues he wanted covered. These focused on the positives – of how he had coached the Bangkwang soccer team, organised sponsorship for the soccer uniforms through friends in South Africa, and how he had successfully lobbied for sewage-free water. He spoke lovingly of his Swiss girlfriend, Elizabeth Kramer Grimm, with whom he has enjoyed the intimacy of exactly one 'contact' visit during their three-year relationship. They had met during one of the pilgrimages to Bangkok's prisons she had made as part of a Christian ministry, and their friendship had blossomed into love. Elizabeth herself had coyly confessed her adoration for him when I accompanied her to Lard Yao, where she had also been visiting Nila Duginov, a Russian-born South African-bred drug mule, who had also been arrested in 1994.

Shani didn't even touch on the turf wars and gang culture of Bangkwang, where supremacy is earned through a particularly brutal Darwinian form of survival, common to maximum-security prisons worldwide. Drug networks, including the deadly Triad and Yakuza crime syndicates, operate from inside Bangkwang, replicating the rituals of their global counterparts in what one could describe as a 'thugocracy'. There is a criminal hierarchy that echoes similar rankings and rites of passage practised on the outside, albeit in a more intensified, more brutalised form, given the spatial constraints. It was only after his release that Shani would disclose his seniority, based not only on his longevity, but also on his proclivity for fighting. Despite his charming veneer, he was feared by many in the prison, he said. And not only because of his physical prowess: he was also a master manipulator who had organised as many objects of comfort that it was possible to accumulate undetected by the authorities in a maximum-security prison. This senior ranking within the inmate hierarchy also meant that the junior inmates cooked and cleaned for him. And his entirely self-taught artistic talent had further elevated his status.

For Shani, incarceration had been a sobering lesson, quite literally: 'I was a drug addict. I was smuggling to feed my habit. But all that changed after my arrest. Being in prison, with every kind of drug available and seeing how people behaved on the shit disgusted me, made me realise how pathetic the whole thing was. I have been clean for 16 years.'

Although smoking was not banned in Bangkwang, unlike in the women's prison, Shani had never acquired the habit, although he admitted having been tutored in bootleg winemaking. He spoke of imaginary art exhibitions, of poetry readings, books to write, paintings to produce, projects to complete. When I enquired why he didn't utilise his art to visually document his experience behind bars, he retorted: 'I live this reality every day. I don't want my art to depict prison life but, rather, to transcend it.'

Such transcendence had been impossible for his family, however. They had also suffered incarceration – not alongside him, of course, but for him. His sister, Joan, particularly, had constructed a wall-less prison that had all but destroyed her physical and mental health. 'At first I thought it would be better for Shani to die rather than remain behind bars in a foreign country for the rest of his life,' she admitted. 'And since his incarceration, I haven't been able to be a proper mother or wife.'

Yet her anguish and anger had also galvanised her into writing letter after letter, lobbying religious leaders, ministers and presidents in an unrelenting crusade to help get her brother a royal pardon. 'I had progressed really far,' she recalled during one of our many heart-wrenching conversations. 'Archbishop Tutu and Madiba, although he was no longer president, had written letters of support.'

In 1998 she even helped draft a prison-transfer agreement with the former director in charge of the directorate for South East Asia at the then Department of Foreign Affairs, Robert McBride. Jackie Selebi, however, who was then director general of the department, dismissed it. So Joan travelled to Thailand for an audience with the king in 1999, to beg for a royal pardon.

'They asked me if I had the support of the Mbeki government at the time,' she said. 'I said no. That was it. Pointless.'

Joan had lost hope of an early release: 'The last time I visited Shani in prison, I knew I couldn't go back there again. It was just too traumatic for all of us – me, my husband, my son and my daughter.'

Shani agreed: 'I prefer for them not to visit. It is just too painful when they leave.'

Nevertheless, Joan's faith in her brother's resilience remained undiminished. 'We would go there to try to give him words of encouragement. But he was the one who gave us strength and courage. And he never lost his sense of humour. He would joke that he had a favourite patch of turf for tanning, which he called Hollywood.' She added: 'And when he was arrested, he swore he would never learn to speak Thai because that would mean he had accepted defeat.'

I asked him whether he had learnt Thai in the end. 'Of course,' he chuckled. 'I have the greatest respect and love for Thai culture. I have made very precious friends here.'

Then he enquired about his ailing mother, whom he had not seen since 1994. His voice faltered. Between the beginning and end of that simple question, time seemed to catch up with Shani

Krebs. His hair was still long and blond, his body still ripped, but his eyes suddenly aged. With his face contorted by grief, he wept raw, choking gasps that seemed to come from a place much bigger than his taut frame.

Those ravaged, heaving sobs evoked the torment of a punishment that, many would agree, far exceeded his crime.

4

LEGAL LABYRINTHS

After my meeting with Shani, the ferry ride back to Bangkok was silent and sombre. The magic of the city I had witnessed from the boat on the way to Bangkwang had dissipated into a uniform bleakness. When Shani had wept, I too had struggled to prevent myself from breaking down. His unflagging optimism and his refusal to sink into self-pity had earned him my enduring respect. This was coupled with an overwhelming sense, on my part, of helplessness – and it wasn't just the frustration of being prevented by the bars and glass from comforting him.

Wading through Thailand's labyrinthine drug legislation requires the cerebral, not to mention legal, skills of a senior counsel. Definitions of and provisions for drug-related offences in Thailand are contained in a plethora of laws enacted under the Measures for the Suppression of Offenders in an Offence Relating to Narcotics Act 2 534 of 1991. The Act defines the term 'narcotics' as being 'any form of chemicals or substances which, upon being consumed whether by taking orally, inhaling, smoking, injecting or by whatever means, causes physiological or mental effect in a significant manner such as need of continual increase of dosage, having withdrawal symptoms when deprived of the narcotics, strong physical and mental need of dosage and health in general being deteriorated ...'

Substances defined as narcotics are classified into five categories. The most serious are heroin, MDMA (Ecstasy), LSD, amphetamines and methamphetamine (crystal meth, otherwise known as tik in South Africa and *ya baa* in Thailand). The second most serious category includes cocaine, codeine, methadone and morphine, while the least serious group comprises cannabis, psychoactive mushrooms and the leaves of the kratom tree – a plant indigenous to Thailand.

Unlike in Malaysia, Indonesia and China, since 2004 there have been relatively few instances of death by lethal injection in Thailand. Until the 1930s, criminals were beheaded, unless the victim was royalty, in which case they were bludgeoned to death. From 1932 to 2003, execution was by firing squad. Since 2004, however, the more humane and considerably tidier lethal injection has been administered. After a five-year lull, the executions resumed in 2009 with the widely televised death by lethal injection of two Thai nationals. They had been sentenced to death in 2001 for possession of 140 000 *ya baa* tablets and their applications for a royal pardon had been rejected. I was to see their final moments, courtesy of clips sent to me by a Bangkok-based cameraman. Their hands were shaking uncontrollably as they penned farewell letters to their families. It was a ghastly sight.

According to Thai Buddhism, one's level of reincarnation in the next life is determined by one's mental state just before death. One can only surmise, therefore, what new life forms would be assumed by the dead men walking in Bangkwang, given the fact that they never receive advance warning as to the specific time of their execution. The guards would simply arrive and usher the condemned prisoners to the execution room, with its blood-spattered walls and crudely pinned-up mug shots, providing a macabre history of the numbers who had entered this chamber, never to re-emerge. Hundreds sentenced to death must live in daily terror of the thud of those grim-reaper boots.

* * *

Those convicted under Thai law of smuggling drugs for disposal or possession for the purpose of disposal are sentenced to death or life imprisonment and a fine of between 100 000 and 5 million baht (about R35 000 to R1.7 million), depending on the quantities of the drugs involved. In the Act, 'disposal' is defined as meaning to 'sell, distribute, give away indiscriminately or exchange'. Possession can result in a ten-year sentence or a fine of 20 000 to 200 000 baht (R7 000 to R70 000). If the quantity exceeds levels specified in the Act, then possession for the purpose of disposal will be inferred. Consumption carries a less severe sentence of three years' imprisonment or a fine of 10 000 to 60 000 baht (R3 500 to R20 000).

Thailand implements its drug laws through a special unit called the Office of the Narcotics Control Board. But regular police are also empowered to enforce the Act, courtesy of a clause specifying that a 'competent official' (defined as 'any official appointed by the minister for execution of the Act' – ie police officers) has the right to question, detain, search for and seize any drugs or any 'properties used to commit an offence', when dealing with a drugs suspect. The law also stipulates that the officer must act in good faith, give his reasons for suspicion, as well as record the event.[1] But 'good faith' is a very grey area in terms of its malleability. Legal recourse is non-existent for those who have been targeted in error, as Thailand has no such organisation as a police complaints commission. Corruption is inevitable, given the Thai police and drug-enforcement authorities' unfettered powers to enter and search any place without a warrant, and to search any person or vehicle if there are 'reasonable grounds' (another suitably malleable term) to suspect that they are carrying or hiding illegal drugs.

Thailand's laws also apply the principle of guilt by association. Such was the case with British citizen Jody Aggett, who travelled to Bangkok in 2001 to visit his Thai girlfriend, Ramphia Lo, with whom he planned to return to England. However, Lo became pregnant and while the couple were awaiting the approval of her British visa, they accepted the offer of a rent-free apartment. Unbeknown to them, the building they stayed in was a notorious MDMA kitchen where Ecstasy tablets were being produced on a massive scale. They were arrested on the basis of the testimony of an informer who did not even give evidence at trial. Aggett was charged after he was forced to sign an untranslated Thai document, which he later learnt was a confession. Together with the couple who had let the flat to them, Aggett and Lo were found guilty and sentenced to 20 years plus the death penalty. Lo gave birth behind bars and was forced to send their baby boy, Ryan, to live in the UK with Aggett's parents. Aggett subsequently appealed to the Thailand Supreme Court on the grounds that his trial had been based on insufficient evidence and procedural defects. It was only in 2007, through the assistance of international human-rights NGO Fair Trials, that the Thai Supreme Court finally quashed both their convictions.[2]

But Aggett's case is very much the exception. And within the net of drug laws and their enforcement, gaping holes abound. This much was explained to me in Bangkok, shortly after I had visited Shani, by Bertil Lintner, a Swedish-born, Thailand-based journalist, author and world-renowned expert on transnational drug trafficking.

'Let's say you are scoring dope from your regular dealer in Bangkok, Phuket, or wherever,' Bertil explained. 'Or it could be a prostitute or *kytoe* [lady boy] supplementing her hourly income. Up until then, they have been reliable. Then they get into debt or get bust for dealing or possession. And they set you up. Then the arresting officer gives you a choice: go to jail, or give him all your money. A portion of it might go to the prostitute or dealer as a reward, or the arrest docket might conveniently disappear.' He added: 'The dealers and cops seem to believe that all farangs are wealthy. Heaven help you if you disprove the stereotype.'

Farangs arrested for drug trafficking are herded, men in shackles, women barefoot and in smocks, into the courtroom. They cannot rely on the supportive presence of a South African

Embassy representative, and unless they can afford a lawyer who can actually understand English, let alone speak it, they must contend with court-appointed counsel without the privilege of an interpreter to explain the judicial process. They aren't even tutored in the meaning of those dreaded words that sound like pistol shots: *bah han* – the death sentence.

*   *   *

'The only knowledge I had of what was going on was when they called my name in court and gestured to me to either stand up or sit down. I didn't even realise I had been sentenced to death until the lawyer conveyed my fate to me in broken English.'

Former beauty-queen finalist Vanessa Goosen was facing me through an opaque glass barrier at Lard Yao Prison. She was the first of the so-called 'mules of 94' to be busted in Bangkok and her arrest pre-dated Shani's incarceration. She spent two years awaiting trial, before being brought before the court without so much as a pre-trial consultation with her legal counsel.

Arrested at Bangkok Airport with 2.7 kilograms of heroin concealed in hollowed-out books in her luggage, she had insisted throughout her incarceration that she had been framed. Along with Shani, Vanessa had become the most high-profile South African incarcerated abroad for drug smuggling.

Vanessa's dilemma was either to face the possibility of her own death and that of her unborn child or to plead guilty and accept the kinder option of a life sentence. In 1997 her sentence of 35 years had been reduced to 30, when the Thai king, in celebration of 50 years on the throne, granted all Thai prisoners a five-year reduction. Her sentence was later reduced to 25 years.

'You have about an hour to decide whether to confess your guilt or take your very slim chances with a lengthy trial in an extremely hostile environment,' she said. 'And should you plead not guilty and are found guilty, your fate will be execution. My death sentence was only commuted to life because I pleaded guilty.' Vanessa continued: 'The wake-up call was the execution of another prisoner in 1996 after she refused to plead guilty. She was killed by firing squad. That terrified me.'

'But what about mitigating factors?' I enquired. Vanessa smiled wryly: 'There is no such thing. The Thai legal system presumes guilt until you are proven innocent and pleading guilty seems the less cruel option because it can take several years for cases to be heard.'

Vanessa was having a bad day, and it had been exacerbated by my news that two more South African women had been arrested a couple of weeks before my arrival in Bangkok. 'What is going on in South Africa?' she yelled, tears spilling down her porcelain cheeks. 'After all the publicity about us, and our efforts to warn other South Africans, haven't they learnt by now?'

I couldn't respond. Until I had the phone call from Shani's sister, my personal level of interest in the fate of drug mules bordered on indifference. I acknowledged the possibility of people being coerced or forced into becoming drug mules or decoys, but, to my sceptical eye, such possibilities constituted more the stuff of neurotic thrillers than authentic scenarios.

Like Vanessa, Dawn van Niekerk was also pregnant at the time of her arrest. The latter had admitted using her pregnancy as a means to avoid the airport X-ray machines – a ploy commonly used by drug mules. It is not that I disbelieved Vanessa's insistence that she had been set up. It's just that in the opaque world of drug trafficking, taking the line that the person found guilty committed the crime was the more comfortable option. To consider otherwise was to acknowledge one's own vulnerability to that kind of duplicity. The agony she must have endured, punished for a crime she insists she did not commit, was beyond comprehension. How does one manage to keep it together, giving birth in a stinking Thai prison, isolated from friends and family, and subsequently being forced to hand the child over to a friend in South Africa?

'So how did you keep hope alive?' I asked her.

'I thought of my child, Felicia. I knew I must be strong for her, for when I would be reunited with her. And it was my faith in God that saw me through even the darkest hours. But there were times when I actually thought I wouldn't make it.'

'I would love to be able to tell your story, to send a warning to other South Africans ...'

My voice tapered off. Vanessa was still sitting in front of me. But her eyes had already left the building, even before I began reciting my lofty mission statement. And when they returned to my face, they were as hollow as my efforts to persuade her that my quest was spurred by something more than my desire for visceral subject matter.

'You know, in 1996 we heard there was going to be a prisoner transfer treaty between South Africa and Thailand that would allow us to at least serve time close to our families. We were so excited. It's not that we were asking for our freedom. We simply wanted to be closer to our families. We were then visited by a delegation from the South African Government. They came there briefly to tell us that we had brought our suffering on ourselves, that there wouldn't be a treaty.'

Her eyes flashed, darkly. 'In that moment they took away our hope.'

Until then, my cursory tuition on the South African Government's attitude towards such an agreement had been primarily through Shani's sister, Joan. Briefly, a prisoner transfer treaty is an agreement between countries whereby, after serving a portion of their sentence in the country of arrest, incarcerated citizens are repatriated to serve the remainder of their sentence in their homeland. South Africa had not entered into a bilateral agreement on the repatriation of its citizens. Without this, South Africans convicted of crimes overseas were doomed to remain incarcerated far from their loved ones, isolated and often forced to endure horrific conditions.

'There are no plans to consider such a treaty,' South Africa's

41

ambassador to Thailand and former DA politician Douglas Gibson had said to me during an interview at the South African Embassy in Bangkok. 'It's a shocking, tragic situation,' he conceded, 'but the South African Government has to respect the sovereignty and laws of other countries, and will not intervene in their judicial processes.'

To justify the country's intractability, Gibson had quoted chapter and verse from the Vienna Convention of 1961, a mothballed international treaty defining a framework for diplomatic relations between independent countries. The specific paragraph he referred to was article 41, whereby diplomats should not interfere in the internal affairs of the state to which they are accredited. But, even to my philistine thinking, there surely existed an insurmountable conflict between elbow-type interference and the need for humanitarian intervention, particularly in cases of human-rights violations. And this clause seemed to fly in the face of South Africa's progressive Constitution, particularly section 35(3), which guarantees the right of every citizen to a fair trial.

If Vanessa's account of her treatment at the hands of Thailand's criminal-justice system was accurate, it was horrifyingly evident that farangs were not afforded even the most basic of human rights. Yet our government seemed to have adopted an out-of-sight, out-of-mind approach. I said as much to Gibson. In response, he assumed the implacable poker-faced expression of the practised politician.

The only possible hope of an early release to which convicted South African farangs could cling would be the largesse of the Thai monarch, a ruler of an unfathomable land. As each year passed, another little piece of hope would be chipped off, like a rock face eroded by a slowly flowing, unrelenting river. And hope has a statute of limitations.

5

THANDO

January 2009

Most prisons reek of decay. There is the fetidness of damp, of
sweat, of stale tobacco exhaled in cramped spaces, but, most
pervasively, there is the rancidness of corroding souls.

Initially, though, Lard Yao women's prison looked like the
antithesis of rot. Manicured shrubs and pastel-hued bougain-
villea created the surface impression of a lovingly tended park.
Fresh-faced women in standard-issue smocks, their hair neatly
contained in braids or buns, proffered the traditional greeting, or
sawadika, with their palms pressed together, heads bowed, eyelids respectfully lowered. Children milled about with the adults
in the waiting area, wolfing down pad Thai or cavorting on the
lawns.

But this family-friendly exterior belied the grim reality of incarceration. In Thailand's prisons, women have it much tougher
than their male counterparts. The kingdom's penal system is
dominated by a rigid patriarchy that regards female inmates
contemptuously, as no better than vermin. Consequently, they
must pay for even the most basic essentials inside prison, like
blankets, sanitary pads and toilet paper. They subsist on a diet
of rice and fish heads. They may not receive supplies from any
source other than the prison canteen and are forced to share a
unit with as many as 200 others. Crammed together when they

sleep, they hoist their legs over the hips of the women next to them. A shuffle to the ablution bucket to relieve a bursting bladder could mean losing one's space and being forced to sleep, literally, standing up.

Visitors are permitted to treat the inmates to in-house delicacies usually denied them, so I had completed the food order form from the prison canteen and had selected a roast chicken, rice and mangoes. Every few minutes, the crackled voice of a prison warder punctuated the air, announcing the names of the inmates awaiting their visitors. Initially it is impossible for a foreign visitor to decipher the names through the linguistic torrent. But, with regular visits, the ear soon becomes attuned to the Thai intonation.

Then the scramble begins – a panicky race to the visitors' section for 20 minutes of contact with the inmates. These meetings are conducted through layers of wire mesh, bars and glass, with a metre-wide gap separating prisoner from visitor. The interlocutors speak through malfunctioning microphones with rusted speakers attached to the wall.

Thando Pendu was one of two South Africans apprehended in October 2008. She was caught for trying to smuggle 48 bags of heroin out of Bangkok Airport. The cargo was strapped to her body like a suicide bomber. It was her second run, the South African Embassy had informed me. Her first had been to Vietnam, and on this second (and last) run she had been en route to China. Her case would only go to trial around May 2009 and until then she was being detained separately from her convicted counterpart. The prognosis for Thando was grim. She wouldn't serve anything less than 25 years.

On the day I visited her she seemed and sounded so much younger than her 23 years. She looked pretty and cheerful; the consequences of her botched drug run seemed not to have fully penetrated. Or perhaps she had already acquired the knack of applying a thin, cushioning layer of psychological gauze over the reality of crime and consequence – both the panacea for, and a symptom of, incarceration. She appeared almost disconcertingly upbeat for a young woman facing, literally, most – if not all – of her adult life behind bars.

'Thank you so much for coming to visit me. The only other people I've spoken to are the staff from the embassy. And I can't understand a word of Thai,' she said breathlessly. 'Are you here to help me?'

I smiled and nodded with false reassurance. Like the others, she was hanging on, delicately, to gossamer threads of hope. I had none to give. After ten frustrating days in Bangkok, I was even further from building a compelling story than when I had left South Africa. Sure, I could tell Shani's tale through his sister. His paintings would also speak eloquently on his behalf, if not about the empirical reality of his incarceration, then at least of an imagination that could somehow transform demons into dragonflies. But apart from some tremulous shots of Shani waving at me from behind bars in Bangkwang's visitors' section and Byron's panoramic footage of Bangkok, I had no visuals and, consequently, squat for a viable TV story. Even my conversation with Vanessa hadn't yielded much more than further confirmation of the plight of South Africans incarcerated abroad for drug trafficking. I still needed an angle.

As I had shoved my way past families trying desperately to communicate with their loved ones through the failing microphones, I became resigned to the probability that visiting Thando would constitute nothing more than a gesture of support for another unfortunate compatriot. There seemed little to distinguish her story from the other South African women behind bars in Bangkok.

For the meeting, I smuggled in my spycam again – more out of habit than practicality. I had hoped to acquire covert footage, if not of horrific prison conditions, then at least of the South Africans chatting to me from behind bars. As with Bangkwang, however, in Lard Yao shooting any footage was impossible, given the murkiness of the glass screen. My only hope of documenting even a snippet of my interview with Thando was to turn the spycam into a makeshift tape recorder. This entailed holding it close to the microphone when talking and thrusting it in front of the speaker when she replied. Unfortunately, the speaker was not adjacent to the microphone, so recording the conversation required a jump to the left and a step to the right, followed by a forward lunge. This brought with it the obvious risk of alerting the warders to my inappropriate cardiovascular exercise. Thando also seemed slightly bemused by my apparent agitation, but, desperate to relate her story, she evidently chose to ignore my bouts of syncopated animation.

Although raised in the Free State township of Thabong, Thando had resided in Port Elizabeth with her boyfriend, Dan, a Ugandan. She had worked as a clothing-store assistant and, despite not having completed her secondary education, she had aspirations of advancing her career. Her Xhosa-speaking mother, Nozukile Pendu, was unemployed and could only speak a smattering of English. As a single parent, she managed to provide for her family of six by selling clothes on the sidewalks of Thabong and Welkom. Her main supplier was a woman called Thembi, who reportedly owned a hotel in Johannesburg and frequently jetted off to South East Asia to purchase designer knock-offs, which she would then sell on consignment to informal traders such as Nozukile.

Through her mother, Thando had met Thembi, who made her an offer that would destroy her life.

'I was visiting my mom about a year ago, and I thought Thembi was the most glamorous woman – her clothes, her jewellery. I wanted to be just like her. I mean, I had never been outside South Africa. I didn't have a passport and here was this woman who had been all over the world. And when she offered me a job in Thailand and the chance to make more money than I had ever dreamed of, I thought my life was made.'

Thembi had promised Thando a job driving ambulances in Bangkok – a patently ludicrous offer, as anyone who has ever negotiated Bangkok's kamikaze drivers will confirm. Ludicrous to anyone, that is, except a naive young woman from the township, who had not completed high school, let alone left the country. When she landed in Bangkok, Thembi was not there to meet her. Thando was soon to discover that driving ambulances was not the career path Thembi had in mind for her: 'There was another South African woman who fetched me and told me Thembi was working in China and that I would see her the following day. When we arrived at the place I was supposed to stay in Bangkok, there were four other young South African girls who, I later learnt, did this thing many times, into China.'

This 'thing' was drug smuggling: 'When I saw Thembi the next day, I asked her about the ambulance job. Thembi told me that the job she does is drugs and that because she bought me a ticket I must now pay her back.'

'I didn't know where I was,' Thando added. 'I couldn't speak the language, and I had no friends. I had no choice.' As an extra security measure, Thando was kept under surveillance by a Nigerian syndicate member called Nonso Okeke, who monitored her every move.

'These guys are what we call "enforcers",' Bertil Lintner would subsequently explain to me. 'Their job within the syndicate is to make sure the mules don't escape or have a change of heart. The syndicates recruit several mules at a time to carry varying quantities of narcotics. They designate one or two as decoys, or sacrifices, who would be arrested by airport customs after a tip-off from the syndicates.'

Meanwhile, the mules carrying larger consignments slip through undetected. 'Usually, the ones with the smallest amounts get nabbed,' continued Lintner. 'The numbers look good for the Thai Government's war on drugs and the "risk" factor is profitable for syndicates because the higher price of the drug is maintained.'

Thando could or would not swallow the condoms. So Nonso, the enforcer, crudely bound the 48 heroin bags to her chest, stuck them up her vagina and stuffed them into her shoes. As the weakest link in their chain of command, she was obviously a liability to the syndicate. So her captors had two options: either dispose of her permanently or go for the kinder option of setting her up. Customs officials were waiting for her at Bangkok Airport. While she was being searched and interrogated, the four other South African mules with whom she had stayed in Bangkok slipped through on their flight to China, undetected.

As Thando narrated to me the details of her ill-fated run, I experienced an epiphany of sorts. It wasn't exactly a Newtonian light-bulb moment. Befitting the anguish of Lard Yao, it was more akin to a slow but steadily spreading cold sweat. I realised that the naive young South African sitting before me, who believed fervently that I could help her, was no more a drug-trafficking criminal than I was: she was a victim of human trafficking.

This realisation constituted the turning point, crossing from the limbo of uncertainty into the land of knowledge. As Thando provided me with the full name and contact numbers of Thembi, the syndicate member who had recruited her in Thabong, I said a thousand, silent hallelujahs and Hail Marys to the deities of technology: without my spycam, there was no way I would have retained even a digit of the details she had provided.

But her disclosures were suddenly punctured by the premature screech of the prison bell. Visitors and inmates had been robbed yet again of an entire ten minutes, a regular malfeasance committed by the prison authorities. In Thai prisons, the bruises and scars of beatings, and the averted eyes, bear testament to the treatment of those who complain too loudly about their jailers. 'Here, if you cry, they just laugh. You must be strong,' Thando explained.

Then, in almost a whisper, her eyes luminescent from unfallen tears, she asked, 'Do you think the South African Government will bring me home so I can at least be near my family?'

The intercom system was mercifully switched off before I could reply.

6

OF MACHINATIONS AND MONGERS: THE GLOBAL WAR ON DRUGS

I now had my story angle and case study, or the beginnings thereof: impressionable, vulnerable South Africans were being duped into becoming decoys, or 'dead cows', for ruthless drug syndicates. They should therefore be judged not as perpetrators of the crime of drug trafficking, but as victims of human trafficking. Developing that argument required a paradigm shift on my part not only towards the decoys themselves, but towards the very principles on which the dominant global discourse on drug supply and demand is predicated.

So, how effective had the arrests of small-fry decoys like Vanessa and Thando been in deterring drug trafficking and countering the global drug problem? They were like sardines in a shark tank. Were their convictions part of a cohesive, consistent and successfully applied macro-strategy? I suspected both the long and short answers would be a resounding 'no'.

Clearly, the trillion-dollar drugs trade has been fuelled as much by demand as supply. The brutal truth is that – whether it is an ageing hippy from the 1960s or a captain of the contemporary corporate world – anyone who has ever used the best hydroponic weed, shnarfed a line of Colombian pure, dropped a cap of Bart Simpson's A-grade acid, injected a 'pink' (or Wellcanol tablet), felt the *lurv* from pure MDMA, or sucked on a mandrax pipe forms an inextricable synapse in the transnational drug-trafficking industry.

The trade stretches from the producers – usually peasant farmers – to the global drug cartels and their middlemen, or dealers. The drugs are distributed to consumers worldwide by the most disposable component of this trade, namely the mules. It seems to me that in trying to prevent drug users from killing themselves with heroin, cocaine or crystal meth, the world has been turned into an unregulated, bloody turf war. Yet each time another drug mule like Shani, or a decoy like Thando, gets apprehended at a port of entry, often with negligible amounts of contraband stuffed into various body cavities, it is hailed by the authorities as another victory in the war against drugs.

This makes no sense. It also smacks of the propaganda some powers use to commit serial violations of less powerful countries' sovereignty through invasions and enforced regime changes. Like its conventional military counterpart, the onslaught on drugs has been predicated on hypocrisy and used primarily for purposes of political expediency and self-interest.

For the first time in ten frantic days in Bangkok, I allowed myself the luxury of conducting some hotel-based research into one of the longest-running crusades since World War II: the global war on drugs. This might seem as an unnecessary detour off a fairly straightforward investigative path, but to me it was imperative to first understand the rules of engagement before I became an active combatant.

I began my research by looking at the early 20th century and the war against Satan's weed, a phrase that conjures up images of Lucifer cultivating his own stash in the backyard of Eden. Satan's weed is one of several names used for cannabis. The term was coined in an American movie financed by a Christian ministry in 1936. The film was intended as a modern Aesopian fable targeting American youth, hence the original title, *Tell Your Children*. The plot revolved around cannabis and its perceived perilous consequences, including loud music, pelvic contortions, rape, murder and the general mutilation of the body and soul inflicted by Satan's weed.

Shortly after the film's completion, an enterprising American producer by the name of Dwain Esper purchased the uncut version. He rechristened the film *Reefer Madness* and it was used by US legislators as an effective salvo in the propaganda war against cannabis. The movie was ultimately relegated to the dumpster of credible documentary film-making. In the 1970s, however, it was resurrected from the cinematic catacombs and rapidly attained comical cult status on college campuses.

Almost 50 years after the launch of *Reefer Madness*, it has been established that cannabis has never killed anyone by direct toxicity/poisoning. Moreover, weed smokers (and by conservative estimates, their global number has exceeded 25 million) generally do not rape, pillage or plunder. They're also often too laid back to get into a car, let alone drive into anyone while under the influence. Among the world's smokable drugs, including crystal meth, heroin and, the most addictive of all, tobacco, there have yet to be cases of cannibas smokers murdering for a pack of Peter Stuyvesant or a cob of Malawi Gold. Nevertheless, despite the proven lethal consequences of that legal, liquid drug called alcohol, which has been linked, incontrovertibly, to mayhem, mutilation and murder, dope is still on the war crimes 'most wanted' list. And despite its proven medical benefits for cancer patients, cannabis remains banned in most countries, including South Africa. Now that's what I call 'reefer madness'.

Aeschylus, the Greek tragic dramatist, declared that 'in war, truth is the first casualty'. Millennia later, the phrase 'war on drugs' has become one of those overwrought clichés, a pompous example of military parlance that peppers official declarations in much the same way that election-campaign speeches are punctuated by power fists punching the air. It is spouted by politicians who declare war while holding peace conferences. The phrase may encapsulate the intention of aggressiveness, but it is a battle fought against an idea, an intangible entity, without any sense of definition, direction or control. And many will argue that it has been a war engineered for failure equally by drug lords and power mongers whose material interests and political ideologies were, are and will always be best served by the perpetuation of this war. In 1996 former president Bill Clinton's erstwhile drug czar, General Barry McCaffrey, said as much, and conceded defeat in the war on drugs.[1]

The UK has also hoisted the white flag on the ever-shifting battle front. In July 2012, British Justice Secretary Ken Clarke told MPs that the UK is 'plainly losing' the war on drugs. And when he was a senator, Barak Obama stated that the 'war on drugs has been an utter failure … We need to rethink how we're operating the drug war.'[2]

That statement was made in 2004, when the US was the world leader in terms of drug-related incarcerations. In a 2014 interview published by *The New Yorker*, President Obama criticised the racial bias attached to marijuana-associated arrests. He emphasised the imperative of drug-policy reform and the significance of new laws legalising marijuana in Colorado and Washington.[3]

Despite the war on drugs, with its anti-drug campaigns, increased incarceration rates and the crackdown on smuggling, the number of illicit-drug users in America has risen over the years.[4] Although consumption has stabilised in Western Europe, the UN Office on Drugs and Crime (UNODC) has warned of an increase in drug consumption in developing countries.[5] This is despite the fact that, in the past 40 years, the US Government has spent over $2.5 trillion on the war on drugs.[6] The billions of dollars of aid pumped into countries in South America and Asia, and elsewhere (like Afghanistan) have resulted in what critics of this policy describe as the 'balloon effect', whereby production is suppressed in one area only to pop up in another.

In the decades since the 1961 UN Single Convention on Narcotic

Drugs, the war on drugs has morphed from a moral, bureaucratic and propaganda battle into a literal one – whether the salvos have been fired at peasant opium farmers, small-time dealers, drug mules, decoys or drug users. A case in point is Thailand's war on drugs. This was launched in 2003 by former Prime Minister Thaksin Shinawatra in response to an explosion in methamphetamine use throughout South East Asia, and Thailand in particular. This drug has proven impervious to the global 'weapons of meth destruction', partly due to the ease with which it can be manufactured and the ready availability of its two main ingredients, ephedrine and pseudoephedrine.

Given the popularity of methamphetamine, South American drug cartels do not need to worry about military-style onslaughts on their coca plantations; nor do Asian warlords need to ponder the limited lifespan of the poppy plant. Ephedrine and pseudoephedrine, used in medications for the common cold, can be easily concocted into meth at home (or in a sophisticated mass-production laboratory). And, like the common cold, meth appears to be here to stay. So ubiquitous has this drug become that the UN estimates that the number of consumers of amphetamine-type substances worldwide today exceeds 56 million, with 21 million of these located in East and South East Asia.[7]

Although Asia's Golden Triangle now produces only 5 per cent of the world's opiates – down from over 70 per cent some thirty years ago – according to the UNODC, it has become one of the major centres for the production of methamphetamine. The industry operates in cahoots with members of the Thai and Burmese armies and police, as well as warlords.[8]

Thaksin vowed to banish not only *ya baa*, but all drugs, from 'every square inch' of Thailand within four months.[9] In a country where corrupt public officials are notoriously complicit in drug trafficking, television advertisements were broadcast to shame those who were sheltering the narcotics trade. However, the Thai Government's modus operandi of naming and shaming included the extra-judicial murders of more than 2 000 citizens, and arbitrary arrests or blacklisting of several thousand drug users and innocent civilians. Thailand's National Human Rights Commission was deluged with complaints of extreme violence, false arrests, improper inclusion in drug blacklists and violations of due process. Although Thaksin declared victory in his campaign against drugs, he conceded that drugs were still very much a feature of Thai life.

The availability of methamphetamine, for example, may have fallen in Thailand, but this was accompanied by a sharp spike in the street price. Those who could afford it acquired it, thereby further enriching the drug lords. Those who couldn't simply switched to cheaper drugs, confirming that while supply had fallen, few inroads had been made into treating demand, which is universally recognised as an imperative for any credible drug strategy.

In reality, it is the narcotics supply chain, rather than the demand, that has been targeted in the war on drugs worldwide. And the 'bottom line' for curbing supply has been motivated not by health matters but rather by the bottom line that defines too many wars, namely profit.

Take the furore around the kratom plant, for example. For centuries, the leaf of this tree had been used in Asia for medicinal purposes and as a herbal sedative. Yet for the past 70 years, kratom has been outlawed in Thailand. This is not for health reasons, but rather because of the economic rationale behind the ban. With the outbreak of the Greater East Asia War in 1942, declining revenues from the profitable opium trade resulted in farmers across the Golden Triangle diversifying into kratom cultivation as a cheaper alternative to the opium poppy plant, from which heroin is derived. However, this attempt at switching to kratom cultivation on the part of the poppy-growing peasantry did not sit well with the Thai Government of the time. This is because opium was a prized currency and lucrative source of taxation throughout the region, including China. In fact, the Chinese nationalist party, the Kuomintang, led by Chiang Kai-shek, dominated the world's heroin trade after the 1927 civil war against communist leader Mao Zedong. Following the nationalists' defeat in the 1940s, thousands of Chiang's troops retreated from southern China and regrouped in what was then Burma (Myanmar). Over the next two decades, Chiang's secret armies assumed control of the established opium industry in the infamous Golden Triangle jungle, where Burma, Laos and Thailand meet. And, ironically, Chiang's warlords turned drug barons were aided and abetted by the CIA, who conveniently turned a blind eye to their distribution of heroin in Vietnam during the 1960s, even though the most lucrative market for the drug was among US troops stationed there.[10]

It just so happens that kratom also provides relief from opiate addiction and, logically, addiction cures are bad for the business of narcotics trafficking. In 2010 Thailand's Office of the Narcotics Control Board proposed decriminalising the tree and its herbal derivatives, stating that its use was an integral part of Thai culture. The board concluded that decades of unproblematic use, and the absence of health and social harm made prohibiting use of the leaf counterproductive. The proposal was defeated by the government, however, and anyone found growing or in possession of the plant in Thailand continues to be subjected to harsh punishment, including lengthy prison terms. Although legal in the US (except in the states of Indiana, Louisiana and Tennessee), kratom prohibition, insists the Thai Government, remains an essential component in the war on drugs.[11] Evidently, consistency is not a prerequisite for efficacy.

Even the loftiest of liberation movements requires the lubrication of hard cash to keep its engines of struggle running smoothly. This is not to imply that behind every revolutionary there is a drug lord. But the saying 'my enemy's enemy is my friend' applies, particularly when the war is ideologically driven.

The Iran–Contra scandal in Central America is a classic example. In 1983 the right-wing Contras were plotting the overthrow of Nicaragua's left-wing Sandinista government. Although US federal funding of the Contras was prohibited, the CIA devised the

Iran–Contra plan, whereby weapons would be exchanged with Iran for cash, with the proceeds being channelled to the Contras. But the greenbacks from the guns weren't enough to fill the deep pockets of America's terrorist allies, so drug trafficking – specifically of cocaine – became a lucrative extra source of income. During this era of coke-fuelled campaigns, either the CIA omitted a due diligence of their allies' finances, failed to convey intelligence of Contra drug trafficking to the US Drug Enforcement Administration or even actively facilitated the trade. This was all done in the interests of defeating the Soviet-supported Nicaraguan administration.[12]

The CIA, allegedly, was not even averse to importing some Central American 'pure' into their homeland. As fantastical as this 'powder' on CIA hands theory might appear, it was given credence in 1996 by means of an article published in the *San Jose Mercury News*, a Pulitzer Prize–winning newspaper. Penned in 1999 by investigative journalist Gary Webb, under the headline 'Dark alliance', the article traced a trajectory of dodgy policy decisions and duplicitous actions that had enabled not only the proliferation of cocaine, but also its more addictive derivative – crack cocaine – throughout the US.

Adding further credence to this angle is the work of Professor Alfred McCoy, an expert on South East Asian history at the University of Wisconsin–Madison. Since the 1970s, McCoy has investigated the CIA and its practice, in country after country, of allying with drug traffickers and providing them with de facto protection from prosecution. McCoy has exposed the self-funding of French intelligence agencies through opium trafficking during the colonial wars in Indochina, and the CIA's recruitment of Burmese drug lords during the Vietnam War and their Afghan counterparts during the war between Afghanistan and the then Soviet Union. 'Faced with the choice,' McCoy stated in 1991, 'the United States Government chose the Cold War over the drug war.'[13]

The twain would always meet, inspiring a cynical double entendre in the name the 'White House'.

As was the case with soldiers who returned from service in Vietnam with full-blown heroin addiction, surveys conducted of over 200 fighter pilots deployed in Desert Storm in 1992 revealed that 57 per cent had consumed drugs at some time during combat. Sixty-one per cent of those who had used stimulants during the operation reported them as essential to mission accomplishment. During the wars in Afghanistan and Iraq, the military slogan 'suck it up' apparently became a phrase more suited to widespread substance abuse among soldiers. Troops suffering from depression and panic anxiety were not provided with conventional debriefing sessions and trauma counselling but rather amphetamines and barbiturates, as well as a cornucopia of muscle relaxants and hallucinogens.[14] Sometimes they were prescribed by qualified medical staff. Mostly, medicines intended to treat ailments from epilepsy to diarrhoea to insomnia were purchased from street dealers (in war zones pills are often cheaper than cigarettes) or stolen from pharmacies and mental hospitals.

In fact, the history of war has confirmed that most battles cannot be fought effectively without a little pick-me-up, whether for factory workers manufacturing bombs around the clock, ground troops marching long hours in hellish conditions, or pilots specialising in suicide missions. During World War II, for example, the drug of choice among Japan's kamikaze pilots was methamphetamine. It made them feel fearless and omnipotent or just too fucked to avoid nosediving into the Pacific. The American troops favoured Benzedrine, a similar compound, which releases adrenalin and makes users see stars and stripes in strange lands. The Nazis were also not averse to a bit of home-cooked meth and even carted their portable drug labs all the way to Stalingrad, probably to alleviate the chill of the Russian winter.

While hunkering in his bunker, Hitler got into chemistry too, reportedly taking a spoonful of speed every day, no doubt to sweeten the bitter medicine of imminent defeat and simultaneously to stave off the shakes caused by Parkinson's disease.

An iconoclastic historian might even ascribe the reason for the Third Reich's defeat not to the superiority of the Western Allies' war machine, but to the unregulated proliferation of hard drugs, particularly methamphetamine, within the German army. But it was undoubtedly Japan that proved to be the land of the rising meth, and the source of its global distribution. Call it revenge for Hiroshima and Nagasaki, or a miscalculation on the numbers of suicide pilots willing to fly high. But, whatever the motivation behind Japan's mass production of the drug during World War II, by 1946 it had a massive surplus of Philopon, the original brand name for meth, which somehow found its way to its enemy in the West. The entire history of World War II and its chilly aftermath could be unpacked and rewritten as the World at War on Drugs. Literally.

*   *   *

In the global war on drugs, failure has been ubiquitous. It has become one of most hyped and costly battles in the history of humanity, a futile crusade, despite trillions of dollars spent on curtailing the supply of drugs and attempting to control their demand.

Despite this, so ingrained has the battle cry become in democracies and dictatorships alike that one would be forgiven for believing that the war on drugs has been around as long as drugs themselves. In fact, the term was coined by the US during one of the icier moments in the history of the Cold War, born out of a distinctly 'West is best' and 'right is might' approach. Although the US Government had fought against drugs for decades (in 1954 President Eisenhower had publicly vowed to 'stamp out narcotic addiction'), the term 'war on drugs' was not widely used until 1973, when President Nixon created the Drug Enforcement Administration, announcing 'an all-out global war on the drug menace'.

By 1975 the Drug Enforcement Administration's attention was

focused on the cocaine industry in Colombia and, later, Mexico. Simultaneously, however, the US Government was faced with multiple challenges: how to achieve victory on not one, not two, but three battle fronts: the Cold War, the drug war and escalating civil unrest. Since then, endeavours have included crackdowns on consumption, as well as catchy slogans and campaigns aimed at youth culture, in particular, which have had as much impact as a shot of placebo in the arm of an intravenous drug taker.

Harm-reduction strategies have been more successful in curtailing demand. However, efforts to shoot down the supply chain by means of increased incarceration rates have backfired. In a devastating critique of the drug war, the multinational Global Commission on Drug Policy pointed out in a 2011 report that worldwide, the 'vast expenditures on criminalisation and repressive measures directed at producers, traffickers and consumers of illegal drugs' have clearly failed to effectively curtail supply and consumption.[15]

Criminalisation has in fact served to empower the global drug trade by securing high profits and augmenting violent competition for this lucrative global market. Although the occasional high-profile apprehending of a drug lord and the arrest of mules or set-up of decoys look good for the stats, ultimately, the simple laws of economics prevail. Drug syndicates generally don't post their income variables on their websites or in annual reports, unless they are fronting as legitimate businesses. But, obviously, a shortage, whether perceived or real, immediately drives up the price of narcotics and, in turn, the demand. More drug revenue for the syndicates does not necessarily translate into profits, however, because disruption of the narcotics supply chain means ballooning expenses incurred by the drug lords to secure delivery. These include more payments to border officials, club bouncers and dealers who coordinate distribution. These costs contribute to an escalation in drug-related violence. As rival drug cartels or their localised distributors – the street gangs – engage in wars of their own to corner this lucrative market, the thousands caught in the crossfire are shrugged off by these 'warriors' as collateral damage.

This is evident in the decades-long escalation of gang warfare in the Cape Flats during a war that, despite temporary peace treaties between rival gangs, remains ongoing and seemingly inexorable. On the one hand, these local wars have been sparked by the stance of a younger generation of gangsters towards the older established leadership, many of whom had returned after long spells in prison to resume their hold on power. On the other, they are part of the ongoing profit-driven contestation of territory, the battle for dominance of the criminal economy, primarily through the drug trade, but also through the distribution of other forms of contraband.

The drug wars on the Cape Flats mirror similar gang conflicts worldwide, fought not only on the streets of South Africa's urban ghettos, but across the African continent, South America, South East Asia, the Caribbean and Afghanistan, where lords of drugs and war have coalesced into omnipotent fiefdoms. It is these hierarchies that ultimately control the rules of engagement. And, as with all profit-driven enterprises, these powerful kings and queens are aided and abetted by their lieutenants, the knights, bishops and impenetrable castles, while the disposable drug mules and decoys are their pawns.

7

DOREEN

January 2009

Winking and flashing like runway lights, the neon illuminations of Bangkok's Sukhumvit Road snake along side streets and alleyways where African and Asian prostitutes punt their wares. The turf occupied by the former typically includes Sois (streets) 3, 4, 5, 7, 9 and 11. Many of the women hail from East and West Africa; some come from further south – Mozambique, Zimbabwe and South Africa. Most of the prostitutes are younger than 25 and barely proficient in English, let alone Thai. As they occupy their assigned street corners, they appear afraid, to judge by the darting glances they intermittently exchange with one another and with their pimps on sentry duty.

In each of them I saw Thando's reflection, a woman alone and terrified, faced with the prospect of death or the equally unenviable choice of smuggling drugs, only to discover that she had been assigned the role of decoy.

Thando's horrifying experience has displaced every preconception I had harboured about the women convicted of committing this crime. Although the prima facie evidence appeared incontrovertibly to weigh against her, if her allegations against Thembi, the woman who had recruited her or, more accurately, coerced her, could be corroborated, then perhaps her case would be reviewed. And if she was a bona fide victim of human trafficking, there must be other South African citizens suffering similar human-rights violations abroad. Such people should be assisted by the South African Government, in accordance with our Constitution. Their convictions should be overturned and they should be set free as soon as possible to return home.

Immediately after my visit to Thando in Lard Yao Prison, I called the South African Embassy. As I related the details of our conversation, I could almost sense their shrugs of impotence. I felt slightly deflated but still buoyed, nevertheless, by my renewed sense of missionary zeal. My next move was to contact the International Organization for Migration, an intergovernmental body established to counter the global trade in human trafficking, which has offices worldwide, including South Africa and Thailand.

But the International Organization for Migration's intervention capacity appeared little more effective than a used condom. 'Our hands are tied because we have no mandate to do anything without the buy-in of both the South African and Thai governments,' explained a staffer. My calls to Amnesty International proved equally fruitless.

'Is non-interference just a feeble euphemism for indifference?' I yelled into a receiver that had already been slammed down at the other end.

I then vented my frustration on a member of a Bangkok-based NGO managing needle-exchange programmes and harm-reduction treatments for the city's many thousands of heroin addicts. 'The heroin trade in Bangkok is controlled by the Nigerian syndicates,' she explained. 'And to get more insight into how they operate, you need someone who's not exactly on the inside, but who knows what's going on and will talk freely.'

She gave me the contact details of a certain Alex, a Liberian national who had been living in Bangkok for several years. Apparently, he had been part of a multilateral trade mission exploring avenues for Thai investment in West Africa. That was in 2000. Although the trip had only been for a few days, like many of his African counterparts, he had remained in Bangkok.

Alex agreed to meet me in Soi 4, at one of the go-go bars in the Nana Entertainment Plaza, dubbed Bangkok's 'sleaze central', for good reason. This three-storey sex mall was full of rubber-limbed Asian women decked out in various guises from coy schoolgirl to dominatrix, the latter wearing outfits made from leather, latex and studs. As Alex shared with me his experiences in Thailand's most populous city, I tried to avert my astonished gaze from a prepubescent girl whose suppleness would put an ancient Shaolin warrior to shame as she performed sexual acts on an assortment of fruit.

Affable and articulate, Alex provided a buffet of information. Although overtly scornful of the narcotics trade, he was not averse to hanging out with the lower-end dealers frequenting the bars along Sukhumvit's Soi 4, even scoring the occasional Moroccan hashish brick from them.

'If you want to understand why and how the drug traffickers operate, how they lure the young girls to Thailand, you have to understand the Nigerian connection,' Alex told me.

He paraphrased the statistics: every six hours, a Nigerian is arrested for illegal – usually drug-related – activities in Bangkok The top guns operate in shadowy, elusive syndicates using opaque *noms de guerre* like Kudos, Tuface and Sim, or more mundane pseudonyms like Steve, Peter, John or Henry. They tend to use religion as their cover – some are self-certified pastors, like an alleged drug smuggler known as Pastor Philip, who apparently runs the New Ministry Bible Centre in Bangkok, or Aaron, who belongs to some Apostolic Mission church.

The top guys are filthy rich and utterly ruthless. When recruiting new members into the drug mafia as runners (the low-end dealers), they entrap and blackmail desperate young Nigerian men, who are sometimes lured here under the false promise of a job, or who come from impoverished areas in search of legitimate work but do not have their legal papers.

'Sadly, they get sucked into the whole scene. There's an attitude of: if you can't beat 'em, join 'em,' explained Alex.

Then, there is the relationship between the Nigerians and the Thais, which Alex described, diplomatically, as 'complicated': 'Farangs cannot establish businesses without a Thai partnership and must employ Thais, in compliance with the law. And many Nigerians land up marrying Thai women, not only because they find them attractive and think they perform sexually like acrobats, which they do, but because it makes good business sense.'

Even the law-abiding Nigerians are reluctant to go to the police or the Nigerian Embassy for assistance because one doesn't know who to trust there. 'Or here,' he added, gesturing towards the unremitting bustle that is Bangkok's nightlife.

It was common knowledge that the international drug trade had for decades been dominated by Nigerian interests. I needed to understand why the global Nigerian narcotics footprint was so vast, so Alex hastily wrote the name and number of an apparently influential Nigerian connection in the Pratunam district of Bangkok. 'Speak to him and then you will understand more,' he said.

* * *

So, the following day, in the epicentre of Thailand's 'Little Lagos', I embarked on a crash course on the Nigerian drug connection. My classroom would be the Baiyoke street market, close to the colossal Baiyoke Sky Hotel in Pratunam. The Baiyoke Sky is to Bangkok what the Twin Towers used to be to New York: at 88 floors, not only is it the city's tallest building, but also the most distinctive feature of the Thai capital's skyline. It also marks the main area for one of the city's all-time favourite pursuits: shopping (and not for sex, for a change). Pratunam is one of Bangkok's most colourful and chaotic areas, noted for its fashion factory outlets, street markets, bazaars and armies of local vendors offering wares at a steal.

Pratunam is also home to a vibrant Nigerian community who

often congregate around the Baiyoke central market, downing beers in groups, or patrolling the doorways to the many bazaars.

I had made an appointment to meet Abubakar Mabolaji, a wealthy Nigerian businessman. Mabolaji apparently wielded considerable clout among the Nigerian expat community and because he is not a drug lord himself, he insisted, he was willing to help me get a handle on the growing global power of the Nigerian syndicates. I was far too eager for his tutelage to question his agenda.

We were to meet at a barber shop. When I arrived, Mabolaji was still in the process of being shaved and sheared, swivelling his rotund form about in a black-leather barber's chair while talking animatedly on his cellphone. When he spotted me hovering tentatively in the doorway, he beckoned me inside and indicated an adjacent chair for me to sit in, while the barber gamely attempted to trim the remaining tufts of hair from under his chin without slitting his throat ear to ear.

'Call me Bakar,' he had insisted when I addressed him by his sur-name. 'I thought we could get some lunch at the Kai Ton Pratunam Restaurant, which serves the best khao man kai (chicken rice) in Bangkok,' suggested the ebullient Bakar, who described himself as a clothing entrepreneur, a euphemism for the thriving knock-off stores he owned in the multi-storey Pratunam Market, where original designs from the US and Europe are expertly copied.

I was keen to meet Bakar to try to understand, from his per-spective, why his compatriots had gained such notoriety as members of drug-trafficking syndicates. In fact, Nigeria has such a dire reputation among international drug-control agencies that it is one of only four countries to have been blacklisted by the US – alongside Myanmar, Syria and Iran – for not pledging sup-port for the global war on drugs. Nigerians now make up one of the largest communities of Africans living both legally and illegally in Thailand. In 2009 they ranked seventh among the top-ten foreign nationalities incarcerated in Thailand. According to recent research, in 2011 there were reportedly an estimated

700 Nigerians in Thai prisons, not to mention more who had died while being detained or imprisoned in Thailand before their extradition back to Nigeria.[1]

But why, in a truly global city of 12 million, inhabited by expatriates from every nation on the planet, are West Africans, particularly Nigerians, singled out as the source of its drug woes? Answering that question entails understanding the history of the Nigerian community, not only in Thailand, but in other host countries as well.

My subsequent research on the Nigerian diaspora revealed that, in the early 1980s, the Nigerian community had gravitated towards Thailand principally as traders – importers and exporters of clothing and precious stones. During this period, and subsequently, Nigeria became one of the Thai kingdom's most profitable importers of Thai rice. Simultaneously, Nigerian organised-crime syndicates began using Thailand as one of their bases of choice for obtaining heroin from the Golden Triangle for distribution to other Asian countries, like Hong Kong and Taiwan, and then onward to the US, Europe and, more recently, Africa.[2]

In the early 1980s, when the war in Afghanistan had disrupted the normal flow of the narcotics trade, the Golden Triangle was a veritable poppy paradise. As the Nigerian syndicates grew in reputation and sophistication throughout Asia, Nigerians were recruited by drug lords and syndicates already entrenched in that region, as well as in South America, Colombia and, from the late 1980s and early 1990s, South Africa. The illicit profits amassed by these cartels were derived not only from their most profitable trade, narcotics, but were also the fruits of 'diversification' into the smuggling of weapons, diamonds and gold, sex trafficking and a variety of other money-making scams.[3]

But recruitment into this illicit economy had not been a collective experience for all Nigerians living in Thailand. As Bakar pointed out, many had experienced hardship in order to attain legitimacy and respect.

'In Bangkok you get all sorts of Nigerians,' he insisted. 'Students, athletes, professors, teachers and legitimate businesspeople, who make a substantial contribution to the economy. But you rarely read about *them*. It's only the Nigerians who are involved in the drug trade that get the publicity, and increase the discrimination against the rest of us.' He continued: 'I believe in assisting my compatriots, who are often left stranded by unemployment.'

On cue, a muscular young man entered the barber shop. 'Mr Abu, begging your pardon,' he entreated. (The West African community endearingly use nicknames with one another.) 'Mr Abu, I'm broke as hell and my student loan only comes through next month.'

Without hesitation, Bakar reached into his Louis Vuitton look-alike wallet and, with mannered magnanimity, thrust a fistful of notes into the student's hands. It was a gesture that I was convinced was for my benefit.

Thanking Bakar profusely, the young man dashed out and I observed the beneficiary of Bakar's largesse passing the baht to another evidently equally needy compatriot.

'I am a friend here to students, to compatriots in prison. And, yes, to some of them, I am a saviour.'

I was about to question the wisdom of Alex's referral, when Bakar touched my shoulder reassuringly. 'And I don't do it with drug money. I am genuinely a self-made man and my aim is to rid the world of this stereotype of Nigerians as corruptors, crooks, con artists and drug traffickers.'

According to Alex, Bakar was well connected at Bangkok's Nigerian Embassy, which was established in 2000. Before then, Nigerians had to obtain a British visa, which was difficult to arrange.

'Many arrive here on fake passports,' Bakar admitted, 'and they get caught out at the airport because they can't speak the language of their so-called country of origin.'

Bakar recounted how he had once received a desperate call from a Nigerian who had landed in Bangkok with a fake South African passport. The tourist standing next to him at customs was also from South Africa and as the passport-control official checked the Nigerian's documents, he indicated to one of his colleagues to call back the South African who had just passed through passport control. 'Speak your language – not English but the other African one,' ordered the official to the authentic South African, who happened to be Afrikaner. I had a vision of a nervous *boere seun* spluttering, '*Goeie more, my broer, ek sê, hoe gaan dit?*', or words to that effect, to which the Nigerian would, of course, have been utterly screwed.

'Naturally, they put him on a plane straight back to where he had come from, but less than three months later, he was back, this time with a Ghanaian passport. He now works in a restaurant and is saving up to study business science.'

But why this widespread culture of finding 'creative' ways to violate the law? I phrased the question circumspectly.

'When most of us came here,' Bakar explained, 'we were struggling for a better life. We never knew we were coming for drug business. We got scammed by our own people. For many of us, the choice was, get deported back to poverty and unemployment, or stay on here and take your chances, doing whatever you can to earn a living.'

And Bakar's own personal experience echoed this struggle. He had decided to leave Nigeria in 1993, at the age of 20, after General Sani Abacha had seized power. The military leader suppressed political opposition and assumed a reign riddled with systemic corruption, misappropriation of public funds and human-rights violations, including arbitrary executions. A golden opportunity presented itself to Baker when an acquaintance of a cousin introduced himself as a travel agent and encouraged Bakar to go to London. In the UK, the agent had explained, work opportunities were plentiful, and Bakar would soon be able to support himself and his family in Nigeria. The travel agent lent Bakar the money for a plane ticket, passport and visa, and promised him a job earning roughly a thousand pounds a month to manage a Nigerian restaurant in Peckham, a London suburb popular with

West African immigrants. The impressionable young Bakar, who had never even travelled to Lagos, let alone London, used all of his savings to pay back the agent, including a hefty 'lender's fee', which he 'begged, borrowed and stole'.

'In my country, there is no such thing as something for nothing. You have to pay for every connection and referral.'

But shortly before the departure date, the agent informed Bakar that a European visa was too expensive and that he would have to 'divert' to Thailand in order to wait for his papers to come through. Another hefty agent's fee later, and Bakar had landed in Bangkok, accompanied by the Nigerian travel agent, who promised to sort him out with accommodation and temporary work while his visa was being processed.

'I'm going to organise us a taxi. You just wait here, my friend.'

That was the last Bakar ever saw of the fake agent, who by then had apparently pocketed thousands of dollars from him. He was swiftly replaced by another Nigerian compatriot who, although a stranger to Bakar, bought him a cup of coffee and, after a couple of phone calls, assured Bakar of a Nigerian support group in the Sukhumvit area that would 'take care' of him. Although Bakar hadn't been coerced into smuggling drugs, he insisted he had been the victim of a Nigerian travel scam – apparently quite a commonplace con used in Nigeria to entrap susceptible young men into becoming career criminals. I couldn't quite weave some of the more melodramatic threads of Bakar's woeful tale into a credible narrative. But I chose to give him the benefit of the doubt. Abandoned in Bangkok, he must have felt almost as vulnerable as Thando when she landed in Thailand – anticipating the job of a lifetime, only to be suckered into enslavement by a ruthless drug cartel.

I briefly recounted Thando's plight. Bakar nodded empathetically. 'When you are in a situation like that – alone, with no money and no home – your chances of survival are small,' he said emitting a sigh, as though reliving the anguish of his experience.

Hitching a ride with the stranger into Sukhumvit, Bakar had

been introduced to some small-time dealers, who served as runners for a major Nigerian–Thai drug cartel. The remuneration was modest, but for Bakar, it provided the portal to a new life, free of the hardships he had endured in Abuja.

'Most of our people in jail in Thailand are the little fish, like the ladies you told me about in Klong Prem,' he said. 'If the big fish get caught, it is a rare thing indeed, because they are the ones walking around with the clean hands. They get everyone else to do their dirty work.' He added, 'I was just very lucky because I met a very nice young Thai lady, by the name of Darika, whose father owned a clothing store and who offered me some legitimate work.'

Although Darika and Bakar got married two years later, their union did not automatically confer on him the status of permanent residency or citizenship. It is business, rather than marriage, that allows Nigerians to renew their visas annually.

'I don't know any Nigerian businessman who has permanent residency here,' said Bakar. 'And my children cannot inherit my wealth, even though I have made a lot of money selling the big designer brands from Europe and the USA.' He added: 'That's why I make it my business to help young men who are just looking for a break, without resorting to dealing in gbana' (the name given to drugs in Thailand's Nigerian community).

* * *

As illuminating as Bakar's story may have been, it did not provide the answers I needed as to why so many Nigerians have gravitated towards the global narcotics trade with such alacrity and success. They have managed to penetrate drug markets in every continent. Their growing ability to cooperate with other transnational drug cartels must be linked to globalisation and shifting patterns of international migration, as well as to the specifics of Nigeria's history and geography.

Expertise on the geopolitics of narcotics was evidently not Bakar's forte. It would only be several months after I returned to South Africa that I would gain greater insight into the genealogy of the global narcotics industry, in general, and the Nigerian influence, in particular. My theoretical knowledge was gleaned primarily from research conducted by Stephen Ellis, an internationally recognised historian, professor in the social sciences at the Free University, Amsterdam, and a senior researcher at the African Studies Centre, University of Leiden. Ellis's work provides a broad historical perspective on why West Africa has become the Silicon Valley of criminal ingenuity, from con artistry, embezzlement and arms smuggling to drug and human trafficking.[4]

As former UNODC Executive Director Antonio Maria Costa put it, drug trafficking, in general, and in West Africa, particularly, is 'not only buying real estate and flashy cars: it is buying power'.[5] Geography is partly to blame, because, as is the case with real estate, the mantra of the transnational drug trade is three words: location, location, location. When the US Drug Enforcement Administration blocked the cocaine routes from Central America and the Caribbean in the 1990s, Mexican, Venezuelan and Colombian traffickers, together with their counterparts in Europe and the Middle East, found alternative markets through and into Africa. The consequences of this 'diversification' included a huge increase in the seizure of cocaine in West Africa, between 2001 and 2007, from approximately 273 kilograms to roughly 47 000 kilograms. Since 2008, trafficking from Latin America through West Africa and onwards to Europe increased significantly. About a six-hour flight to Europe, six and a half hours from South Africa and about nine hours across the Atlantic Ocean from Latin America, West Africa enjoys geographical proximity to several world markets, which makes it a suitable staging post for drug trafficking.

Furthermore, not only is Nigeria conveniently located for illicit trade between South America and Europe, but the internal dynamics of its sociopolitical topography have also rendered it eminently suitable for the international contraband market. These include flimsy monetary controls and law-enforcement mechanisms, and rampant corruption.

'Many Nigerians do not have the same morality towards narcotics as you do in the West,' Bakar had explained. 'To them, it's a victimless activity – simply a trade involving willing sellers and willing buyers, and, despite the fact that it is illegal, it is viewed as a legitimate means of wealth distribution from [Nigeria's] north to the south, not to mention worldwide.'

And it would seem as though this attitude spread swiftly across the region. Foreign and local traffickers have developed new routes in West Africa, establishing new narcotics hubs, particularly in Ghana, The Gambia, Guinea and Guinea-Bissau. Once hailed as a potential model for African development, Guinea-Bissau is now one of the poorest countries in the world.[6] Collusion between the army and organised-crime syndicates extends to drug traffickers using military premises to stockpile cocaine awaiting shipment to Europe. According to UNODC documents, these consignments are transported by private planes from Guinea-Bissau's military airstrip.[7]

In the oil-rich Niger Delta, there have been numerous reports of local militias smuggling crude oil to tankers moored offshore, (who are paid in cash, weapons and cocaine), particularly in towns such as Warri and Port Harcourt, two major delta cities, perpetuating the pattern of collusion.[8]

But the trafficking business in the West African region, and specifically Nigeria, did not sprout overnight. In fact, the development of the drug trade in Nigeria spans over half a century. According to Ellis, the first documented case of West Africa as a depot and transit point for heroin smuggling dates from 1952.[9] In that year, parcels of the drug were transported by a Lebanese syndicate from Beirut to New York via Kano, in northern Nigeria, and Accra, Ghana, using couriers on commercial airlines.

However, the roots of West Africa's emergence as a major transit point for a more broadly based trade in illegal drugs go back to the 1960s, the hippy era in Europe and the US.[10] It was during this period that a mass market for drugs was on the rise. The first reports emerged of cannabis being exported from Nigeria to Europe by airline passengers stashing small amounts in their personal luggage. This small-scale smuggling, conducted by enterprising individuals, would help sow the seeds for the powerful drug-trafficking syndicates of the future.

During this time, Ellis explains, despite being the region's only major oil producer, Nigeria was experiencing acute financial difficulties – the consequences of global vagaries and its own profligacy in earlier, more favourable times. Together with its neighbours, Nigeria was forced to borrow money on a massive scale from the International Monetary Fund and the World Bank, as well undergo a large-scale reduction in expenditure and downsizing of its bloated public sector. The enforced austerity measures plunged many people into financial dire straits, forcing them to seek other forms of remuneration through the second (informal) or third (criminal) economies. Rural communities with low levels of education began migrating to the towns in search of alternative employment. The more sophisticated urbanites, particularly those proficient in English, looked further afield in their search for new frontiers of opportunity. Many were students who were supposedly benefiting from postcolonial perks like bursaries and scholarships, but who did not receive their study grants. An alternative form of income generation, therefore, had to be devised.

However, according to the US Drug Enforcement Administration, the transnational trade was primarily carried out not by cash-strapped students, but by Nigerian naval officers undergoing training in India.[11] They bought heroin there and sent it back to West Africa to be repackaged and re-exported by couriers, or mules, whom they had recruited among the Nigerian student community. The meteoric spike in the Nigerian drug trade in the 1980s has also been attributed to regional conflicts spawned by the Cold War, which diverted the world's attention from the growing drug scourge.[12]

It is certainly the case that, by the early 1980s, Nigerian syndicates were dominating the main areas of narcotics distribution. They would travel to South America or Asia to buy small quantities of cocaine or heroin, which they would conceal in their personal luggage, and which would then be forwarded to a recipient either in West Africa or another transit country. And, as with any successful business, as their global sphere of influence expanded, so too did their powers of delegation. In fact, Nigerian syndicates are credited as being the first to devise the body-packing and swallowing method of transport, on a large scale anyway. To ensure the secure passage of their cargo, not to mention the prospect of expanding their economic sphere of influence, many traffickers took up residence in producer countries like South America, for cocaine, and Asia, for heroin. This enabled them to adopt a much more profitable, hands-on control of the distribution chain. Their relocation was often facilitated by the political and military instability afflicting their host countries. For example, thousands of Nigerians converged on Asia's Golden Triangle during the civil wars of the 1980s, and 99 per cent of the Nigerians who came to Thailand during that time were involved in drug-related business.[13]

Nigeria's own contradictory history in the war on drugs often served to help, rather than hinder, its expansion. In 1990, almost immediately after its inception, the country's National Drug Law Enforcement Agency (NDLEA) was mired in scandal with its own officers implicated in the narcotics trade.[14] In 1991 the agency's former boss Fidelis Oyakhilome was fired after being accused of having an affair with a Lagos socialite, who was subsequently convicted for drug-related crimes. The NDLEA also came under global fire when it embarked on a violent crackdown on drug smugglers in 1994. Special criminal tribunals were established to try drug mules, while a new law mandated NDLEA officers to arrest anyone who could not account for their wealth.

Nigeria's military government also attempted to impose the death penalty for drug trafficking – an echo of 1984, when three drug merchants were publicly executed by firing squad.[15] But this 'take-no-prisoners' approach to the drug problem prompted an international outcry. Meanwhile, the syndicates were constantly adapting and improving their methods, attracting the attention and earning the respect of cartels from other countries. Colombian drug bosses, for example, began making overtures to Nigerians during the 1980s to mitigate the effects of oversaturation in the US.

In the last three decades, many Nigerian drug-trafficking operations have graduated to the status of multinational enterprises, lording it over their competitors in the trade. With business associates in both producing and consuming countries, their global footprint has become vast. It is estimated that 40 per cent of heroin entering the US is smuggled in by Nigerian syndicates. They are also said to control the narcotics trade in many parts of England, especially in the north-west, which is home to growing immigrant communities. Estimates of their control over the Asian markets are in the region of 90 per cent. India has also acquired favoured-country status among these syndicates, particularly in Mumbai, where more than 2 000 Nigerians reside. A small but industrious Nigerian community operates in Afghanistan, where Boko Haram enthusiasts may receive military training while simultaneously partaking of the thriving export trade in cannabis and heroin.[16] In partnership with the Chinese Triads and rebel armies ruled by warlords turned drug barons, these syndicates have also diversified into dealing in counterfeit commodities, diamond, gold and weapon smuggling, and, in particular, human trafficking.[17]

As far back as 1995, a senior US anti-drugs official, Robert S Gelbard, described Nigerian drug networks as 'some of the most sophisticated and finely tuned trans-shipment, money-moving and document-forging organisations in the world'.[18]

Gelbard had issued warnings concerning West African cartels established in South Africa, which were exploiting the country's political transition and porous borders, while consolidating their influence on the narcotics industry in South East Asia.

Particularly since 2000, the scale of illicit consignments to and from South Africa has increased so dramatically that huge shipments smuggled in private yachts or planes have become increasingly common. However, the classic mode of transportation – using mules – still remains the syndicates' favoured method of transportation.[19]

So, what is the secret of the Nigerians' international success in this trade? According to Ellis and the UNODC, the Nigerian drug trade and its hierarchy of operatives have been characterised by a distinctive 'business' structure that lends itself to forming cooperative relationships with rival cartels from other regions. Unlike the more corporate style of the American mafias, the Nigerian syndicates appear to be more informal, and are organised along familial and ethnic lines, thereby making the cartels less pervious to infiltration. This also makes it even more difficult to identify, apprehend and convict a central kingpin, simply because there are so many. Furthermore, the deliberate looseness of the chain of command means that the low-ranked members have no contact with the top guns and no knowledge of their identity.[20]

The operations of the larger syndicates are also supplemented by smaller-scale freelance operations, resembling a so-called 'adhocracy', in which experts are drawn from different disciplines into ad hoc project teams.[21]

And crucial to the success of Nigerian drug syndicates are their highly flexible modes of operation, as they constantly form and re-form their business relationships from among a wide pool of acquaintances, affiliations and allegiances.

To earn their stripes, the kingpins of the syndicates must be able to purchase their drug supply cheaply at source. This entails setting up contacts with the drug lords who control production of the crop, be it in South America or Asia.[22]

The second prerequisite for success is a reliable contact in the receiving country, be it Asia, North America, Europe or South Africa. This, unfortunately, is where the Nigerian community gets its criminal stereotype. Even though most of the millions of Nigerians residing outside their homeland have legitimate occupations, the existence of this vast diaspora nevertheless provides the medium through which traffickers operate most effectively.

The third determinant of a drug baron's worth is the ability to maintain a low profile and not attract attention. Not for these enterprising businessmen the usual materialistic and flashy accoutrements of success. They might well own palaces in tax-free principalities and cruise on yachts, but they don't flaunt their ill-gotten gains with the crudeness of a Kardashian, the vulgarity of a Middle Eastern petro-terrorist or the flamboyance of a Colombian peasant turned cocaine baron. They tend to be a lot subtler in terms of their financial transactions and very selective in the amount of capital required to finance operations.

And it is their modus operandi that makes them frustratingly mercurial. For the purposes of transportation, Nigerian drug lords work with a second tier, whom I describe as CEOs, or cross-enterprise operators, otherwise described by Ellis as 'strikers'.[23] As the name suggests, the striker 'strikes', or brokers the deals via an excellent network of contacts, be they for forged documents, weapon smuggling or drug trafficking. Attaining this position is no mean feat and often entails working one's way up through the ranks as mule and street dealer. The role of this middleman, or illegal labour broker, requires specialised negotiation skills. He receives a fee for performing this type of service on behalf of the drug lord, and might also be outsourced by several syndicates simultaneously as an independent consultant or contractor.

The strikers might also recruit the couriers or delegate someone to do so in the source country (South Africa, for example, as in the case of Thembi, Thando's recruiter, who targeted young women from Welkom's Thabong township). They are paid a recruitment fee for each mule and decoy – between R5 000 and R10 000 – and might accompany them to the airport. The couriers will also be met by handlers at each point of departure and destination to ensure that the drugs are properly swallowed and the correct quantity delivered. Bona fide mules will never fraternise with the top brass of the narcotics hierarchy. They are usually recruited in social environments by their casual acquaintances, even childhood friends who themselves have been recruited as mules. They are often financially, emotionally or sexually seduced into becoming couriers. The incentives for participating in and controlling this trade are obvious: although mules earn a small fraction of their superiors' income in the chain of command, they are paid in hard, tax-free cash earned in a relatively quick turnaround time, and there is the possibility of a fast track to the top for greedy or desperate individuals.

Once recruited, a change of heart is not an option. As was the case with Thando, the couriers are kept under constant surveillance by an enforcer for days or weeks before they eventually make the trip. As a decoy, Thando represents the most desperate, exploited category of courier: the innocent victim of duplicity who has no self-agency. But even mules who have willingly agreed to smuggle the drugs dare not change their minds. Unable to seek assistance from their country's embassy, they may also feel too afraid to turn to the police or customs officials at their point of departure.

Perhaps the most effective means of securing the cooperation of susceptible couriers is through faith. There are literally thousands of religions, secret societies and cults in Nigeria and the Nigerian diaspora. Forms of worship range from conventional Christianity to a bizarre array of deities. Couriers or mules are often escorted to religious shrines to swear an oath of allegiance – not to the drug lord, but to the Lord and saviour, Jesus Christ. Their mission is therefore spiritually ordained and they are programmed, cajoled or coerced into believing they are God's emissaries. Betrayal of such a role, therefore, is nothing short of sacrilege. It is punishable by death, or the mule is set up as a decoy, a dead cow for piranhas.

* * *

Even before my theoretical initiation into Nigerian Syndicates 101, I was convinced that Bakar and Alex's crash course on contraband had provided me with enough information to allow me to infiltrate one of the drug syndicates operating in Sukhumvit – or so I naively believed. After meeting Bakar, I called Alex and he agreed to meet me again, but this time the designated meeting place would be at my hotel.

'Being seen too often in public, chatting to you, a white farang journalist, could be risky,' he cautioned. I assured him that I had maintained an appropriately low profile in Bangkok, but he was not convinced.

'You have been to Bangkwang and Klong Prem prisons to visit South African mules. You are not a regular visitor, unlike many of the women whose husbands are based here or who visit as part of a religious delegation. So you have definitely attracted attention. What's more, there are syndicate members who visit the mules to make sure they are not spilling the beans.'

Inwardly I squirmed when I thought of my visit to Thando at Lard Yao a few days before and my syncopated dance around the microphone and speaker system.

'If it is so dangerous, why have you agreed to meet me again?' I asked Alex testily when we met at the Atlanta Hotel.

'Because shocking human-rights violations are being perpetrated against women, particularly the South Africans. Yet your government does nothing to assist them. Perhaps by exposing how they are manipulated, threatened and beaten into becoming couriers, you will make your government take notice and take action.'

Lowering his voice conspiratorially, Alex added: 'Some of the visitors are definitely on the payroll of the syndicates. They might be boyfriends of the incarcerated couriers or they might even be operating under the pretext of belonging to some ministry or another. They act as financial and emotional emissaries between the women and their families thousands of miles away. The families deposit money in their bank accounts. Often it never reaches its intended beneficiaries.

Some of these visitors have even been known to arrange for mules in prison to marry syndicate members or inmates from Kenya, Nigeria or Congo, so that the mules can then be extradited with their "husbands" to these countries – all of which have prisoner transfer treaties with Thailand, unlike South Africa.'

The fate that would befall the women once they landed up in these countries was rarely followed up by their families, Alex explained. While some appeared to genuinely make a new start, others continued muling, developed drug addictions, resorted to prostitution to feed their habit, or simply disappeared.

Alex continued: 'And to increase their transnational narcotics reach, the syndicates usually target vulnerable young women – sometimes of Asian descent, but increasingly from Africa. The members either get them to fall in love with them, get them hooked on drugs or delegate "recruiters" to coerce or trick them, like Thando, the woman you told me about.' He added: 'All these methods of entrapment are definitely on the increase and those girls don't stand a chance.'

By way of example, he told me about a South African woman, a prostitute and *ya baa* junkie, whom he knew only as Doreen. She had never disclosed her full name to him, but sometimes she spoke wistfully of her youth in rural South Africa, he said, and the circumstances that led her into a life of prostitution and addiction in Sukhumvit.

Doreen's story had a tragic refrain – a situation to which Thando possibly would have been forced to succumb, had she not been set up as a decoy and arrested.

Apparently from Motherwell, in the Eastern Cape, Doreen was about to begin her first semester at a college in Port Elizabeth. But her educational aspirations were derailed when, seeking a part-time job, she was introduced to a certain Veronica, who offered her a job selling designer knock-offs. Drug abuse had dulled Doreen's youthful memory and, Alex informed me, she could no longer recall the woman's surname. But still tattooed on the increasingly opaque edges of her brain was the name Steve, a dashing West African 'spiritual healer' who had fallen on hard times, whom she had met through Veronica. He was squatting in a hotel on Govan Mbeki Avenue, Port Elizabeth.

I was familiar with that cesspool of a street and its occupants buzzing about like a swarm of mosquitoes. In 2005 *Special Assignment* producer Jessica Pitchford had broadcast two exposés on the sex and drugs trade taking place there. At the time, the Belvia Hotel was a particularly notorious hunting ground for Nigerian drug syndicates targeting susceptible young women from the margins of the province, both black and white, and luring them into prostitution, drug addiction and trafficking. Although the Port Elizabeth police were aware of their activities, they were routinely accused of complicity by making arrests that would be thrown out of court due to shoddy investigations, or by confiscating drugs only to sell them back to the syndicates involved.

Alex also recalled Doreen mentioning the names Christian and Austin, two senior syndicate members, who frequented Port Elizabeth's streets of bawd in search of girls as young as 11 to be recruited as sex workers, drug mules or both. Alex hadn't known what to make of the information, but had made a mental note of certain details, which he was only too eager to pass on to me. At the time, neither name held any significance for me. It was only subsequently, in 2010, when I learnt of the arrest of a certain Christian Ndukauba and Austin Okeke on charges related to human trafficking, that Doreen's contacts assumed greater significance. The arrests of Ndukauba and Okeke were largely thanks to the efforts of a joint provincial task team comprising the police, the National Prosecuting Authority (NPA), NGOs and social-development agencies. The team had been established in 2009 to investigate the rise in human trafficking in the run-up to the 2010 FIFA World Cup. However, the entire syndicate could not be apprehended because four of the suspected traffickers and their mules had absconded long before – to Bangkok. It is possible that Steve and Doreen had been part of that band of fugitives.

Alex told me that by the time she did her first drug run in early 2008, Doreen was trapped in an abyss of sex-and-drugs trading from which she would probably never emerge. Steve had showered her with jewellery and promises of a glamorous life if she would just assist him one time with some 'cargo delivery'. It would be risk-free and merely entailed a 12-hour flight from Johannesburg to Bangkok, a luxurious vacation on the island of Koh Phangan during the popular Full Moon Party and a R10 000 cash bonus. She had never been on a plane before and was already heavily addicted to crack cocaine, so she didn't require much persuasion.

* * *

I was waiting for Doreen in a watering hole frequented by West Africans called Jacky's Pub, in Soi 3. My spy camera was deftly positioned to the left of my cleavage. The camera was attached to my breast pocket by a clip resembling that of a marker pen. Only to those well versed in the art of covert technology would the lens be visible, eyeballing and recording the scene.

I had diligently rehearsed my cover story: ageing hippy; caught up in the hedonism of Thai island life; out of money; debts piling up at home in South Africa; $10 000 would see me right.

Alex had casually slipped the information to his hashish dealer that an 'older' South African woman, desperate for cash, might be willing to do a run. And it seemed that Steve would deploy his South African–born girlfriend, Doreen, to check out my credentials. Three hours before our designated meeting, Alex sent me an SMS: 'Be at Jacky's @ 8 pm.'

Before I could even respond, he had texted me again: 'Do not call or SMS me ever. Skype only.'

My gratitude towards Alex had turned into apprehensiveness. When it came to dealing with Steve, or whoever this slippery syndicate member might be, I was definitely on my own.

As she weaved her way towards me in Jacky's Pub, Doreen looked no different from the thousands of other *ya baa* addicts in Bangkok. Excruciatingly thin and clattering unsteadily on her heels, she was nevertheless beautiful, with delicate features only partially camouflaged by layers of crudely applied make-up. She wore her ebony wig in a bob with wisps framing her heart-shaped face and oversize sunglasses. I extended my hand towards her. She neither responded nor removed the sunglasses, even though the Bangkok sun had long set, its orb casting crimson, orange and lilac tones through the smog.

'Apparently you are from South Africa and short of cash.'

I launched into my tale of woe, only too aware that once contact had been made, I had become 'marked', both by agents of the US Drug Enforcement Agency, who worked in tandem with the Thai authorities, and the syndicates themselves. This is also what makes infiltrating the syndicates so difficult: the walls of the Drug Enforcement Agency are porous, and the network of intelligence is vast. By now, both sides could have photographed me and even if I altered my usual route back to my hotel, someone, either an agent of the Drug Enforcement Agency or a syndicate enforcer – or both – would be able to follow closely behind.

I also knew not to ask too many questions. But without crucial biographical details, Doreen's story, only partially patched together for me by Alex, remained too fragmented for me to investigate further.

According to Alex, in 2008 Doreen had flown to Bangkok, where she was dispatched to the Rose Inn Hotel, on Soi 3, opposite Jacky's Pub. There she had been met by a Thai man, who removed the modest suitcase she had brought with her and replaced it with a backpack. The following day, she had boarded a bus, with the backpack filled with 5 kilograms of heroin. She had then taken a ferry to Koh Phangan, where she disembarked in Haad Rin, the island's nightlife capital and home to the Full Moon Party, which attracts tens of thousands of revellers from all over the world.

Once there, she had been met at the harbour by a local taxi driver. He had been instructed to take her to the nearby Drop In Club Resort and Spa, whose reputation, I subsequently learnt, is murkier than its sewer-like swimming pool. There, she was swiftly relieved of her illicit cargo. Then she had taken the 30-minute boat trip to nearby Koh Samui, with its resort-style airport, from where it was a quick flight back to Bangkok. Steve was waiting for her. She had passed her initiation.

Facing her at Jacky's Pub, I realised the intractability of her situation. And, potentially, of mine.

'Doreen, I know how it all started. At the Belvia Hotel,' I whispered.

Her vapid expression suddenly sharpened. 'Who are you?' she hissed.

'I am a journalist. I'm here to help you. I can take you to the South African Embassy. They will protect us.'

'Are you mad?' she whispered. 'He watches me all the time. I can't even go to the shops alone. Do you know what he, they, will do to you? And if you survive after what they do to you, you won't want to live anyway.'

She removed her shades and I couldn't suppress my gasp. Her left eye was a patchwork of bruises – indelible evidence of how scores are settled and dues are paid in this trade.

Her second drug run had been far riskier than the first. This time, Steve had forced her to swallow 50 pellets of heroin (about half a kilogram, with a value estimated at around 1 million Hong Kong dollars) before booking her onto a flight to Hong Kong.

'He beat me up because I didn't want to do it any more. He told me I'd got off lightly, that the next time I disrespect him he will have me killed or set up.'

Steve was now sauntering towards us, gold chains glinting against his tight white T-shirt.

'You ladies getting along good?' Doreen swiftly donned the sunglasses. I nodded.

'Let me escort you to your hotel and we can get to know each other,' he offered while caressing Doreen's cheek.

'Love to,' I somehow managed a smile. 'But my hotel doesn't allow men to accompany us inside.'

The night air was cool, but it was circling my throat with the pressure of a tightening noose. No one would ever find me. Byron Taylor, the SABC cameraman, had expressed patent disapproval of my reckless efforts to infiltrate the syndicates operating in Sukhumvit. He was about to return to South Africa. And I, truthfully, had no exit strategy.

Then Steve's eyes drifted to my cleavage. In rapid succession, he frowned, smirked and grabbed the spy camera, swiftly removing the memory card from its minuscule slot on the side. 'What is this shit? You film us?'

Doreen began to scream – not so much a scream, but more of a wail – and for a second she was the focus of Steve's attention. I bolted out the door, shoving my way through the throngs along Sukhumvit, into Soi 4 and towards the skytrain at Nana Station, which whisked me to Soi 2. I ran through another side street, thankfully one without go-go bars, horny tourists, hookers or drug merchants, past the Cavalry Baptist Church and towards the Atlanta Hotel, whose entrance sign, 'No sex tourism or drugs allowed', beckoned like a talisman.

8

KOH PHANGAN

January 2009

My terrifying encounter with Doreen and Steve had yielded little information. I didn't manage to find out Doreen's surname, let alone obtain contact details for her family in the Eastern Cape. I had no way of knowing where she lived in Bangkok and whether or not she had even survived Steve's wrath after he had exposed my cover. I felt sick at the thought of Doreen being subjected to further torture because of my reckless attempt to infiltrate Steve's syndicate. In future, instead of fumbling my way into and stumbling out of precipitous situations, I vowed to be more circumspect in my investigative approach.

The one concrete lead I had on Doreen was that she had travelled to Koh Phangan and had stayed at the Drop In Club Resort and Spa in the town of Haad Rin, where the Full Moon raves take place. I wanted to retrace her journey, to find out if anyone at the hotel recalled anything about her and her drug contacts on the island. Even the most minuscule of recollections might help me assemble a more comprehensive dossier on Doreen and the drug syndicate that had ensnared her. But without an image of either Doreen or her ruthless boyfriend-cum-enforcer-cum-pimp to show to anyone at the Drop In – Steve had confiscated my spycam the previous evening – I wasn't optimistic that I would receive any details worth chasing up.

Nevertheless, I decided to go to Koh Phangan and not solely for the sake of the investigation. Truth be told, I desperately needed a break from Bangkok. The morning after my escape from Steve, I had checked out of the Atlanta Hotel, after another sleep-deprived night, courtesy of the kamikaze moths self-immolating against the ceiling light. Each time I switched it off, the mosquitoes would launch a full-frontal ankle attack. I had run out of repellent but did not risk venturing out of the hotel for more, lest I bump into another 'Steve'.

In fact, I was loath to go anywhere alone in Bangkok. I was starting to identify with the sense of vulnerability probably experienced by women like Thando and Doreen. My growing paranoia was not assuaged by the humidity in the city, which was beginning to feel oppressive. I longed for the balm of seafood, surf and sun – the signature attractions of Thailand's islands. Furthermore, Koh Phangan's raves were legendary, for both positive and negative reasons. If music is the food of love on the island, then sex and drugs are its cocktails. My curiosity was spurred, therefore, by both a hedonistic impulse and a desire to explore the laissez-faire approach to the invasion of narcotics and sex on this island, an attitude that clearly contradicted Thailand's official policy of zero tolerance.

So, the following morning I headed there aboard a ferry that almost seemed submerged with the collective weight of expectation. Hundreds of sun-kissed backpackers and 'gappers' (students on a gap year) were in search of the ultimate trip: Koh Phangan's Full Moon Party, which draws the greatest crowds in Thailand's rave scene – around 25 000 to 30 000 a month. The parties are notorious for hallucinogenic drugs, such as Ecstasy, space cookies or, for the retro-hippies, LSD.

Narcotics are to Koh Phangan's beach parties what massage parlours are to Bangkok: ubiquitous. Before, during and after the parties, everything from hashish and cocaine to methamphetamine and heroin is available at the bars along the beach where the Half Moon, Black Moon, Full Moon and Jungle raves take place.

Like the drugs, the price of accommodation in Koh Phangan varies according to availability. The closer the date to the Full Moon Party, the more exorbitant both become. I had opted for the Drop In Resort and Spa, but not because it was avidly recommended. On the contrary, many tourists had labelled it the island's 'drop-out' resort, and for valid reasons, as I would soon discover. It was the kind of hotel that Koh Phangan's more discerning class of cockroach would choose to avoid but was a magnet for every other species of flying, swimming or crawling beast from the pages of *National Geographic*. The hotel's two-legged occupants were hardly of the human A-list variety, either. They were predominantly a motley crew of bedraggled backpackers drowning perennial hangovers in cheap beer and whining about the surly hotel staff, the pervasive stench, the parlous state of the bedding and the perilously flimsy walls that seemed to shake with the slightest breeze. The Drop In was cheap, though, and just a few minutes' walk to the main beach. It had also been Doreen's drop-off point for the heroin in her rucksack, which she had been ordered to deliver with the promise of $10 000 and a dream vacation.

Had she changed her mind, where could she turn? She wouldn't have known who to trust on the island and clearly the Drop In was the last place she would be able to seek refuge. During Full Moon, especially, the beachfronts and the alleyways of Haad Rin resemble the side streets of sin in Bangkok, Pattaya Beach or Phuket. The monthly rave provides a viable market for small-scale drug trafficking by Thai, Vietnamese and farang prostitutes – a veritable United Nations of sex workers of every nationality and sometimes ambivalent gender.

And if Bangkok offers the true girlfriend experience, then in true bargain-basement style, Koh Phangan provides a special: two for the price of one, as the khatoeys (Thai lady boys) are sometimes described. My first close encounter of the khatoey kind happened at the Drop In bar. After browsing the street stalls laden with an assortment of authentic artefacts, trendy trinkets and overpriced knock-offs, I had stopped off at the bar. Inside, several lady boys were vying for the attention of an attractive Australian surfer who initially ignored them and began chatting to me. The Australian had, surprisingly, chosen Koh Phangan, which is not ideal for surfing, over the more popular swells at Koh Lanta, in the Krabi Islands, almost 1 000 kilometres from Bangkok. But he couldn't resist the lure of the Full Moon rave, he explained to me.

Meanwhile, a couple of West African prostitutes had targeted a portly German entrepreneur, whose penchant, he confessed with inebriated candour, was for mulatto 'wors'. The 'wors' – or, rather, the whores – had perfected the craft of the coy coquette with their chat-up lines, 'Hey, Mista, you velly, velly handsome. Me like you velly much.' By the following morning, however, they would have either fleeced their 'tricks' of thousands of baht or fed them copious quantities of MDMA – or both.

From what I had learnt about Doreen's situation, narcotics are employed as both the hook to entrap and keep susceptible young women in the world of prostitution, and as effective sexual lubricants for their clients. Many of Thailand's sex workers, like Doreen, wear the signature expression of the addict. If it's an addiction to *ya baa*, their darting eyeballs are as empty as a ventriloquist's dummy, or appear to be immobilised beneath a thin, glazed gauze. Heroin sucks the soul out of the eyes and turns the pupils into bottomless pits. The needle marks are rarely visible until the addicts remove their shoes, exposing the filigree around their ankles and between their toes.

It was not yet dusk, but the games were already in full swing. By then, the German tourist had staggered off with his 'Marilyn-mulatto' – all décolletage and platinum-blonde wig. The other prostitute had clearly sized up the Australian surfer, whose focus on me had been diverted by a seductive khatoey. I withdrew discreetly. The khatoeys are notoriously brutal when it comes to snaring their spoor. This one was petite with waist-long flaxen locks (blonde is the hue of choice for the South East Asian sun-kissed set) and an enticing dragon tattoo breathing fire up her arm. She had draped it around the Aussie's shoulder and he, obviously unaware of her sexual identity, was behaving like the Bruce who had bagged the hottest Sheila in the room. But just as they were about to leave together, the Nigerian prostitute loudly 'outed' her rival.

'Mista, you like the lottery? You wanna play with balls? 'Cos that's all you gonna get.' Before the astonished surfer could reply, the khatoey had stubbed out her cigarette on the Nigerian woman's cheek.

The latter recoiled, bellowing in agony. The Australian bolted from the bar and at that point was probably prepared to swim to the Krabi Islands. Waving the smouldering cigarette like a syringe, the khatoey advanced menacingly towards her foe, who was cowering in a corner of the bar, which had by now become rapidly depleted of customers. She hissed and spat. Then, with a feminine flick of her locks, she flashed a smile at the rest of us, her eyes surveying the scene for another prospect. Ah ha! Found him. She shimmied over, breasts thrust forward and eyes lowered diffidently, strategically.

The following morning, the German tourist staggered back into the Drop In bar. He was on his way to the airport at Koh Samui, horribly hung-over from his antics with his Marilyn-mulatto the night before: 'She told me she was supporting her orphaned sisters in Lagos and that the youngest was suffering from breast cancer. She had been saving up to send her to Germany for a mastectomy but was short of about 50 000 baht. I am not an idiot. I wasn't going to donate all my money so I offered her 30 000. She seemed grateful and burst into tears. I cried too, as she seemed sincere. And we had the best sex I have ever experienced. Or maybe it was the MDMA. Pure fucking Ecstasy. I must have passed out. The next morning, she was gone with all my dollars.'

Unsurprisingly, this is not the Koh Phangan advertised in the tourist brochures. Nor do encounters like this define the island, which boasts pristine beaches and snorkel-friendly surf. But, although the Koh Phangan brand might not have been built on the butt of sex tourism, unlike Pattaya Beach, for example, drugs are nevertheless the elixir of the Full Moon pilgrims, the lotus eaters of South East Asia, in search of the ultimate hedonistic experience.

By evening, the crescent-shaped beach had metamorphosed into a frenzy of between 15 000 and 30 000 ravers, gyrating to 15 sound systems from which the world's best DJs were blasting trance, Goa, drum 'n' bass, dub, reggae, commercial hits, house, techno and every other conceivable genre from 1970s rock and 1980s pop to 1990s first-wave acid trance and electronic body music.

There was a ring of fire through which revellers dived like circus seals through hoops, hopefully without incendiary consequences. Mix in the body paint, fireworks, glow sticks, tasty buckets and the popular 'shroom shakes, and the Full Moon rave becomes an orgy of unrestraint. What Durban Poison is to KwaZulu-Natal, mushrooms are to Koh Phangan. They are the island's principal indigenous psychotropic attraction. Mushroom shakes are openly advertised in the pubs of Haad Rin at 500 baht a shake. They are all the rage in a bar above Sunrise Beach, nicknamed Mushroom Mountain.

At the parties, sex, drugs and booze flow with equal velocity, followed by urine and vomit – expelled into the ocean, onto the sand, and among the discarded bottles, pipes and capsules. The ablution facilities have been converted into quick-sex booths. There's even an aquatic version of the 1980s thrash-metal parties: throwing oneself off the rocks at the southern end of Haad Rin headfirst into the surf. Hundreds do it; most survive.

And long after the last reveller had 'slurched' off to sleep or passed out on the beach, long after the weary locals had cleared the shards of bottles and drug paraphernalia, the drug fest continued. Late into the night, at the numerous Rasta bars, the wafts of marijuana smoke intermingled with the odours of alcohol, tobacco and sweat.

And this reality, except perhaps in Thailand's remote north, constitutes the contradiction of a country on the one hand steeped in the meditativeness and discipline of Buddhism and the religion's art, literature, ethics and morality, while, on the other, pandering to the whims of tourists in search of the perfect package deal: an island paradise where the water is warm, the women are easy and the booze is cheap. Whether the tourist is in search of water sports, getting wasted or getting laid, or all three, Thailand offers a nirvana of options. The Thai authorities are, understandably, in a quandary. Tourism is Thailand's largest economic sector and provides more than 4 million jobs a year. In the context of its socio-economic woes, the country dare not risk alienating the mainspring of its economy.

Although it makes bad business sense to clamp down hard on every cannabis smoker and drunken tourist, Thailand's punitive laws are still enforced, which means that any farang who is busted must be made an example of. In Koh Phangan, undercover cops regularly trawl the beaches during the Full Moon parties, mingling with the throngs and selling dope. It is public knowledge that bribery is commonplace. Although there have been moves to transform the image of Koh Phangan Island into a zero-tolerance, drug-free brand, the quest appears doomed to failure. It couldn't be otherwise, given the complicity of the authorities and the local economy in perpetuating the island's chief source of income.

*   *   *

I was starting to understand how trapped Doreen must have felt. She had performed her first drug run on an island awash with drugs, and with hordes of tanked-up tourists and cops on the take. I could imagine her initial excitement in South Africa, as she fantasised about her free vacation in paradise. But I couldn't even begin to contemplate her horror at the realisation that she had, in reality, embarked on the first leg of an indefinite holiday in hell. Like Thando, she hadn't stood a chance.

My close shave with Steve in Bangkok had made me think that, in a way, those who had been caught on their first drug run, like Thando, had arguably been served with a softer, albeit unenviable, punishment. For Thando, 25 years in an overcrowded prison seemed a more benevolent punishment than Doreen's form of incarceration. During my visit to Thando, she had spoken longingly of her boyfriend, Dan, and her family, especially her mother, Nozukile. Sure, she was frightened and hopelessly unprepared for the consequences of the crime that she insisted she had unwillingly committed, but she exuded a sturdy sense of self and, most importantly, of hope. Doreen possessed neither of these traits. Her trip of a lifetime had degenerated into a life – possibly death – sentence of addiction, prostitution and abuse. Unless Thando succumbed to suicidal despair or a fatal illness in prison, she would almost certainly survive her sentence. Unless Doreen was rescued from her ordeal and rehabilitated, she probably would not.

There seemed nothing I could do to mitigate her pain or to make Steve accountable for his crimes. But as Bangkok's Suvarnabhumi Airport receded into a blur, I resolved to track down Thando's recruiter and the syndicate responsible for her plight.

9

NOZUKILE

February 2009

Nozukile Pendu spoke haltingly, while her second oldest, Sipho, Thando's sister, helped us by playing the role of translator. We were sitting in the lounge of Nozukile's two-roomed RDP home in Welkom's Thabong township. The space was occupied by two armchairs adorned with doilies camouflaging the frayed armrests and a dresser supporting a television set. I noticed among the faith-filled wall hangings several photographs of Thando. She was preening for the camera, dressed in evening wear, snug inside a white, fur-trimmed coat. They were images of a photogenic, care-free young woman for whom the future beckoned brightly.

On my return to South Africa from Thailand a couple of weeks before, I had made contact with Thando's boyfriend in Port Elizabeth. Thando had given me his number. My spycam had recorded his details, as well as those of her mother, Nozukile. In October 2008, both had been notified of Thando's arrest by the then Department of Foreign Affairs; both had been, under-standably, horrified and confused by the news. It made no sense that Thembi, the woman who had promised that she would look after Nozukile's oldest child in Bangkok, would be guilty of such a betrayal. Nozukile had immediately called Thembi to demand an explanation but Thembi had feigned ignorance. Thando's boy-friend had agreed to fly to Gauteng, courtesy of *Special Assignment*, and accompany me to the Free State to spend some time with the Pendu family, to follow the trail to Thembi, which would lead, hopefully, to the syndicate complicit in Thando's arrest.

My interest in Shani Krebs and Vanessa Goosen had become clipsed by Thando's case. I still wanted to tell their individual stories, but I sensed that, as isolated as they both felt, and as worthy as their personal biographies were as subject matter, each had much greater agency than an impressionable, unedu-cated, township-raised young woman. Shani and Vanessa regu-larly received letters, money, visitors and love. Vanessa even had several long-distance suitors, one of whom subsidised her daughter Felicia's trips to Thailand to visit her.

Thando had no one. Even if her mother could have afforded to travel, she would not have been able to navigate her way through Bangkok alone. And there's no way I wanted to accompany her, for fear of being detained at the airport. I had broken Thailand's penal laws by smuggling a spycam into a prison. The story was due to be broadcast on *Special Assignment* later that month and it would probably generate some interest from the Thai Embassy, which I had also contacted for comment after my return. Initially, the embassy had agreed to my request but a few days later, an embassy representative had emailed a terse refusal. I had also been warned by the South African Embassy in Bangkok that Thando had waived any right to media exposure and that if I publicised her name, I would risk increasing her vulnerability at the hands of Thailand's sometimes egregious penal system. I suspected that, still traumatised and disorientated after her arrest, and faced with sheaves of documentation and a mountain of red tape, Thando would probably have had no idea of what she was signing. And the most significant investigative threads of the story had been woven from Thando herself. Although she had been entirely unaware of my covert recording, I had informed her that I was a journalist and requested her permission to publicise her plight, to which she had unhesitatingly agreed.

So, without exposing Thando as the unwitting source, I had

decided to include snippets of our covertly recorded prison conversation in the programme. That decision, once the *Special Assignment* programme had been broadcast, would possibly have earned me a place on Thailand's list of undesirables. I wasn't about to risk instant deportation, as had happened with William Bosch and Sean Allen, or get hauled into prison for committing lese-majesty like the hapless Harry Nicolaides. Perhaps I was exaggerating the risks in my imagination, but at that stage I was more comfortable erring on the side of caution, given my reckless track record in Bangkok.

Nozukile had agreed to being interviewed, with the proviso that I protected her family's identity, a condition to which I had, of course, acceded. We had also agreed to withhold Thembi's name in the programme until Nozukile had laid a charge against her. At that stage, I wasn't even sure what offence Thembi could be charged with. I only knew that I needed to find out more about her relationship with Thando.

'Thando was such a good daughter, so generous and positive in her attitude. And now her life is finished.' Nozukile's eyes conveyed her unrelenting guilt for being unwittingly responsible for the horrific fate of her daughter. 'If I had not given Thembi permission to take her, she would not have gone. Yes, she wanted pretty clothes, the good things in life, but she went because of me, so that she could also make my life easier.'

Yes or no: a choice made in a New York minute, a mere instant, had determined the young woman's fate. In her anguish, Nozukile could not begin to comprehend the intricacies of seduction that form part of the trafficker's arsenal to entrap the vulnerable, the naive and the downright desperate. Like sexual predators, traffickers need not apply direct force or coercion, initially anyway, to catch their prey. All that is required is the appropriate bait, be it emotional or financial. In Thando's case, it was both.

As her boyfriend explained to me, Thando had been 'groomed' over several months to become a courier. She began making frequent trips to Johannesburg, where she stayed at Thembi's hotel. She would breathlessly tell Dan about her adventures in the big city. Thembi introduced her to restaurants, nightclubs, designer clothes and jewellery. For a women from the township, the lure of this lifestyle must have been irresistible. Even if there were warning signs, Thando would have ignored them. Had Nozukile not permitted her to leave the country with Thembi, I harboured no doubt that she would have gone anyway.

But Nozukile remained inconsolable in her belief that it had been her fault. 'She called me once shortly before she was arrested to say that she had earned R10 000, which she had given to Thembi to bring home for me. I didn't even ask how she had made so much money so quickly.' She added, 'I never received a cent of it.'

Augmenting her pain was the fact that the woman responsible for her daughter's incarceration still lived a short distance away in one of Thabong's more upmarket streets. 'I see her sometimes driving by in her fancy black car. And everyone now knows what she has done. Thando was not the only one, but Thando is the only one who got caught.'

*   *   *

Nozukile, Thando's boyfriend, a cameraman and I cautiously pulled up next to the face-brick house. Two cars were parked in the driveway, a white Mercedes-Benz and a black Volkswagen Polo.

'That's her car!' exclaimed Nozukile. 'She's inside.'

My first impulse was to pull a doorstop manoeuvre, the journalistic term for cornering somebody for an unexpected interview. However, given the emotiveness of the situation, such an approach might have developed into a dangerous conflagration. I wasn't sure to what extent Thembi posed a personal threat, whether she might be armed, who was with her and, most importantly, how Nozukile would react to the woman who had destroyed her child's future. Before I could even issue any directive, we heard a door slam and saw the Mercedes reverse out the driveway. Swifter than a rapid eye movement, Nozukile leapt out of our vehicle. I had no option but to follow her, while the cameraman shot our confrontation from the car.

Understandably, the driver of the Mercedes, a rotund man, probably in his mid-40s, looked bemused, then alarmed. As I began to explain the reason behind our unexpected visit, he alighted from his vehicle and, clearly recognising Nozukile, shouted, 'Thembi isn't here. Now get out.'

Nozukile suddenly let rip in isiXhosa, which I later understood to mean: 'Liar! Her car is here. This is the car she bought with the soul of my daughter!' She grabbed a fistful of gravel from the driveway and hurled it at the Polo. The man lunged at Nozukile, slapping her face and attempting to grab her hair.

Nozukile responded like one demented as all her grief and rage erupted in a swift, retaliatory kick to her attacker's groin.

Rushing towards them both, I yelled, 'No! No!', grabbed Nozukile, pushed her behind me and squared up to the man, who was now cowering in pain.

'You touch her again and I shall have you arrested for assault. We have you on camera. In fact we should have you arrested right now.'

He stared at me with genuine perplexity. And while my outrage at his assault on Nozukile was not feigned, my pretence at self-confidence belied the panic I, too, was starting to feel. I hadn't yet identified myself as a journalist. We could be arrested for trespassing and, because of Nozukile's stone throwing, malicious damage to property. However, this was not the moment to back down. As I eyeballed him with what I was hoping was an expression of righteous disgust, I added: 'You're already in a lot of trouble over the drugs. Don't make it any harder for yourself.'

My bravado paid off. His mouth agape, and eyes darting left to right like ping-pong balls, he protested: 'What? No, no, I'm not involved with drugs.'

'Well, your wife is. And we demand to speak to her.'

'We are not married. What has she done?'

I beckoned to the cameraman: 'Take Nozukile back to the car. Please stay with her. This gentleman and I need to talk.'

It would be unsafe for me to accompany him inside. I needed to remain within range of the cameraman, now parked on the opposite side of the street, should the conversation become heated.

In more measured tones, I explained that I was here to question Thembi about her alleged involvement with a drug syndicate and her coercion of Thando into becoming a mule. Again, he denied any knowledge of drugs or Thembi's involvement with drugs.

'To show I am not lying, I will even take you to where she is,' he offered. He fumbled for his cellphone and dialled a number. 'Thembi, what the fuck is going on with you?' he shouted into the receiver, before continuing the conversation in isiXhosa.

'Okay,' he said to me when the phone call was over. 'She is at the taxi rank. I will take you there. She has agreed to meet with you.'

He then made a bizarre suggestion: 'We can go in your car and I will park my car directly in front of the gates, blocking her, so that if she is hiding here, she won't be able to take her car if she wants to run away.' There wasn't time to deconstruct this odd non sequitur uttered by a man whose name, in the fracas, I had yet to learn.

As we weaved our way through the throngs crowding Thabong's potholed streets, our navigator volunteered some information. His name, he said, was Albert. He was a teacher and had been involved with Thembi for several years. Recently he had become suspicious of her, particularly as she had never invited him to stay with her at the hotel she purportedly owned in Johannesburg. He had heard rumours of her involvement with a Nigerian man and was now considering ending the relationship.

We arrived at the designated meeting spot. Albert phoned Thembi again. 'Where are you? What? No this is rubbish, man. Oh, okay, see you there.' Apologetically, he turned to the cameraman, who was driving the car, while I recorded our conversation from the back seat. 'Thembi asks if we can rather meet at another spot. It is about five minutes away. I'll show you.'

I nodded, but I was starting to prickle with unease. We had already been driving for about 20 minutes, and had gone around almost the entire perimeter of Thabong. Albert was animatedly conversing with the cameraman in isiXhosa, wildly gesticulating with one hand while indicating with the other the direction in which we needed to drive.

'Albert,' I ventured. No reply.

'Albert, you better not be fucking with us.'

He didn't respond.

'Is Albert your real name?'

'Yes, yes. My name is Albert, but I'm not giving you my surname.'

It suddenly hit me. We had been led on a detour to buy Thembi enough time to abscond or possibly remove incriminating evidence from their house. I silently berated myself for my naivety.

'Give me your phone now,' I barked. 'And turn around,' I instructed the cameraman. 'We are going back to the house.'

I pressed the redial button on Albert's phone. There was a voicemail message: 'The number you have dialled does not exist.'

Our most prudent course of action would have been to drive directly to Thabong Police Station to lay a charge of assault against Albert. But Thembi was our target and we needed to foil her efforts to get away. When we returned to the house, with the help of Nozukile's canny sense of direction, Albert opened the passenger door and dashed up the driveway towards the kitchen, with Nozukile in furious pursuit. As I ran towards them, a high-pitched voice joined the fray. It was Thembi.

'Get out of here, all of you!' she shouted.

Albert bellowed: 'Why have you caused trouble for me again, you filthy whore?'

He punched Thembi on the side of her head, knocking her to the floor. She whimpered as his shoe connected with her ribs.

'Leave her alone. I'm calling the police!' I screamed as I searched for my cellphone, which was in the car.

'Now you all fuck off or I will shoot you.' From Albert's tone, I suspected this was no scare tactic.

'Okay, let us just calm down. No violence, please,' I implored. 'I simply want to talk to Thembi, to give her a chance to set the record straight.' Turning to her, I told a whopper of a lie: 'We are doing you a favour, because both the SAPS and the Thai police are already investigating you.' I held her panicked gaze, paused for dramatic effect, and then uttered 'please'.

Slumped in an armchair, Thembi suddenly seemed very small. Her hand was massaging the spot where Albert's shoe had connected. I almost wanted to touch her shoulder, comfortingly. Then I noticed the golden chain mail draped around her wrists and neck, the miniature chandeliers glistening from her ears, her coiffed hair, the haute couture contours of her dress, her artificial nail tips, manicured, buffed and polished siren red. Thando's plea, shortly before the prison bell had commenced its torturous wail, came back to me: 'Please tell my mom that I'm sorry. I love her. I didn't know ...'

Another New York minute.

Thembi sighed. 'Okay, I will speak, but only with you.'

*   *   *

Long ago she might have been pretty. But years of excess – too much make-up, too much 'gravy' – had smudged the fineness of her features. She eyed me warily as I perched on a couch in the lounge of her house. I secretly switched on the spycam that was peeking coyly from my pocket. Could she tell that I was faking a sense of authority I didn't really possess? And I wondered who she thought I was. Hopefully a cop and not just a pesky journalist.

The following extracts were taken from my covertly recorded interview with Thembeka Veronica Nwabude:

'Why was Thando in Bangkok? What was she doing there with you?'

'I don't know what you are talking about.'

Thembi shifted restively, fingers scratching between the folds of her décolletage, as though picking at an invisible spot.

'Thando was staying with you when she was arrested for drug trafficking. You forced her to carry the heroin and you were responsible for her being bust.'

'No, no. Not me! I wasn't even in Thailand when she was arrested. I was in China. The first I heard of it was when her mother contacted me from Thabong. I was also very shocked.'

'How many times have you been to Asia this year? Twice, three times?'

Silence.

'Perhaps your passport will refresh your memory.'

'I don't have a passport now. I lost my passport. I am waiting for a new one. I am supposed to be back in China.'

'A common ploy, of course. You conveniently lose your passport. Unquestioningly, Home Affairs replaces it and the suspicions of customs officials are not alerted by the multitude of foreign entry stamps in your passport.'

'No, really you are wrong. I go to China to buy clothes. I know nothing about Thando, really.'

'Please, Thembi. You are the only one who can help her. She is going to remain in prison, possibly for the rest of her life. She's 23 years old. She's a little thing.'

'I'm telling the truth.'

Thembi then stood up and walked across the room. My spy camera followed her as she agitatedly rearranged the bric-a-brac – an unexpectedly modest collection of ornaments – adorning the television cabinet. I continued: 'She has told the embassy and the police everything, so whatever your involvement, you now have a small window of opportunity to help her, to maybe get her sentence reduced.'

'I'm willing to help but about what?'

'She needs you to acknowledge that it was not her fault, that she was forced into this, by the syndicate.'

'No, not me. I'm telling you the truth. I knew nothing. It was her mother who told me she was caught.'

'How could you not know? She was staying with you, together with four other South African mules. And there was another woman who met her at the airport.'

'Huh?'

I attempted an alternative interrogative approach: 'When Thando was staying with you in Bangkok, what was she doing?

'Nothing.'

The scratching now extended across to her armpit.

'Do you know there is a warrant out for your arrest in Thailand? The Bangkok police know more about you than they do about Thando. The only way they will go easy on you is if you tell me the truth about who is the top guy in the drug syndicate. And if you assist the cops with their investigation, if you testify for the state, you will be protected. No charges will be brought against you.'

Thembi's face stiffened. She held my stare, challengingly.

Poker-faced, I continued. 'You knew Thando's mother, Nozukile, was unemployed, that Thando had a limited education. That's what made her all the more vulnerable to your deception. That's why she agreed to go to Thailand, to help improve her family's situation, especially her mom's. How can you live with yourself knowing you have destroyed not only one life but that of an entire family, and – given the fact that you have been doing this for several years – probably many families? How can you start to make this right?'

For a second, it seemed that my words might have connected with whatever threads remained intact in an otherwise frayed moral conscience. She sank back into the chair and sighed. 'It's true, she was with me, she was there in Thailand. I can't say it's false. But, about the smuggling, really, I was not there, believe me. I was also very shocked when I heard about that.'

'She was staying there with you for a month before her arrest! You were her guardian. How does a young woman who has never travelled beyond South Africa's borders, knows no one in Bangkok and cannot speak the language, get caught up in drug trafficking?'

Again, silence.

'And what about the other South African girls staying with you?'

'Who?'

'Four of them.'

'Staying with me? No!'

'And the woman who fetched Thando from the airport because you apparently were unable to meet her?'

Again, that impenetrable stare.

'And you never returned to Bangkok from China after Thando was arrested? You flew home to South Africa?'

She swallowed. 'I went back to Bangkok.'

'So why didn't you visit Thando in prison? After all, she had been staying with you, up until her arrest?'

'Because I don't know Bangkok. I didn't know where to find her.'

'Yet you travel to Bangkok frequently.'

'No, I only stay there on my way to China. I stay in a flat, then I travel to China, then I come back.'

'The apartment is owned by a Nigerian, isn't it?'

'No.'

'Can you give me the address in Bangkok?'

'I forget it, but I can show you the dresses I bring back from China to sell in Thabong.'

I followed her into a bedroom decorated in white, rose and lavender frills, and heart-shaped embroidered pillows. I felt a little unsettled by the feminine decor, unlike the vulgar opulence I would have expected from the boudoir belonging to a rapacious member of a global narcotics syndicate. Apart from her flashy car and gaudy body trinkets, nowhere in this residence was there visible evidence of the material fruits Thembi must have reaped from her role in this illicit enterprise. From the cupboard, she pulled out a single designer suit sheathed in a Hugo Boss cover.

'Is this what Thando was supposed to bring back to sell?'

'Yes.'

'So you bought her a ticket to Bangkok to bring back knock-offs you purchase in China. That doesn't make sense.'

'No, she wanted to go herself to Bangkok but she didn't have enough money for a ticket.'

'So a woman who has never been out of the country wants to go to Bangkok and you provide her with the ticket and a passport. And what did you get in return?'

No response.

I was now nipping at her heels with the shrill persistence of a terrier.

'She couldn't swallow the heroin pellets, so you and the syndicate set her up. I suppose the only other alternative was to kill her. A kinder fate, you probably thought, was to make her the decoy, the sacrifice, the one who gets bust with a smaller quantity while the others slip through. And when you went to China, you had arranged for her to fly to Hong Kong with the other mules, except that, unlike the others, she was not going to make it through.'

'She went to Hong Kong? When?'

'You know she was on her way there when she was arrested. Before then, you had sent her to Laos.'

Thembi looked away, shaking her head.

'No, I was not there, really, God knows, I was not there.' Then the bravado: 'So, tell me, where did I get these things, these drugs, from?'

'The police told me where you get them from,' I faked. 'You are not directly involved in the distribution. You do the recruiting or, as in Thando's case, the entrapment. Thando said you occasionally do a drug run yourself, for some extra pocket money.'

She laughed: 'No, not me.'

We had reached a predictable impasse and I felt depleted. She had repeatedly contradicted herself and lied, initially about her responsibility for luring Thando to Thailand, not to mention her feigned ignorance of Thando's involvement in drug smuggling.

But I had no proof, and Thembi could easily ascribe the inconsistencies and contradictions in her responses to linguistic miscommunication: English, after all, was not her first language. I had only the allegations put to me by a terrified young woman trapped in a Thai prison and those of her despairing, almost destitute, mother to implicate her.

I made one last-ditch desperate attempt to extricate something incriminating: 'Okay, Thembi, if you have nothing to hide, you will cooperate with us. I want your details: mobile number, ID.'

She dutifully wrote the digits on a piece of paper I provided, mumbling, 'I have nothing to hide. I know nothing.'

Then I remembered. Thando had told me Thembi's surname: Nwabude.

'What is your surname, Thembi?'

'Mfenqe.'

'Please write down your surname.' I shoved my hands into the rear pockets of my jeans to control their trembling.

Thembeka Veronica Nwabude, aka Mfenqe, had unwittingly provided the first concrete, and potentially crucial, piece of evidence that she might have something to hide.

* * *

26 February 2009

An online search via a professional tracing service initially yielded modest but promising returns: Thembeka Veronica Nwabude, aka Mfenqe, travelled under two passports, and had lived in Gauteng, the Eastern Cape and the Free State. There was a default judgment against her name, but no information that definitively linked her to a transnational drug syndicate operating between South Africa, Thailand and China.

That is, until I sent an image taken during my covertly filmed interview with her to Alex, my Liberian contact in Bangkok. He had spotted her there at least twice in the last year, he wrote to me. Alex then emailed me a photograph of Thembi cavorting at one of the Nigerian bars in Sukhumvit, in the company of several men, one of whom was Steve, Doreen's captor and pimp from the Eastern Cape. Almost incoherent with elation, I called Nozukile and Thando's boyfriend. I told them about the imminence of Thembi's demise and the certainty of Thando's release.

Nozukile uttered a single word: 'Hallelujah.' Then, her daughter, Sipho, took over, informing me of at least two other young women in Thabong who had also been coerced by Thembi into drug trafficking. Nozukile would make contact with them and their families, she promised. But, fearful for their lives, they might be reluctant to speak.

I then emailed my findings to the NPA, the Department of International Relations and Cooperation (DIRCO), Interpol, the South African Embassy in Thailand and the International Organization for Migration.

The only acknowledgment of receipt that I got was from Anna Mokoka, the then consular attaché at the embassy, who had initially alerted me to Thando's case. Mokoka sent me an email on 27 February 2009 saying that she would 'pass on the information to everyone'.

That was the last correspondence I was to receive from the South African Embassy in Bangkok.

10

PATRICIA

By her own admission, Patricia Gerber is a conventional housewife and mother. She adores her three children. In her spare time, she does embroidery and makes porcelain dolls. It suits her dogged temperament to repeatedly position the materials, and to model and sculpt features from formless matter. The dolls she crafts are life-sized, the details of their bows and frilly bonnets intricately woven and their verisimilitude to real baby girls belies the fragility of the material that moulds them. That is Patricia Gerber: delicately meticulous, tenacious and possessed of an enduring desire for bows that are symmetrically tied and for neat endings. She is also shy, she confesses, and doesn't find it easy to converse.

Since 2005 Patricia has turned her attention away from embroidery and doll making. Her energy is now directed at confronting heads of departments, ministries and entire governments. And she has learnt to live in grief. Since 2005 each waking moment and every ounce of energy in her petite frame have been focused not only on bringing home her own son, Johann – who was imprisoned in Mauritius – but on lobbying to release every South African incarcerated abroad.

'That woman has an agenda,' Dayanand Naidoo, then director of consular services at the Department of Foreign Affairs, had told me during an interview in February 2009. Although extremely engaging off the record, on camera Naidoo had spouted the official line with the frozen impenetrability of the programmed politician, in a manner that would not tolerate counter-argument, riposte or any of the rubber bullets I had stashed in my journalistic arsenal: 'In terms of the Vienna Convention of 1961 ...'

I knew by now the rules of that decrepit agreement by rote: 'respect for sovereignty'; 'non-interference; 'judicial processes'. Between recited sound bites, after instructing the camera to be switched off, both Douglas Gibson (whom I had interviewed at the South African Embassy while I was in Bangkok) and Naidoo had uttered compassionate comments about South African citizens arrested abroad. These momentary lapses into humanity would then be masked behind facades that seemed to resemble the art of the embalmer more than living, breathing human beings.

Naidoo had visibly bristled when I mentioned a lawsuit I had heard was being brought against the Department of Foreign Affairs, as well against as the Department of Correctional Services and the Department of Justice by a certain Patricia Gerber from George, in the southern Cape. The intention of her case was to force the South African Government to furnish reasons as to why it would not consider entering into a prisoner transfer treaty with any other country.

'She definitely has an agenda,' he repeated.

'Of course she would have an agenda!' was my retort. 'She is a mother and she wants her son to be close to her while he serves his sentence, so that she can at least visit him. And that goes for every other South African family suffering from the incarceration of their children, siblings and parents overseas.'

But my time was up. And with that implacable mask Naidoo had politely dismissed me. I had nothing personal against him. Like any other government functionary, he was simply 'doing his job'. Articulating any opinion that might alter the structure of the policy tower, no matter how faulty its foundations, was not part of his job description.

* * *

Still heady from the recent success of my impromptu sting operation on Thembi, Thando's recruiter, I made contact with Patricia Gerber and arranged to meet her in George, where she lived with her husband, Johann (senior) in a leafy, affluent suburb. On numerous occasions Patricia had been mentioned to me by Shani's sister, Joan, who had described her as a feisty woman who would stop at nothing to bring her son home. I'd subsequently heard about the court application she was about to bring against our government and, although I admired her tenacity, I was initially sceptical about the outcome. How could a private citizen with limited financial resources challenge the state on policy issues and hope to win? But Patricia had elicited the support of several legal heavyweights, renowned human-rights lawyers, and constitutional and international law experts. These included Wim Trengrove, professors John Dugard and Max du Plessis, as well as Advocate Anton Katz, all of whom had written compelling arguments concerning South Africa's constitutional obligations to all its citizens, both within and beyond our borders. They underscored section 35 of the Constitution, which asserts the rights of South Africans arrested, detained or accused of committing a crime not to be compelled to make any confession or admission that could be used in evidence against them; to be brought before a court as soon as is reasonably possible; to be detained in conditions that are consistent with human dignity; to communicate with, and be visited by, their family; to have the right to a fair trial, which includes the right to be tried in a language that they understand or, if that is not practicable, to have the proceedings translated.

I was convinced that Thando's treatment, along with hundreds of South Africans in foreign prisons, was in flagrant violation of the Constitution. Notwithstanding the emotional resonances behind Patricia's plea for a prisoner transfer treaty, I was sure that she would be able to strengthen the theoretical framework for such a treaty to be implemented in the near future.

After meeting Nozukile, I had had several telephone conversations with Patricia, during which she had rattled off a litany of complaints about the intransigence of Foreign Affairs and the indifference on the part of our embassies towards South Africans imprisoned abroad. I was curious to meet this woman who, from the little I knew of her, didn't fit the profile of a typical human-rights activist. But that was one of Patricia's many formidable strengths: her ability to confound expectations. The second was her pit-bull-like tenacity. The third was an uncompromising belief that somehow she would succeed in bringing home not only her own child, but all of the South Africans locked up abroad – there were well over a thousand of them.

'In the beginning, it was only about Johann,' Patricia admitted to me when we finally met at her home in 2009. 'But I began exploring, and I realised that there was something even more important at stake than the desire for a mother to be near her child. I learnt that all was not as it seemed, that there were sinister reasons behind many of our citizens being arrested overseas for drug smuggling, and that a battle for justice needed to be waged on behalf of every South African imprisoned abroad.'

In August 2005, Patricia's 20-year-old son, Johann, had been detained in Mauritius for drug smuggling. Johann's own account of his case initially reads as one of the more bizarre narratives in the convoluted anthology of drug runs. Yet the more one examines the circumstances surrounding drug mules and the sacrificial lambs of the drug trade, the more credible his account of events becomes.

Johann had been contacted by a young woman who had sent an SMS to Johann's older sister, asking her for his mobile number. She invited Johann for coffee. When they met for the first time, she had enticingly told him of an all-expenses-paid holiday she had enjoyed in Mauritius. She offered him a similar trip to paradise. All he would have to do, she assured him, was take money out the country on behalf of some offshore investor and hand it over to someone on the island. The suspicions of the young

Johann, who had never even been to Cape Town, let alone out of the country, were not alerted.

He told his mother that he had been invited to Mauritius, but did not reveal the terms under which he would be travelling. It was only two months after his arrest, when Patricia had finally tracked down his recruiter, who was working in a shopping mall in George, that she learned of the forex ruse.

'I introduced myself to her and she immediately said she would tell me everything,' Patricia recounted. 'Of course, she denied knowing anything about drug smuggling but said she had taken over currency to Mauritius and that this was the bait that lured Johann.'

Patricia continued: 'The drug run happened three weeks after Johann had met the young woman. Johann caught a bus to Cape Town, but he did not know that he was expected to swallow heroin pellets until it was too late for him to back out. When he protested about taking drugs overseas, the syndicate to which she belonged warned him that they knew where his family lived and that should he back out, his family would bear the consequences.'

'Was Johann himself using drugs?'

I tentatively asked the question because I had become familiar with the dogged loyalty shown by the families of convicted drug mules, like Shani's sister, Joan, and their refusal to believe that their loved ones might have been complicit in their own demise. To a woman like Patricia Gerber, living in a sedate seaside town, drug addiction would be an affliction that happened to other people's children, not hers. But in the four years since Johann's arrest, Patricia had acquired a street wisdom that has equipped her emotionally for any possibility.

'I have no idea if he ever experimented,' she said. 'But I am convinced that he would never have got involved, voluntarily, in drug dealing or trafficking.' She added, 'When I gave the information about his recruiter and the syndicate to the police – names, telephone numbers and addresses of those who coerced him – they did nothing to either apprehend her or the syndicate members.'

I asked whether Johann could have alerted the authorities, either at the airport, or once he had passed through customs, or on the aeroplane, to request their assistance.

'When he was in prison he told me they had warned him that he was being watched constantly. He was also accompanied on the flight to Mauritius by another young woman called Thelma, who happened to be the best friend and flatmate of the recruiter. Thelma carried nothing, but she was to accompany Johann to make sure he didn't get away or alert the authorities.'

With 920 grams of heroin pellets in his stomach, Johann caught the flight to Mauritius with Thelma, his handler. After landing, he was sent to a hotel but given nothing to expel the pellets. Then, after being instructed to meet contacts at a certain location, he was informed that the plans had changed. He had stomach pains and was told by a contact to go to a pharmacy to purchase medication to expel the pellets. By then, he was feeling sick from the drugs in his stomach and terrified that they would leak and kill him. Thankfully, he managed to expel them. There was still no one waiting to collect the heroin. The plans kept changing and they kept leading him on a wild-goose chase. Patricia said, 'He was so traumatised, so exhausted that eventually he threw all the drugs into a flower bed at another hotel.'

Someone was clearly watching, because shortly after his attempt to dump the heroin, the police swooped on the hotel and arrested him, together with Thelma. She told the police that Johann had brought the drugs over, and protested her innocence, but, like Johann, she was also convicted and sentenced. Her sentence was seven years, two years shorter than Johann's.

According to Patricia, the Mauritian police drafted a statement that read more like a confession and which was clearly signed under duress.

'Johann was placed in solitary confinement, in a windowless cell, in total darkness for 23 days, where he was told he would remain unless and until he signed it. It was that "confession" that convicted him when his case finally went to trial two years later.'

The two years he had already spent in prison awaiting trial were not taken into account in his sentence.

Johann's version of events, conveyed to the police by his desperate mother, were greeted with derision by Senior Superintendent Devan Naicker. During a 2007 interview with M-Net's investigative programme, *Carte Blanche*, Naicker claimed that intelligence sources had confirmed that Johann was a drug addict and that he had racked up a hefty debt with his drug merchants, which he settled by muling.

'When we'd asked [Johann] if he'd been forced, whether a gun had been held to his head, he said "no",' Naicker had insisted. But when asked whether he had actually taken a statement from Johann, Naicker conceded that he had not. Naicker subsequently went on to head the Hawks Narcotics Unit.

The South African syndicate members implicated in Johann's case were never investigated, interrogated or charged. Patricia had been notified by South Africa's Department of Foreign Affairs and instructed to give them any information pertaining to Johann's recruiters and syndicate connections, but after a month she had still not been contacted by the South African Organised Crime Unit of the SAPS or Interpol, so she started asking questions: 'I contacted the Department of Foreign Affairs to find out when we would be notified about the investigation, only to be told that we must not investigate on our own, as this could be very dangerous and we could be killed by the drug-syndicate barons.'

She continued: 'I went to the public prosecutor in George to find out what charges could be brought against the syndicate. I was told there was nothing I could do.'

Undeterred, Patricia began the painstaking process of understanding everything possible about the Mauritian penal system. She discovered:

- At the time of Johann's arrest, there were 27 South Africans in Mauritian prisons. Many were still awaiting trial, some for as long as five years; most of them were women.

- In many of the cases, the Mauritian Anti Drug and Smuggling Unit (ADSU) had been alerted by its South African counterpart, the Organised Crime Unit, beforehand of their arrival in Mauritius and had been waiting for them. However, no effort had been made to apprehend them before they left, even though it was known they were carrying quantities of drugs through customs at OR Tambo International Airport.
- Many of these South African citizens were not drug mules, but were recruited under false pretences, coerced or blackmailed into becoming decoys. Ninety-nine per cent of those detained in Mauritius were first-time offenders. Once they were arrested, the South African Government and their consular representatives in Mauritius adopted an out-of-sight, out-of-mind approach.

* * *

In October 2005, two months after Johann's arrest, Patricia flew to Mauritius to visit her son and make contact with ADSU to enquire whether Interpol was investigating the syndicates who had recruited the decoys arrested in Mauritius. She was told that Interpol does not get notified and does not investigate these matters.

But Patricia was privy to some of the operational methods and collaboration between ADSU and its South African counterpart: 'ADSU's deputy superintendent, Padiachy, informed me that intelligence on the drug syndicates responsible for couriering heroin into Mauritius was given to his friend, an officer at the Organised Crime Unit in Pretoria by the name of Superintendent Jan Rehder. Deputy Superintendent Padiachy also told me that all the South African mules arrested in Mauritius are connected to the same syndicate.'

On 25 November 2005, Patricia contacted Superintendent

Rehder: 'I introduced myself and told him my son was detained in Mauritius, to which he replied, "Oh! There are many such cases." I told him that I was given his mobile number by Deputy Superintendent Padiachy in Mauritius. The phone went quiet on his side and I thought he had hung up. He then said that he could not talk to me, as he was not in the office. I asked if he would be in the office on Monday and if I could call him then. He said that I could.'

Patricia continued: 'On Monday 28 November 2005, I called him around 10 am. When he answered his mobile and heard it was me, he shouted, "What do you want from me?" I told him I was phoning to get information regarding my son's case and was told that "it has nothing to do with me".'

In early December 2005, Patricia was approached by an Interpol spokesperson, Senior Superintendent Tummi Golding. According to Golding, the global policing body did not possess a single file of any South African detained in Mauritius. This was a bizarre admission, given Patricia's repeated attempts to notify Interpol. Golding then asked Patricia to contact the families with whom she had interacted, and ask them to make statements concerning the detainees. They were to meet in Cape Town for this purpose. Yet, according to Patricia, after faxing a letter of confirmation as to when she would be in Cape Town to meet with Interpol, she received a call informing her they did not require any statements from either her or the other family members. The stated reason: Interpol does not investigate such cases.

Patricia supplied me with a list of the Interpol officials with whom she had spoken, all of whom confirmed the above, namely that the Organised Crime Unit of the SAPS, not Interpol, investigates cases of transnational drug trafficking. If this was the case, the former were clearly not doing their job and the latter were somewhat confused about theirs.

Augmenting Patricia's disquiet was the whereabouts of a confidential letter she had faxed to the Cape Town office of the deputy minister of Foreign Affairs, Sue van der Merwe. In the letter,

Patricia had requested an investigation into the reasons why – given that the mule and decoy recruitment took place on South African soil, as did the crime of smuggling the drugs – South African citizens were not apprehended by South African border-control police before boarding flights to Mauritius. Was it the result of some cosy arrangement between the SAPS, customs officials and the Mauritian authorities that the mules, and decoys in particular, would get arrested overseas?

Predictably, perhaps, she never received a response from Van der Merwe. She subsequently learnt that her missive had been intercepted and redirected to the Pretoria office of the Department of Foreign Affairs.

'From an intelligence perspective, letting the decoys go through without apprehension, only to be bust when they land, just doesn't make sense from an investigative perspective,' said a contact from the former South African Narcotics Bureau (SANAB), with whom I had collaborated on numerous drug stories in the past. 'Your best means of busting the syndicate top guns is to follow the trail upwards from the mules. So if you know they are carrying drugs and are about to board a flight, you figure out a way of subtle interception, or put them under surveillance, at the airport, or on the flight, when they land, when they make the drop. You don't just let them leave, knowing they are going to be set up and locked up, and the key thrown away.'

Although the mules and decoys have only a limited comprehension of their role in the transnational narcotics industry, interrogating them would nevertheless provide vital intelligence, enabling the police to unpick the syndicate hierarchy, one link at a time, along the entire supply chain.

'Even if they aren't aware of every component in the chain of command, sure as hell they are going to be able to lead you to the next link and the next will lead you upwards,' explained my SANAB source. His logic was inescapable: for every decoy arrested, several mules pass through; for every decoy, there must be a recruiter – someone either familiar to the decoy, or a connection of a connection, or a stranger who provides the bait in the form of a trip overseas, or a lucrative employment opportunity, or a seemingly innocuous request to deliver a package to a friend overseas. Once the recruiter is found, the path becomes less circuitous: every recruiter has at least one mule making the occasional drug run. The mules making the runs do not usually get bust. They are the ones carrying substantially larger quantities of drugs than, say, the 920 grams of heroin found discarded by Johann Gerber outside a Mauritian hotel. And for every mule that makes a drug run, either with a handler or alone, there is a contact or handler on the other side. The handler's job is to relieve the mule of the cargo, which will then be weighed and repackaged, ready for distribution among drug consumers. With the correct intelligence and surveillance, the police could nab the recruiter and handler, simply by shadowing the mule.

So why don't they do this?

My SANAB contact shrugged: 'Maybe they think the mule is small fry. Letting him or her fly out of South Africa is easier than undertaking a more complicated investigation that demands time and resources. It's so much easier to let them land in the long arm of the law in another country. And it means one mouth less to feed in our prisons.'

Patricia had reached this disquieting conclusion herself. She began to investigate why substantial leads to the trail uncovered by her own son's arrest had been ignored. Was it because the supply chain was too insignificant to warrant expending any investigative energy? Or, more ominously, was it because the leads might reach the upper echelons, those with political clout? The downright defensiveness and unmasked belligerence of Foreign Affairs officials and police officers suggested the latter. But without the certainty of knowledge, Patricia's questioning continued relentlessly, years after her son's conviction.

'This is not just about my son, Johann,' she insisted. 'This is about every South African incarcerated abroad for drug trafficking. Many are innocent or set up, I believe. And those who have willingly committed this crime, I am not advocating we let them off the hook: they broke the law, they should be punished. But we, as their families, are also being punished. We are incarcerated alongside, in a prison without walls, but a prison nevertheless.'

She told me about the suicide in 2005, of Karel Burger, a South African citizen awaiting trial in Mauritius. After his death, his body lay for four months in a Mauritian mortuary before finally being cremated because his family could not afford to provide him with a decent burial.

'I shudder at the thought of what his family went through, imagining his fear, loneliness and pain,' she said.

Patricia returned to Mauritius on 3 April 2006 to visit Johann and meet with the South African High Commissioner at the South African Embassy in Mauritius. She protested that South African citizens were being subjected to severe human-rights violations by being detained for years before their cases went to trial, that prison conditions were deplorable and rehabilitation non-existent. She also criticised the embassy's feeble efforts to even marginally alleviate the plight of their citizens.

'The high commissioner became extremely angry with me and shouted that he detests it when someone insinuates that they sit on their backsides,' she laughed ruefully.

Then, later that month, it seemed as though the South African authorities were spurred into conducting some form of investigation. This was prompted by the letter Patricia had faxed to the then deputy minister of Foreign Affairs, Van der Merwe, who instructed the national police commissioner and Interpol head, Jackie Selebi, as well as Inspector Martin van der Merwe of Organised Crime in George and Ludwig Odendaal from Bloemfontein to travel to Mauritius to take statements from all the South Africans incarcerated on the island. However, both Van der Merwe and Odendaal were subsequently excluded from the team. On 25 July 2006, the remaining delegation was joined by Senior Superintendent Devan Naicker, Superintendent Jan Rehder and Senior Superintendent Brian Oppalt from the Organised

Crime Unit in Pretoria. The task team remained in Mauritius from the morning of 25 July until 29 July. They were accommodated in a five-star resort. During their investigation they spoke to a total of six South African detainees, but did not take a single statement.

Yet in September 2006, Naicker stated that soon after their return from Mauritius they had arrested the syndicates respons-ible for sending the South Africans to Mauritius in the first place.

Patricia disputes this: 'Without statements, there is no mandate to investigate and, secondly, the people who recruited my son are all still free. They were never even questioned by police.'

She added: 'I knew then that I had to take this as far as I could, to expose the duplicity and fight for the rights of fellow South Africans, particularly their constitutional right to a fair trial.'

In the space of a year, this shy middle-class housewife and mother became the spokesperson for hundreds of families whose loved ones were in prison, not only in Mauritius, but worldwide. She also became an expert on South African law and a formidable combatant of every official – both South African and Mauritian – who she believed had the power to shift government policy on South Africans incarcerated abroad. Every conversation with ministers and law-enforcement operatives was recorded, every letter diligently photocopied. She built up a dossier of malfea-sance, corruption, incompetence and sheer indifference on the part of public servants and police officials mandated to address the plight of their citizens locked up in a foreign country.

She provided her information to the Scorpions and the NPA. The response was a resounding silence. It was then that she decided to take on the South African Government in a bid to pressure it to sign a prisoner transfer treaty with Mauritius.

'Mauritius was keen to sign such a treaty, as had been Thailand, Brazil and India the previous decade. It was just our government that refused to budge.'

* * *

After two years of approaching every government department and receiving no response, Patricia decided to seek legal advice. Her determination to bring the government to task was fuelled by two separate incidents involving drug smuggling, both on board SAA flights. The crews of both flights were detained at Heathrow when drugs were found in their luggage. But instead of being arrested in London, standing trial in the UK and, if convicted, forced to serve their sentence in the country where the crime was committed, these suspects were flown back to South Africa and were arrested on home soil.

It seemed incomprehensible that while the police allowed so many South Africans carrying drugs to leave South Africa without any intervention, preferential treatment was given to suspected drug smugglers because they happened to belong to the crew of South Africa's national carrier.

'That just reinforced the government's double standards,' Patricia wryly commented.

In August 2009, Patricia filed an application against the Government of South Africa for its failure to properly consider her request that the government enter into a prisoner-exchange agreement with the Government of Mauritius, or to provide sufficient reasons for its decision not to do so.

Then, in January 2010, while the court was deliberating on the merits of Patricia's application, the Sheryl Cwele drug-trafficking case hit the news. Not only was Cwele a prominent member of the Hibiscus Municipality in KwaZulu-Natal, she was also the wife (albeit the then estranged and subsequently divorced spouse) of the minister of state security, Siyabonga Cwele. The latter was one of the architects of the 2013 Protection of State Information Bill (a draconian piece of legislation designed to muzzle the media and stifle the public's access to information on the grounds that such information should remain a matter of state security).

The general response to Cwele's arraignment was one of incredulity. Here was the wife of an influential politician, who held the key to state secrets, embroiled in crimes with a notorious Nigerian drug syndicate. This could seriously compromise the minister's office, it was felt. Equally gobsmacking was the fact that Minister Cwele lacked the integrity to fall on his sword in the wake of what was a dismal failure on the part of national intelligence to catch even a whiff of his wife's nefarious activities.

And it was not South African police investigations that exposed Cwele and convicted her and her accomplice, Nigerian drug dealer Frank Nabolisa. (For years, the latter had been a regular 'delivery man' to Johannesburg's northern suburbs and had notched up a reputation for distributing top-grade cocaine. Nabolisa had apparently cosied up with SAPS officers with a nose for South American snow.) It was the evidence of two young women, Charmaine Moss and Tessa Beetge, but mainly the courageous testimony of Beetge's mother, Marie Swanepoel, which finally brought Cwele and Nabolisa to account.

Cwele had attempted to recruit Moss as a mule, with the promise of employment. Moss had ultimately seen through the ruse. However, Beetge had fallen for it and had subsequently been arrested in Brazil for drug trafficking. Text messages exchanged between the convicted mule and Cwele, presented to the police by Swanepoel, provided the incontrovertible proof of Cwele's crimes. Swanepoel had served as her daughter's proxy in court, providing eloquent evidence that corroborated and complemented the damning cellphone and email documentation she had had the foresight to keep. Cwele and Nabolisa were each sentenced to 12 years' imprisonment. Both appealed and their terms were increased to 20 years. However, the Constitutional Court reversed their sentences to the initial 12-year duration. But, unlike Beetge, who, until her release in March 2014, had suffered in a Brazilian prison, far from her devoted mother and children, Cwele would serve her prison term close to her loved ones. (In 2013, when Swanepoel suddenly succumbed to illness and died, her heartbroken daughter was not even able to attend her funeral.)

The injustice of it enraged Patricia and her anger was aggravated by a call she received in February 2010 from Colonel Izak Ludick, the investigating officer on the Sheryl Cwele/Frank Nabolisa case.

'He told me he is the person who calls the foreign airports and tells them that he has information that a certain South African citizen is in possession of drugs and then they are arrested,' Patricia explained. 'I told him that he was defeating the ends of justice ... Why was he not arresting them before they left South African soil or when they returned, instead of notifying the foreign airport so they get arrested in a foreign country?

'He cut our conversation short and told me he would ask his secretary to give me his fax number and if I had any information, I must send a fax.' She added: 'I am still waiting for the secretary to contact me.'

On 29 and 30 March 2010, Patricia's application was finally heard. The presiding judge took almost nine months to pass judgment before her case was dismissed with costs. She filed an application in December 2010 for leave to appeal the judgment in the Constitutional Court.

On 11 February 2011, without even going to court, the Constitutional Court judges dismissed Patricia's application for leave to appeal because there would be no prospect for success.

Patricia's attempts to force the government to enter into a prisoner transfer treaty were by no means the first lobbying efforts on the part of private citizens. As Shani's sister had told me, she had drafted a treaty in 1998, together with Robert McBride, which Selebi had unceremoniously dismissed.

And subsequently, in 2000, an opposition Member of Parliament had attempted to move a private member's bill on the transfer of offenders between South Africa and other countries. This was documented in research published by Jamil D Mujuzi, a lecturer at the University of the Western Cape's Faculty of Law. In order for such a treaty to be ratified, there must be consensus between the three ministries directly affected: DIRCO, the Department of Justice and the Department of Correctional

Services, as well as between South Africa and the proposed country. Although the bill presented in Parliament was supported by some officials from the Department of Justice, the Department of Correctional Services vehemently opposed it because, according to Mujuzi, the bill 'did not provide for the cost of the prisoner transfer, and it was not clear if the Correctional Services Act was to be amended to empower the minister of Correctional Services to administer the law relating to the transfer of offenders'.[1] The ANC also expressed hostility towards the possibility of such an agreement on the grounds that it would be 'problematic since it would allow for prisoners' sentences to be reduced', there were the 'financial implications of housing South Africans presently imprisoned overseas' and 'there was some concern over which crimes would be covered under the draft bill'.[2]

The authorities' reluctance to adopt a prisoner transfer treaty is despite the fact that South Africa has been signatory to two international treaties: the UN Convention against Transnational Organized Crime and the UN Convention against Corruption. Both treaties encourage countries to sign prisoner transfer agreements.

So, if South Africa is obliged to comply with the recommendations of these two treaties, why the ongoing intransigence? The Sheryl Cwele case had confirmed Patricia's suspicion that it suited certain individuals in government to keep drug mules and decoys arrested for drug trafficking out of South Africa because the paths leading from their recruitment, drug trafficking and arrests might lead to the doors of the politically connected.

Patricia has remained unbowed. Learning to utilise the media like a seasoned pro, she has participated in live television broadcasts and radio chat shows, and written articles published both by the local media and their Mauritian counterparts. She has doggedly forced police and government representatives to acknowledge that conditions in many of the prisons in which South Africans are currently detained, including those in Mauritius, Thailand, Hong Kong, Brazil, Peru and Venezuela, do not comply with basic principles of human rights, as prescribed by South Africa's Constitution and organisations like Amnesty International.

She has also established a website, Locked Up in a Foreign Country (www.lockedup.co.za), to expose the horrors endured by South Africans locked up abroad, and to serve as a deterrent to the naive, the desperate and the greedy.

Her crusade has taken a harsh toll. The legal fees for the court application have consumed virtually all the Gerbers' savings, forcing her and her husband to put up their bucolic home for sale. Her health and that of her husband have also suffered.

13 December 2012

The news was not good. The doctor had just informed Patricia that she needed to see him the following day – three days after another biopsy had been performed on her breast – and that she should bring along her husband.

On 18 December 2012, five days after our interview, Patricia Gerber underwent a partial mastectomy. She had asked the South African Embassy to inform her imprisoned son of her impending surgery. On 17 December Johann had been permitted to call her from prison. He was distraught at the news of her illness but, as always, she reassured him.

We chatted again in George's Mediclinic, where she was undergoing further tests to determine whether the cancer had spread. Fortunately, it is stage one.

'I know I will get through this,' she insisted. 'I'm not afraid of the diagnosis. I'll take whatever treatment is meted out to me. It's just that I want my son home with me. And I'm scared I won't see him again.' Her voice cracked.

In that moment, the titanium will of the woman who had

launched a relentless crusade to force the South African Government to sign a prisoner transfer agreement seemed to buckle. I drew her close to me as she cried softly on my shoulder.

11

SABELO

February 2010

It had been a year since I reported my findings on Thembeka Nwabude/Mfenqe to the NPA, the South African Embassy in Bangkok and Interpol. My information contained Thembi's multiple passport numbers and surnames, her telephone details, the covert prison recording of my conversation with Thando, as well as my recorded confrontation with Thembi. I had even elicited the collaboration of an informant in Thabong: an illegal gold prospector who had fallen on tough times and relied on the small change I meted out in return for occasional nuggets of intelligence. But there wasn't much in the way of information on Thembi's movements. She seemed to be lying low. She was operating a tuck shop in the township, across the road from a local high school – the ideal recruitment ground for young township women with limited means and *Top Billing* dreams.

As confirmed by telephone calls that I made under the pretext of having called the wrong number, Thembi hadn't changed her mobile number, which indicated she had been neither sufficiently unnerved by my interrogation nor fazed by any threat of further criminal investigation. Meanwhile, the NPA's Charmaine Labuschagne and I had been exchanging correspondence. However, the NPA was powerless to intervene, Charmaine had explained, unless charges were laid against Thembi and an arrest made. The investigation was not so much in a state of limbo as in paralysis.

That is, until Sabelo Sibanda switched on SABC3 and watched the repeat broadcast of 'Time of the farang (foreigner)' – a *Special Assignment* programme I had produced shortly after my return from Bangkok in February 2009. Although I had withheld Thando's identity, the narrative had served as the thematic fulcrum of the programme. My angle – that her case should be reclassified as one of human trafficking – had generated considerable interest and controversy. After all, this was not the conventional approach to drug mules and it raised uncomfortable questions, not only about the South African Government's constitutional obligations to its citizens incarcerated abroad but also about its reluctance to enter into a prisoner transfer treaty on humanitarian grounds.

Born in South Africa but raised in Zimbabwe, Sabelo was an internationally respected human-rights lawyer, who had represented victims of severe human-rights violations, including detention without trial, and torture, perpetrated by Zanu-PF. He had been based in Musina but at the time of the *Special Assignment* repeat broadcast, he was working for the Johannesburg Legal Resources Centre and just happened to be attending a conference on human trafficking held at the SABC in Auckland Park. He immediately raised Thando's case as a classic example of coercion, transportation and exploitation – the three criteria identified by the UN and the International Organization for Migration to classify victims of human trafficking. A *Special Assignment* colleague of mine, Busisiwe Ntuli, was attending the conference and she gave him my details.

I was elated when he contacted me. I believed that Sabelo's reputation as a formidable legal brain and humanitarian champion would most certainly add credence to the link between human trafficking and drug trafficking. On our way to Welkom, Sabelo was emphatic about the imperatives for reviewing Thando's case: 'It is obvious that Thando had no criminal intent. But what was she to do? A young, uneducated woman in a foreign country, surrounded by people she thought were her friends, mentors, but who are actually dangerous criminals. She can't speak Thai and she can't contact the embassy because her every move is being watched by a ruthless syndicate enforcer. As she said in the tape recording, she can't even go to the shops alone. And she is there with other young women who are being used for the same purpose but who, unlike her, are possibly willing participants. And when she refuses to swallow the heroin pellets, the syndicate knows she is their biggest liability: the weakest link in the chain.'

Sabelo was also convinced that by ignoring Thando's situation, and that of hundreds of South Africans, the government was flouting not only section 35 of the South African Constitution, which protects the rights of arrested, detained and accused South Africans, but also the rule of law and the principle of legality. Its rationale for refusing to sign a prisoner transfer treaty was, at best, disingenuous and, at worst, nonsensical.

Sabelo continued: 'The government is not obliged to sign a prisoner transfer treaty and might very well have sound reasons for not doing so. But to justify its refusal in terms of the Vienna Convention's clause on non-interference in the judiciary of a sovereign state makes neither legal nor moral sense. The one has nothing to do with the other.'

In fact, it is precisely because of its policy of non-interference that a prisoner transfer treaty would be the logical step forward. At the very least, repatriation of its citizens, even to correctional services at home, would contribute towards fulfilling the state's constitutional obligations by providing an alternative for South Africans in countries that still carry the death penalty or where horrific prison conditions exist. Also, in terms of its own 2005 White Paper on Correctional Services, the government advocates the promotion and fulfilment of human rights, as well as the need for rehabilitation and reintegration of offenders back into society. This cannot be achieved if citizens remain imprisoned in a foreign land for the duration of their sentences.

Sabelo wanted to globalise the relationship between drug trafficking and human trafficking, and to galvanise the South African
Government into protecting the rights of its citizens, not only
within our borders, but also beyond. He fervently believed that,
particularly in the case of Thando, even if a review of her status
could not be accomplished in Thailand, at the very least she
should be allowed to serve the remainder of her prison sentence
at home.

We had arranged to meet Nozukile and her cousin, Jabulani
Khubone, who was proficient in English, outside the NPA offices
in Welkom. I barely recognised Nozukile: hair coiffed, make-up
meticulously applied, wearing full-length traditional dress, she
looked almost regal in anticipation of the moment in which
she would witness justice being done for her daughter. Sabelo
had already met her several weeks before in Thabong and had
reassured her that Thando would not be forgotten, and that,
if necessary, he would make representation to President Zuma
himself, the SADC leaders and the UN. But, first, Nozukile
needed to lay a charge against Thembi. Charmaine Labuschagne
had interviewed Nozukile the week before, and had advised her
to lay a charge of drug trafficking and kidnapping. Charmaine
warned her, however, that it would be risky to open a docket at
Thabong Police Station in case Thembi was well connected – a
valid concern, given the fact that she was apparently feared by
many in Thabong.

At the time, long-awaited legislation on human trafficking had
yet to be passed. A bill was drafted in 2006, but since then it had
been gathering dust in the vaults of Parliament. At the beginning
of 2010, the bill on the Prevention and Combating of Trafficking
in Persons had been passed by the National Assembly onto the
Parliamentary Portfolio Committee of Justice and, finally, onto
the National Council of Provinces before it was due to land on
the desk of President Zuma for signing. Yet the bill had remained
with the National Council of Provinces for two years. Meanwhile,
incidents of human trafficking, particularly of children and young

women from neighbouring countries into South Africa, and even from the rural hinterland, had spiked alarmingly. The complexity of the crime had been demonstrated in the myriad of ways in which it had manifested: through sexual exploitation, forced labour and, more recently, drug trafficking. Although South Africa is a signatory to the UN Protocol on Human Trafficking, which identifies the three criteria for classifying victims of this crime that Sabelo had referred to in the case of Thando, South Africa is not compelled to enforce these protocols at home. This is despite the fact that the circumstances of several convicted so-called mules, like Thando, fit this classification.

Charmaine and her assistant greeted us affably, but as we were about to sit she dropped a clanger. Apparently, although she couldn't remember the actual date, a man from Thabong had recently laid a charge of drug trafficking against Thembi.

'Who is he? With whom did he lay the charge? Has Thembi been arrested?' I asked.

Charmaine shook her head. 'No, there was some, um, irregularity.'

Charmaine called Welkom Police Station and was put through to an officer, a certain Captain X. The conversation that followed was disconcerting, to say the least: 'What do you mean you didn't ask for his name or his address? And why wasn't the charge followed up?'

I gestured to Charmaine that she should request to see the captain. I harboured a growing suspicion as to the identity of the complainant. I suspected it was Albert, Thembi's lover in Thabong. There had probably been another violent spat and Albert had exacted revenge by pimping Thembi to the police. But after make-up sex, he had probably retracted his allegations.

The captain arrived shortly after the telephone conversation with Charmaine, and both Nozukile and I noticed that Jabulani looked visibly concerned when he appeared. Without dwelling on the police officer's gross dereliction of duty, I enquired why he hadn't taken down the details of the complainant.

131

'Uh, he's made complaints before because he was having a fight with her and then withdrew them.'

'But didn't you think to at least take down his details because there might have been some measure of truth to his allegations?'

The captain glared at me but said nothing.

'There is another complainant who wishes to lay a charge against the same woman.' Charmaine struggled to contain her irritation. 'Make sure you take down her details properly when she comes to the station.'

Charmaine then motioned to the police officer to leave.

'The levels of corruption are very worrying,' she said, as he slammed the door.

After the officer had left the room, Jabulani blurted out, 'I know that man. He takes bribes.'

Charmaine nodded but proceeded to caution me: 'I respect the fact that you have an investigation to conduct and a programme to broadcast, but at this stage, given the sensitivity of the situation, I would appreciate it if you made no mention of what just happened in this office in your programme. It could compromise an already complicated case.'

I reluctantly acquiesced. The main priority was for Nozukile to formally lay charges of drug trafficking and kidnapping against Thembi, which she did.

Afterwards we celebrated over KFC and ginger beer.

'We thought that because Thando is not someone famous, influential or rich, she would be forgotten,' said an elated Jabulani. 'But now we know she will be helped.'

'Thank you,' said Nozukile, embracing Sabelo and me.

* * *

'It is an obscenity for a democratic government to sacrifice the human rights of its citizens to the altar of diplomatic and trade relations,' Sabelo said to me during the ride back to Johannesburg.

He added: 'There are two courses of action: we need to make representation to the Thai Government to change Thando's classification from perpetrator of drug trafficking to victim of human trafficking. Alternatively, the South African Government must sign a prisoner transfer treaty with Thailand, so that she can return home.'

Three months later, members of Bloemfontein's Crime Intelligence Division visited Nozukile to take another statement from her. Simultaneously, a certain Colonel Gerber, from the Organised Crime Unit in Bloemfontein contacted me and offered to meet me in Cape Town with members of his team to discuss the case against Thembi. I prepared all my evidence pertaining to my findings on Thembi's drug-trafficking role, which I handed to him, over prego rolls and a beer at a Portuguese tavern in Green Point. Why I should recall the culinary trivia of that meeting is beyond me, but what I do know is that, after the meeting, I was never able to enquire about developments, or the lack of them, in the investigation into Thembeka Veronica Nwabude/ Mfenqe. My calls to Colonel Gerber's personal mobile number went immediately to voicemail and he responded neither to my increasingly shrill SMSs, nor to the desperate messages I left for him at Bloemfontein's Crime Intelligence Division.

Initially I was completely nonplussed by his evasiveness. But, by June 2010, it had become evident through media reports and confidential sources that Bloemfontein's Organised Crime Unit was nostril-deep in the stench of its own corruption. In May 2010, for example, six Free State police officials and eight Nigerians were arrested on suspicion of belonging to an international drug syndicate linked to an international network. The suspected officers were charged with deliberately losing or destroying dockets and transporting drugs in official police vehicles. Gerber, who had a reputation for honesty, probably had his hands too full cleaning out the effluent in his own back yard to be able to focus his energies on the malfeasances of a mid-level drug syndicate recruiter in a Free State township. I had to acknowledge that Thando Pendu, imprisoned in a country thousands of miles away, would not feature high up on the priority list of Bloemfontein's Organised Crime Unit.

As for Sabelo, there was no further direct contact between us, save for a diminishing number of phone calls, which eventually ceased altogether. He had resigned from the Legal Resources Centre to focus all his energy on Zimbabwean nationals who were victims of severe human-rights violations in Zimbabwe. I certainly couldn't blame him: Sabelo had always been motivated by a relentless, uncompromising sense of justice, and his first priority was his own people. However, that did not mitigate my disappointment. I needed someone like him with both the clout and the will to globalise Thando's case and, by extension, those of other South Africans who had unwittingly been lured, or coerced into the narco-lair. The buoyancy I had felt after Nozukile had laid charges against Thembi was rapidly deflating.

My confidence in maintaining Thando's presence in South Africa's collective consciousness had also waned. I was subscribing to the cynicism of the media cycle. I rationalised that the vagaries of journalism entailed catering to the limited attention span of a nation in the throes of a form of post-traumatic stress, caused in part by an unrelenting onslaught of bad news on substance abuse in South Africa. Consumption of crack cocaine, heroin and, more recently, tik had spiked terrifyingly, particularly among the youth. Fuelled by society's zero-tolerance veneer towards substance abuse, the South African public, I suspected, would probably not buy into the argument that some of those arrested as drug mules were actually victims of human trafficking.

There were other stories to tell and different battles to fight, I figured. Apart from the occasional funds I transferred to Bangkok for Thando, at the request of her still-devoted boyfriend, her story was packed in Tupperware and stashed in my mental freezer, labelled 'story on ice'.

Sometimes I would receive distraught calls from Nozukile, in faltering but agonisingly intelligible English: 'Thando! What are you doing about Thando?'

I also received a text from Thando's sister, Sipho: 'U tell us you want to save Thando, that u r interested in da truth. But u r only interested in da story.'

I did what any survivalist in the techno age would do: I erased her message, hoping that the literal act of deletion would expunge it from my conscience.

After all, I am just the messenger …

12

THROUGH THE LOOKING GLASS, DARKLY

January 2012

'Two years is a long time in a wilderness of mirrors.'

So wrote Ivor Powell, a friend and former colleague at the *Mail & Guardian*. In 1999 Powell had swopped journalism for the role of senior investigator for the now defunct Scorpions. He was also the author of the controversial Browse Mole report, an explosive, albeit officially discredited, investigation conducted during 2006 into the possibly dodgy sources of funding for the then Deputy President Jacob Zuma. The report had caused a political storm when it was leaked and Mbeki's office went into PR overdrive to minimise the political fallout. An investigation was conducted, not on the veracity of the information, but on the source, led by Siyabonga Cwele, who headed the Joint Standing Committee on Intelligence. Whatever the conflicting narratives surrounding that report, I had no doubt of Powell's unwitting role. He had been the fall guy in a merciless battle that had pitted Mbeki's coterie against Zuma's cabal, and the Scorpions, South Africa's elite crime-busting unit, against the more potent machinations of politics and cadre cronyism.

While one cannot unring a bell, one can certainly smother the sound under a cushion of conjecture and lies, especially when truth is often a battle of perceptions. Powell's phrase 'a wilderness of mirrors' seemed to encapsulate my own increasing sense of disorientation, dismay and unease. While the events he described bore no direct relationship to my own investigations, they underscored the intertwining of the criminal-justice system with South Africa's intelligence services and their entrenchment as the principal means by which to secure and sustain political hegemony. The sobering moral of Powell's tale seemed to be that the act of pissing off certain politicians was at the top of the priority-crimes list, ahead of rhino poaching, drugs and human trafficking. I felt suitably warned.

Since Sabelo Sibanda had accompanied me to meet Nozukile in February 2010, my investigations into human trafficking had ceased. My focus had shifted predominantly to coverage of service-delivery protests, particularly in the Western Cape. This change of investigative lanes was partly for pragmatic reasons. The SABC was traversing yet another troubled rite of passage, fiscally speaking. Big-budget assignments entailing overseas travel were being eschewed in favour of more localised stories, produced in a quicker turnover time, and mainly predicated on 'development' angles. Simply put, this journalistic approach entailed documenting the conditions within the country and the challenges affecting the future of South Africa as an emerging nation, as well as highlighting proposed government projects to encourage growth and development. But while such stories can serve as powerful tools for local education and empower-ment, the dangers inherent in development journalism include succumbing to attempts by government to exert its influence on story content and to suppress information that is deemed to be unsupportive of the ruling party.

It wasn't only within the SABC's increasingly Fawlty Towers

that the choking potential of censorship was being felt. The reconception of the infamous Protection of State Information Bill in 2010 by President Zuma's security cluster, particularly Siyabonga Cwele, served to reinforce the threat of a noose tightening around the neck of media freedom.

At that point, I wasn't particularly keen on sticking my own neck out any further. What had initially appeared as a relatively straightforward assignment, an investigation into South African drug mules incarcerated abroad, like Shani Krebs, had become a project characterised by opaqueness. Drug trafficking intertwined with human trafficking was certainly not a new phenomenon, but while it was one matter to access global statistics on these crimes, for me it was entirely another to learn first-hand of desperate South Africans like Thando Pendu being deceived into becoming decoys for drug syndicates. Yet the clear determination I had felt after hearing Thando's tragic story of deception was becoming a smudged horizon line blanketed by smog.

Like John Foster Dulles, the 1950s Cold War–era counterintelligence chief who had coined the phrase 'wilderness of mirrors', I was experiencing increasing difficulty separating disinformation from truth. Concrete leads and credible contacts had disintegrated like chalk dust beneath a blackboard duster. I hadn't yet succumbed to the paranoia that can afflict even the most sanguine of drain sniffers, but I was starting to suspect that if I rapped too assertively on doors that had been slammed on my efforts to find some restitution for South Africans like Thando, I, too, might be banished into the wilderness of journalistic exile.

I harboured no elevated sense of my own significance, journalistic or otherwise, but I had long felt unnerved by the subtle and not-so-subtle fault lines reshaping South Africa's political cartography. The treatment of Ivor Powell and the way his report had been received had reinforced my sense of disquiet. As a journalist, I was witnessing political battles that fed off ongoing fissures in the ruling party, replete with mendacity, filibustering and accusations of conspiracies, into which I – along with my colleagues in the media – was often drawn. In short, I feared the growing preponderance of larger egos in lesser men, whose conduct was in danger of reducing the Rainbow Nation to murky shades of grey.

Many South Africans believe, somewhat ingenuously, that South African history can be carved, like the Christian calendar, into BC ('Before Change') and AD ('After Democracy'). However, even during the years just before and after 1994, while the country still glowed in the light of liberation, the spectres of both reactionary and revolutionary authoritarianism were hovering. Deals were being made with the devil, the secrecy of which did not seem to be bound by a statute of limitations. Unanswered questions surrounding the assassination of Chris Hani, the arms deal, and the degeneration of a culture characterised by transparency and open-door rapprochement into one of defensive plutocracy, even kleptocracy – these were just some of the unsightly stains seeping through democracy's duvet.

Then came the discrediting of the NPA, Zuma's victory over the Mbeki camp at Polokwane and the subsequent withdrawal of corruption charges against the then future president of our democratic republic. This was followed by Mbeki's ignominious ousting before the end of his presidential term, and his foe's ascent to the most powerful post in the land. Zuma soon surrounded himself with a security cluster comprised of loyal brigands from his exile years as head of Intelligence. In the wake of the Nkandla scandal, many would now argue that the stage was set for a licence to lie and loot. Although buttressed by the South African Constitution, a vibrant media, active civil society and an independent judiciary, our rule of law, whereby justice is meted equally and fairly to all, was being insidiously undermined through interference, particularly when the politically powerful or connected were implicated.

In the interim, the National Intelligence Agency had been pitted against the Scorpions, contributing to the dismantling of the latter and the further fracturing of the NPA's credibility.

The decline of the prosecuting authority's independence has been widely attributed to its leadership crisis, which began after Advocate Vusi Pikoli, former NPA Director of Public Prosecutions, was dismissed for attempting to arrest and prosecute former Police Commissioner Jackie Selebi for corruption. Despite several attempts to postpone proceedings, Selebi's trial eventually got under way. It was not, however, a case in which the truth would out, but rather a trial characterised by lies and prevarication, in which drug lord Glenn Agliotti was let off the hook in exchange for testifying against Selebi, his former friend. Selebi was ultimately convicted and sentenced to 15 years. However, his sentence was subsequently converted to medical parole, prompting a public outcry and widespread accusations of political interference.

The relationship between Agliotti and Selebi has been extensively documented by the media: South Africa's erstwhile national police commissioner and head of Interpol in the pocket of a narco-banker and trafficker. Nothing novel about that in the global annals of corruption. However, the pact between Selebi and Agliotti, and the debacle characterising both of their trials (the latter's for the murder of mining magnate Brett Kebble) magnified the crevices in our criminal-justice system and the culture of cronyism that had begun to erode the NPA's ability to act decisively against South African drug cartels and their international allies. The devil's deal with Agliotti underscored this. The unabridged anthology of Agliotti's nefarious dealings has yet to be published. But one of the more widely covered claims to his infamy had been his involvement in a shipment of 1.2 million mandrax tablets, with a street value of over R100 million, which was exposed in 2002. Although convicted for his complicity in that deal, in exchange for his testimony against Selebi, Agliotti never served a day behind bars.

Agliotti's entrepreneurial interests would subsequently include receiving and repackaging narcotics, as well as other contraband, via his import company, in conjunction with his trans-shipment business. In 2006 the Scorpions exposed the latter when they busted an Agliotti-linked organised-crime syndicate in Alberton, seizing more than a ton of compressed dagga and over 700 kilograms of hashish. The sources of the consignment – with a street value of over R200 million – included Swaziland, Lesotho and Iran. However, this stash represented merely the proverbial tip of a literal iceberg: the illicit cargo included crystal meth, otherwise known as 'ice', alongside the more traditional commodities of the contraband trade, such as mandrax and cocaine. Court documents of the marathon trial, which lasted until April 2011, alleged that the syndicate had been operating since 1997 when the two major players, Stefanos Paparas and Lesley 'Bob the American' Curtis, met in Swaziland, where they were both, allegedly, already embroiled in the narcotics trade. Curtis was allegedly affiliated to an Afghanistan kingpin, while Paparas and his father, Dimitrio, supposedly held keys to the gate of Glenn Agliotti's shipping business. Two more South Africans, with extensive knowledge of smuggling routes in southern Africa, were also recruited, as was Stanley Poonin, a Lenasia businessman, who allegedly provided the transport for the local distribution of the drugs.[1]

For ten years, the syndicate allegedly eluded the authorities in Canada, Paris, Dubai and Bangkok, until their arrest at a warehouse in Alrode, in 2006. Ironically, it was the Scorpions' investigation into Brett Kebble's murder that led them to the multimillion-rand stash. In what became dubbed the 'Paparas trial' and 'the biggest drug trial in South Africa', Agliotti cut another deal with the NPA. In terms of section 105A of the Criminal Procedure Act, he admitted contravening section 5(b) of the Drugs and Drug Trafficking Act and, in exchange for his freedom, agreed to testify in the trial of his co-accused.

Five years later, in a shock judgment, all three accused in the Paparas drug-trafficking trial were acquitted due to a broken chain of evidence and the unreliable testimonies of Agliotti and Clinton Nassif, who were both later charged, tried and acquitted of Brett Kebble's murder.

So how had the state scuppered such a major opportunity to

bring to justice organised-crime leaders involved in racketeer-ing, trafficking and even murder? Who was complicit, co-profiting and for how long?

These were the rhetorical questions posed to me in 2011 by Trevor Bailey, a retired undercover cop. Bailey had been at the forefront of investigations into dodgy diamond, gold, arms and drug deals conducted by members of both South Africa's old guard and liberation movements, in cahoots with organised-crime cartels. Although he had left the force in 1992, Bailey maintained that long before his departure the stage had been set for the granting of political quid pro quos by certain individu-als whose names would become synonymous in post-apartheid South Africa both with political power and crime.

'It was an expedient arrangement and had nothing to do with ideals or ideological affinities,' Bailey explained. 'It was a rela-tively simple arrangement – "We need cash to fund the liberation struggle and you need a foothold to expand your own 'business' interests, now and in the future. Let's talk."'

The principal target of Bailey's investigations had been Vito Palazzolo, who had ingratiated himself both with the apartheid government and ANC leaders. In 2009 the fugitive banker from Switzerland and alleged Mafia heavyweight, was sentenced to nine years *in absentia* for allegedly laundering drug money linked to Sicilian Mafia bosses Bernardo Provenzano and Salvatore 'Toto' Riina. Palazzolo had been nicknamed the 'pizza man' because of his complicity in the 'pizza connection' investigation, which exposed a $1.6 billion heroin- and cocaine-smuggling operation between 1975 and 1984, using New York pizza outlets as a cover.[2] Since his arrival in South Africa in 1986, on a false passport obtained from a fellow inmate at a prison in Switzerland, Palazzolo had evaded prosecution, at first through protection afforded him by the apart-heid regime (specifically by the National Party's East London MP, Peet de Pontes, who was convicted of fraud and racketeering for facilitating Palazzolo's original South African passport and docu-mentation). He also befriended Oupa Gqozo, then military leader of the Ciskei. In fact, so tight were Gqozo and the pizza man that the former had granted Palazzolo citizenship of his puppet state. The transition to democracy was accompanied by the dismantling of the homeland, or Bantustan, system – the cornerstone of apartheid's 'separate development policy' – and the granting of South African citizenship to all homeland 'citizens'. As the holder of Ciskei citizenship, therefore, Palazzolo was the recipient of a South African passport and he rapidly became close to the new political and economic elite.

To prevent the rot spreading, in 1996 Nelson Mandela ordered an investigation into police links with Palazzolo and other crime bosses. The man hand-picked to head this Presidential Investigative Task Unit, was André Lincoln. By the following year, the unit was itself under investigation by old-guard policeman Leonard Knipe, on the orders of South African Police Commissioner George Fivaz. In 1998 Lincoln's team was disbanded and Lincoln arrested for fraud, theft and his allegedly improper relationship with Palazzolo. After Lincoln's arrest, the probe into Palazzolo was taken over first by Piet Viljoen, followed by a multi-agency team, which included the prosecution authorities, the Scorpions and the National Intelligence Agency. At the time, Dumisani Luphungela, an operative of the National Intelligence Agency in the Western Cape, was the agency's representative on the team's management. However, in 2002 Luphungela, by then head of the National Intelligence Agency in the Eastern Cape, was suspended following allegations that he had taken a bribe from Palazzolo.[3] His alleged double dealing was exposed by Knipe, who had since joined a private-investigation firm owned by Fivaz, who had retired as police commissioner. Knipe and Fivas just 'happened' to be doing a security installation for Palazzolo when the information came to light.

In 2006 David Malatsi, former MEC for Provincial Environmental Affairs and deputy social-development minister of the Western Cape, was found guilty of corruption for accepting a R100 000 bribe from Count Riccardo Agusta, a close friend of Palazzolo.

This was to secure approval for the development of the R550-million Roodefontein Golf and Country Estate, in Plettenberg Bay.[4] Agusta went on to purchase Palazzolo's Franschhoek estate amid allegations that his company was linked to the allegedly corrupt sales of helicopters in the controversial arms deal.[5] Malatsi's suspension from office exacerbated the spat that had been dubbed post-apartheid's cold war between old-guard cops and their ANC counterparts. In fact, relations between several erstwhile political enemies had become so icy that many in the National Intelligence Agency regarded the enmity as a greater risk to national security than South Africa's burgeoning criminal networks and disquieting culture of political nepotism.[6]

Because the sources of political-party funding are protected by law, it is impossible to determine to what extent party and campaign sponsorship serves as a route for legitimising corruption and money laundering, and whether political-party benefactors represent criminal interests. In the case of Palazzolo, it is widely alleged that out of gratitude for his financial largesse during election campaigns, he received special protection from the ANC government, despite extensive police investigations into his alleged involvement in gold, diamond and drug smuggling. More than ten years ago, Palazzolo began disposing of his South African interests, transferring them to his sons and shifting his regional base of operation to Namibia, where he allegedly owned farms and mining rights. He had close ties with the Angolan and Namibian governments.[7]

It was only in March 2012 that, by default, he would finally be nabbed in Thailand by the Italian police, who had been on his trail for decades. Despite his protestations of innocence, a Thai court ordered his extradition to Sicily for retrial. But until he finally gets deported, Palazzolo has apparently exchanged the power of pizza connections for pad Thai and become the big pecorino of Bangkwang maximum-security prison. Not a shabby status for a man who still insists his principal skills lie in banking, not bilking.

Bailey cannily observed that Agliotti was cut from the same cloth as the pizza man: charming, dapper, dangerous and extremely powerful, and with some of the new South Africa's most high-profile politicians in his pocket. Jackie Selebi had obviously been one of them. As mentioned, in his capacity as director general of the Ministry of Foreign Affairs, a post he held from 1998 to 1999, Selebi had shot down at least one attempt on the part of members of Foreign Affairs to sign prisoner transfer treaties with other countries. And, in June 1999, during discussions between South Africa, Brazil and India concerning prisoner transfer agreements, Selebi insisted that his department would no longer sign treaties advocating the transfer of South Africans convicted for crimes abroad.

*   *   *

Even before Selebi had assumed the helm of diplomatic relations with South East Asia, however, the South African Government seemed to have adopted a contradictory approach to the issue of its citizens incarcerated abroad.

'It was an era of such possibility, this open-door policy towards a world that had locked us out because of apartheid, an opportunity to build trade and diplomatic relations,' recalled Roel Goris, South Africa's first ambassador to Thailand, referring to the halcyon days following South Africa's first non-racial democratic elections. In 2012 I had contacted Goris and he had agreed to be interviewed for another *Special Assignment* investigation into drug trafficking.

'And, then, the spate of arrests ... all these young South African men and women ... one after the other, many of them literally on the eve of our democracy. It was horrifying, heartbreaking. We were completely unprepared for how to deal with it,' said Goris.

The incarceration of South Africans in foreign lands for drug trafficking was nothing new, however. Before 1994 several had been arrested, including high-profile names like South African gospel singer Deborah Fraser. Apprehended in Brazil in 1986, Fraser was released a year later only after the intervention of a delegation of South African artists.[8] During the era of South Africa's pariah-hood, these intercessions were inevitably low-key and conducted out of the public spotlight.

But that obviously changed with AD, or 'After Democracy'. After 1994 the trickle of South Africans caught in Thailand alone became an unprecedented deluge: Vanessa Goosen, Shani Krebs, Dawn van Niekerk, Nila Duginov, Octavia Malevu, Catherine Nobantu Mnyengeza, Gladys Naidoo, Eugene Noboto, Bongekile Ncala, Eugene Nwaneri, Sean Allen, William Bosch, Uwes Dauberman and William Geldenhuis.

These people were strangers to one another, but most had a common denominator: an association with Nigerian syndicates either operating from South Africa, Thailand or both countries. And both countries, still basking in the glow of their new relations, were uncertain about how to cope with the situation. Said Goris: 'The Thai authorities were very shocked by these arrests, as was our government, especially at a time when we were signing bilateral trade and diplomatic treaties. Madiba's leadership had heralded a policy of forgiveness and reconciliation, not only between former foes but towards all South Africans. So, very much on the agenda was the signing of a prisoner transfer treaty that would enable South Africans convicted of crimes overseas to serve two-thirds of their sentences in South African prisons, close to their families. I was mandated to look into this and draft a treaty.'

The Thai Government was also supportive of a treaty, Goris emphasised. He extracted the most practicable components from existing treaties between Western democracies and presented his draft at a meeting of heads of departments at the Department of Foreign Affairs. The response left him shaken.

'It was completely shot down. I was told that South Africa could not afford to be seen to be soft on drugs, that our prisons were already overcrowded, and that these people must stay where they are.' He added: 'I understood the rationale behind their arguments, but what they refused to consider was that it wasn't only about the individuals themselves. Their families were enduring unimaginable anguish.'

Goris subsequently left the diplomatic corps and quit politics altogether. As mentioned previously, by the time Mbeki came to power, another draft prisoner transfer treaty had been placed before Selebi by Robert McBride. Together with Joan Sacks, McBride had been instrumental in drafting it. Selebi had literally torn it up, recalled Joan. And McBride had corroborated her account, as well as the pragmatics behind such a treaty. 'Forget the humanitarian component, for a moment,' he had advised. 'From a solely intelligence perspective, it made sense to bring home South Africans imprisoned overseas, instead of leaving them there for decades. They would, at the very least, be able to provide information and evidence on the syndicates that had recruited them.'

Selebi subsequently exchanged his diplomatic post for the more prestigious mantle of South Africa's top cop, national police commissioner, and from 2002 until 2006, he was head of Interpol. In 2004 he disbanded SANAB, the specialised narcotics unit inherited from the apartheid era. Whatever the ideological leanings of the bureau, the unit had excelled in covert intelligence gathering and investigations. It made little sense therefore to incapacitate the very organ trained to counter the narcotics supply chain.

Selebi knew naught about policing. As the product and beneficiary of the post-apartheid culture of cadre deployment, operational expertise was evidently not a prerequisite for the job – something unprecedented in any democratic policing agency. Selebi's ignorance was matched only by his arrogance, an undisguised penchant for expensive shoes and a yen for mixing with the cream of the world's criminal classes.

For example, a *Noseweek* article published in May 2007 recounted how a 'notorious smuggler' of electronic goods by the name of Imram Ismail had established close ties with Dawood Ibrahim, an internationally infamous drug trafficker, who, at the time, was credited with being the most wanted man in India.[9] Ibrahim first came to South Africa in 1994, after having been deported from Zambia for suspected drug trafficking. He spent the next three years hobnobbing with some old spies, as well as members of South Africa's new political and social elite. His social peregrinations were diligently documented in publications such as *City Press*, the *Mail & Guardian* and *Noseweek*.

In the *Mail & Guardian* website of 11 May 2007, Sam Sole, Nic Dawes, Stefaans Brümmer and Zukile Majova wrote: 'Ismail was close to Pakistani national Rehan Syed, who was suspected of involvement in smuggling drugs and other contraband and was investigated by the police for dealing in stolen cars, a case in which Selebi himself allegedly got embroiled.'[10]

As had also been exposed in a *Noseweek* article that was published at the same time as the *Mail & Guardian* story, Selebi and Ibrahim had both been guests of Ismail at a World Cup cricket match at Centurion in 2003, 'a year before Selebi was made Head of Interpol. Ismail also moved in the same South African circles as Vijay "Vicky" Goswami',[11] the self-confessed erstwhile business partner of soccer tycoon Irvin Khoza. As reported in several South African publications, a Lear jet operating from Lanseria Airport during the 1990s, allegedly owned by Khoza, once belonged to Goswami.[12]

The southern African underboss for Ibrahim, Goswami belonged to the Indian Kanu Mafia and was their drug-smuggling kingpin in Africa before he was imprisoned in Dubai on drug charges in 1995. After being deported from Zambia in 1994 for alleged drug trafficking, Goswami had gravitated to South Africa, where he spent the next few years mixing with high society, while allegedly expanding his narcotics and money-laundering businesses. He was sentenced to life imprisonment for smuggling 843 kilograms of mandrax and establishing two factories in Dubai to manufacture the drug. In December 2012, he was released on parole. In

November 2013, the *Mail & Guardian* reported that he was allegedly planning to return to South Africa to reclaim property he had acquired before his departure for Dubai in 1995.[13]

Goswami was also linked to a lighter-weight drug dealer called Robert 'Rocks' Dlamini. The latter belonged to a Soweto-based drug cartel whose principal source of income – apart from carjacking and gunrunning – was smuggling mandrax tablets from India. Dlamini disappeared in 1995, after a R1.5 million drug deal went sour and shortly afterwards, Goswami fled South Africa. Another of Dlamini's comrades, Chris Meela, died in mysterious circumstances shortly after being admitted to Johannesburg General Hospital with pneumonia in 1998.[14]

Then, there was Chika Odimara, a Nigerian drug lord who also consorted with Selebi, as well other select members of the inner circles occupied by both the old guard and the new. According to several media articles, he was particularly chummy with corrupt staff members at the Department of Home Affairs, who produced identity documents for Nigerian illegals allegedly embroiled in cocaine trafficking.[15] Odimara had been the recipient of one himself. He also allegedly cajoled crooked senior bank officials to siphon funds from company accounts to finance cocaine smuggling between South Africa and neighbouring countries, using teenage girls as drug mules. This was in 2001, and Odimara's thriving drug-trafficking trade had been operational for several years in both Gauteng and Colombia.

At the time, I was investigating Odimara's links to a Johannesburg-based lawyer by the name of Welile Thabethe, who had defended Trevor Tutu, Desmond Tutu's son, in 1999 on tax-evasion charges. A journalist with the Independent Group and I had simultaneously, albeit separately, received documentation detailing a request allegedly penned by Thabethe in 1994 that Odimara be permitted to enter the country to attend a 'roof-wetting party'. This was puzzling, given the fact that Odimara was already in possession of a South African identity book. Thabethe confirmed that he had invited Odimara to his house in 1994 but had had no further contact with him. However, these claims were contradicted by media reports of several cars being registered in Thabethe's name, which were allegedly bought by Odimara. The Nigerian's alleged transnational crime spree was subsequently suspended by his deportation from South Africa in January 2001.[16]

By then, the rot spawned by police corruption had set in. As criminologist Liza Grobler documents in her 2013 book *Crossing the Line: When Cops Become Criminals*,[17] in the last 15 years the system has become toxic, rendering the phrase 'crime intelligence' oxymoronic in the extreme. Ever since the late 1990s, Grobler writes, budgets earmarked for vital intelligence resources have been systematically plundered for political and criminal expediency, entrenching a culture of dysfunctionalism and distrust.

Even in an imperfect world, intelligence services should have clear mandates and regulations, minimising manipulation and abuse of our security apparatus. Of course, in the murky world of spooks, deceit is all too often the dominant discourse. But by 2000 the fractious relationship of the conflicting factions between and within the National Intelligence Agency, the SAPS and the Scorpions had reduced effective intelligence gathering to a crudely paranoid battle of spy vs spy.

The unfortunate consequences of increased political interference in South Africa's intelligence and police services can be located in the debacle around the suspension, reinstatement and renewed suspension of former crime-intelligence boss Richard Mdluli. In 2011 Mdluli was suspended, facing charges of fraud and corruption, as well as his alleged involvement in the murder of his ex-lover's husband, Oupa Ramogibe. Although an inquest cleared him and he was reinstated, Mdluli was again suspended in 2012, pending the court application to review the withdrawal of the criminal and disciplinary charges against him. In September 2013, the North Gauteng High Court ordered the reinstatement of criminal and disciplinary charges against him. This ruling was rapidly followed by the suspension of the acting head of police, Nhlanhla Mkhwanazi, for having withdrawn the charges against him in the first place. As one might say in a cynical variation on a struggle theme, '*o escândalo continua*' (the scandal continues) ...

Long before Selebi shut down the specialised drug-fighting unit in 2004, confidential documents attested to the systematic undermining of SANAB's ability to function effectively against the more than 250 international criminal cartels operating openly in South Africa. For example, a 1996 SANAB report noted that of South Africa's 97 key points of entry, a mere 17 were controlled by the SAPS, customs and immigration, and 33 airports were not covered by any of these agencies. SANAB's findings were that South Africa had turned into a trading and transit route for the worldwide drug cartels and organised-crime syndicates, resulting in increased weapons dealing, mineral smuggling, human trafficking, prostitution and other criminal activities within and beyond South Africa's borders.[18]

This much was underscored by several reports published, for example, in 2007 and 2011, by the UNODC.[19]

And within a 'target-rich environment', as South Africa is often described by international law-enforcement agencies, government can quickly squander its limited crime-fighting resources and achieve only marginal results if it uses them to pursue the wrong targets.[20] Predictably, arrest statistics would rise temporarily, and a few of the dealers and couriers would be successfully prosecuted. But without effectively utilising information or intelligence to identify the size and nature of the threat, assess its consequences and design an effective strategy to impose the most damage on the criminal organisation, the fundamentals of the illicit infrastructure would remain intact.

A case in point was Mauritius in 2000. By that year, the island had joined the pantheon of drug destinations earmarked by transnational drug syndicates using South Africans as mules or decoys, or both.

'Drug addiction in Mauritius – particularly from heroin – had become a major problem,' revealed a contact from the Organised Crime Unit, who had been with SANAB before its disbandment and who requested anonymity. 'The drugs would be sourced along the Golden Triangle or from Pakistan, and transported to South Africa as a transit stop. From here, the mules would smuggle them into Mauritius. But we were told very specifically not to apprehend the South Africans before they left for Mauritius, even though we knew they had drugs on them.'

I asked my contact who had instructed SANAB to act thus, and why. Suffice it to say, the orders came from high up. And who was holding the reins at Interpol and SAPS? Selebi, of course!

He added: 'It was easier this way. It made the drug mules Mauritius's problem, not ours.'

Meanwhile, South Africa was becoming a gangsters' paradise – a veritable thugocracy where Russian, Italian, Asian, Israeli, Nigerian and Moroccan gangsters consorted with their local counterparts, forming alliances with street gangs and security bosses in order to carve the topography of this country into criminal fiefdoms.

This may read as a simplistically linear summary of South Africa's underworld trajectory over the last couple of decades. But it was enough to make me realise that, viewed from the prism of a bewildering chamber of distorting mirrors, it seemed that the more I sniffed into political sewers, the more I would become ensnared in a web of intrigue from which there would be little prospect of escape.

*   *   *

My quest to get Thando's status reclassified had been resuscitated by Sheryl Cwele's arrest for drug trafficking and the courageous disclosures provided by Moss, Beetge and Swanepoel. But my emails to DIRCO were not even acknowledged. And I was 'advised' by my anonymous contact that any further media exposure of South Africans imprisoned abroad would rebound badly on my efforts to draw attention to their plight.

'Best you don't ruffle feathers and let the criminal-justice system take its course,' he warned me. He leaned closer, conspiratorially: 'And you don't fuck with President Zuma's security cluster. There is a cabal that is intent on protecting certain interests that have naught to do with state security.'

In retrospect, his warning was eerily prescient.

I kept my mouth shut. I waited for due process to take its course: for the law-enforcement agencies, human-rights lawyers and global activists to contact me. They didn't. Sheryl Cwele, ex-wife of the minister of state security, had been implicated in an international drug-trafficking scandal. Selebi had been convicted for corruption because of his allegiance to one of South Africa's drug kingpins. However, leads provided to assist investigations into the transnational drug-trafficking trade and their connections to human trafficking were being ignored. When I ventured to elicit some form of follow-up to the investigations I had launched into the link between drug and human trafficking, through the medium of *Special Assignment*, instead of the positive response I had hoped for, the reaction was either indifference or antagonistic parochialism.

If I truly believed in the future of our constitutional democracy, like a born-again avatar I would have to dust off and re-don my dulled investigative armour. But before I could re-enter the arena of transnational drug trafficking, I would need to understand historical aspects of the narcotics trade in South Africa BC and AD. This would entail revisiting the treacherous realms of gangs, nightclubs, drugs, bouncers and smuggling, which, in the last 20 years, had been infiltrating the corridors of political power and were in danger of irrevocably dislodging our democracy.

So, like a dog whose nose retains the smell of a bone recently buried, I began to dig again.

13

A BRIEF GUIDE TO ORGANISED CRIME IN SOUTH AFRICA, BC–AD

There remains an abiding myth among many South Africans that organised crime (and its most lucrative income generator, narcotics trafficking) is primarily a feature of post-apartheid South Africa. The recurring refrain goes something like this: greater openness, weakened policing and porous border controls, as well as incompetence and corruption in the public sector have created a parasitic relationship between South Africa and international crime. On one level, this is true, but the explanation conveniently ignores the fact that the stage had been set decades before the end of apartheid for the consolidation and expansion of an indigenous criminal underworld operating within and beyond our borders.

The reality is that the major difference between 'pre' (BC) and 'post' (AD) is the diversification of the narco-menu and its merchants.[1]

Before 1990, South Africa's drugs trade was predominantly based on mandrax and locally produced marijuana. At the time, the sights of law enforcement were too closely set on the colours of red (ideology) and black (ethnicity) to take much heed of the hues of green ganja and white pipes. This colour selectivity rendered the authorities extraordinarily inattentive to the risk posed by international traffickers, who flocked to the country from Eastern Europe, India and the rest of Africa, particularly during the 1980s. It also rendered law enforcement wilfully colour-blind to the illicit activities of our boys protecting our borders.

During the decade spanning apartheid and post-apartheid South Africa, some of my information had been gleaned from the most authoritative verbal libraries. These included local watering holes and the most reliable of informants, prompted by Jack Daniel's and Johnnie Walker, not to mention other entertaining lubricants. Such spirited company regaled me with riveting accounts of larceny, committed at the bidding of the apartheid government. Among them were inebriated malcontents from 32 Battalion turned Executive Outcomes; Civil Cooperation Bureau assassins who reinvented themselves as reptilian private investigators; diamond and drug pirates from Port Nolloth; shit-faced ex-Selous Scouts and French Foreign Legion members; as well as legless, but now harmless, former Koevoet recruits who still refer to South West Africa and Rhodesia with teary-eyed nostalgia.

These former combatants fervently believed that PW Botha's stroke of misfortune heralded the sell-out of southern Africa to the wilderness. (In fact it was PW who landed up in the Wilderness, literally, in the Western Cape's Garden Route.) In reality, southern Africa, and some countries further north, had been sold out long before then: of timber, diamonds, gold, ivory, rhinos and marine resources.

And, of course, drugs.

Organised crime was as ingrained into apartheid as the Mixed Marriages and Group Areas acts. More than 100 front companies involved in state-sponsored criminal activity were uncovered during the Truth and Reconciliation Commission. Access to many of the secrets of the apartheid state and its subsidiaries, however, has been obstructed by the shredding of documents, particularly military and intelligence records, which occurred before 1994.

Some of those tens of thousands of records do still exist in Zimbabwe, Zambia and Tanzania, and even in Russia, buried like acorns before the hibernating season, stashed abroad as insurance policies by resourceful double agents and former bureaucrats. But the blades of the shredding machine cannot obliterate the data processed and stored by human memory, particularly of those who operated within the murky terrain of intelligence gathering and dissemination – either on behalf of apartheid or against it. Sometimes the twain would meet. To my knowledge, however, no list of spies in high places in the liberation movement, those activists involved in alliances of convenience with their arch-enemies, has ever been made public. Too many newspaper reports linking the doyens of freedom with free-market kleptocrats have become incomplete dossiers, while those accused continue to cavort publicly with the cream of criminal society.

What I do know is that some of the crimes seeping like rising damp from one era to the next, committed by apartheid's apologists, weren't even that well organised. They were opportunistic, avaricious and downright crude, aided and abetted by proponents of civil war intent on stuffing their already bulging pockets (and body parts), while planning acts of sabotage should the 'commie terrorists' assume the mantle of political power.

Much has already been researched and written about state institutions like the Broederbond, which choreographed leadership roles in the most influential tiers of the private and public sectors, and flourished through corruption, capitalised on the arms and oil embargoes against South Africa, and whose members amassed vast amounts of money in overseas tax havens. Studies have also been conducted on the boere mafia, a moniker coined to describe politically conservative criminal cartels. These local Afrikaner mobsters modelled themselves on John Gotti, the American gangster who became the boss of the New York Gambino Mafia. They formed an unholy trinity with crooked apartheid-era banks, which laundered their dirty lucre without so much as a raised eyebrow, and members of the security forces with an entrepreneurial bent. It was the latter, in cahoots with their right-wing political connections who became deeply embroiled in ivory poaching, gunrunning, diamond and gold smuggling, and drug trafficking – primarily in dagga and mandrax.

According to experts on criminal cartels and their methods of enterprise, these crime syndicates share several characteristics, including a hierarchy and designation of control; sophisticated fronts or legitimate business interests, established to launder their illicit gains; and a ruthless, take-no-prisoners approach to enemies and competitors alike, unless a deal was brokered with the latter, whereby the 'market' would be divided between rival syndicates.[2]

In addition to apartheid-era crime syndicates there were also individuals without any political or ideological allegiances, who, for pure financial gain, smuggled consignments of dagga or mandrax via Mozambique, Swaziland, Lesotho and Zambia, bound for the international market. Some were known by names that would be appropriate in the pages of a modernised Damon Runyon story: George the Duke, Stan the Man and Kaptein Caprivi. Few of these 'Goodfellas' were busted or did time. Many made millions and built legitimate careers in asset management, car dealerships, the taxi industry, second-hand clothing and even game farms from the proceeds.

Furthermore, international isolation did not prevent South Africa's 1960s and 1970s generation from tasting, tripping on and trafficking the psychotropic fruits of the hippy era – LSD, opium, cocaine, quaaludes and heroin – as they travelled to London, Amsterdam, Marrakesh, Torremolinos and Goa. During the decades preceding liberation, otherwise law-abiding young travellers were sometimes not averse to carrying a brick or two of compressed Durban Poison or Swazi Skunk in their backpacks, just in case picking grapes in France, olives in Italy or tulips in Holland proved too onerous a workload.

Some of these part-time smugglers lived the dreams of *On the Road*, Jack Kerouac's lyrical Beat Generation opus, and James Michener's *The Drifters*, attempting to emulate the characters of his era-defining novel on freedom, fucking and getting fucked up. South Africa's political pariah-hood held some advantages for citizens from a country largely isolated from the global drug-trafficking world: they could contribute to this rapidly thriving trade with relative impunity because small-time South African traffickers were not a priority for the authorities, whose focus was on suppressing political resistance and on winning both the propaganda and military war against the enemy.

But whether they were opportunistic 'businesspeople' or cash-strapped students, these smugglers were small fry compared with the highly organised rackets established during the 1970s under the auspices of the South African Defence Force (SADF). In 1977 the SADF published a white paper based on the directive issued by Prime Minister PW Botha that South Africa faced a 'total onslaught' in virtually every area of society. The threats were the red, or communist, peril and *die swart gevaar* (the black danger) – terrorist organisations operating in neighbouring countries, whose allegiances lay either with the Soviets and their Cuban minions or the Chinese. These threats, said the apartheid administration, could only be countered by a 'total strategy' to be fought on two fronts: through war against Marxist terrorists operating from neighbouring states and, internally, by crushing any civil resistance in the townships in the wake of the 1976 Soweto student revolts.

The total-onslaught strategy provided the perfect opportunity for senior members of the SADF, chiefs of staff and their foot soldiers to enrich themselves through some nefarious means. Their allies in the Mozambican and Angolan pro-Western political rebel movements and the Rhodesian Selous Scouts helped them poach ivory, and smuggle weapons, minerals and precious metals, as well as distribute cannabis and mandrax around the subcontinent.[3] The purpose of this trade was partly to pay for South African aid in weapons and other services, partly a destabilising strategy and, indubitably, for the more base aim of self-enrichment.

The trafficking of ivory, in particular, has been documented by one of South Africa's most experienced and respected soldiers, Colonel Jan Breytenbach, who also pointed an accusatory finger at his brothers in arms regarding their drug, weapons and diamond deals. After leaving the SADF Special Forces in 1975, Breytenbach led the infamous, but expertly trained, 32 Battalion in the war against the MPLA – Angola's Marxist liberation group – and their Cuban allies, along the Caprivi Strip for two years. In November 1989, he gave a damning newspaper interview in which he accused UNITA, the South Africa–backed Angolan rebel movement, of smuggling many forms of contraband, in complicity with SADF senior personnel.[4]

The smuggling pipelines through Angola, Mozambique and Zambia spread throughout South Africa and even into Botswana and Lesotho.[5] These cross-border routes were developed with the knowledge of, or endorsement by, the military and special-operations units immersed in clandestine work. The trafficking of contraband along these routes was hailed as an effective destabilisation tool and a source of valuable information (as well as money), not only on the subcontinent, but on the home front as well.[6]

In particular, the history of mandrax trafficking and consumption in South Africa illustrates the efficacy of these multi-pronged objectives. Mandrax, or 'buttons', is a synthetic drug manufactured from a chemical process whose active ingredient is methaqualone. In the 1960s and early 1970s, mandrax was a medication prescribed as a sleeping pill, sedative or palliative for anxiety attacks and high blood pressure. At the time, it was proclaimed as a miracle cure: safe, non-addictive and highly effective. That is, unless it was combined with dagga and alcohol, which produced alarming, even life-threatening, side effects resembling narcolepsy and Tourette's syndrome, and could result in psychological and physical addiction. It was conse-quently banned worldwide, but continued to be manufactured in clandestine laboratories in India, Pakistan, Kenya, Tanzania, Zambia, Swaziland, Mozambique, the Far East and South Africa. Packaged in 1 000-tablet units, illegal mandrax was trafficked in false panels of cars, spare wheels of trucks, false fuel tanks or in containers of second-hand clothing and other import–export commodities.

Although it was widely distributed throughout South Africa, the most lucrative markets for mandrax in the 1970s and 1980s were among the dispossessed communities of the Cape, who had been forcefully removed from their homes in District Six and elsewhere, dumped in dour structures built on sand, in a wasteland known as the Cape Flats. The rising popularity of this drug is inextricably linked to the growth of gang culture in these ghettos. Mandrax became the gangs' principal form of currency, fomenting brutal competition on the part of its manufacturers and merchants to dominate the market.

The township gangs, however, were not the sole sources of mandrax distribution. Despite the disclosures made during the Truth and Reconciliation Commission, which started in 1996, and some horrific exposés of right-wing forces hell-bent on annihilating the anti-apartheid struggle, embarrassingly little has been revealed of how the South African security underworld dipped their fingers into the narcotics pie during apartheid. However, one name remains synonymous with the manufacture and widespread distribution of illicit drugs for ideological purposes: Wouter Basson, dubbed 'Dr Death'.

Basson was one of many health professionals who acted unethically during apartheid. But whereas numerous doctors confessed and received amnesty at the Truth and Reconciliation Commission in June 1997, Basson chose not to come forward, as he seemed to believe he had done nothing wrong. Yet since the 1980s Basson had been accused of masterminding the local manufacture of mandrax, as well as the distribution of Ecstasy, another synthetic product that gained its status in the pantheon of designer drugs that were introduced into South Africa during the 1980s. Now practising, ironically, as a cardiologist in Cape Town, in December 2013, Basson was finally found guilty of unprofessional conduct by the Health Professions Council of South Africa (HPCSA) for coordinating the production and stockpiling of mandrax, Ecstasy and tear gas 'on a major scale'.[7]

At the time of writing, sentence has yet to be passed. The HPCSA judgment has been seen as a victory by many, who felt that Basson had literally got away with murder for more than two decades. Others felt it was too little, too late. And there were some who argued that, as a soldier, Basson had merely been obeying orders and should therefore not be held personally responsible. These conflicting opinions were broadcast in a *Special Assignment* investigation, produced in March 2014 by my colleague Richelle Seton-Rogers.

Before the HPCSA trial, which spanned six years, from 2007 to 2013, Basson had appeared on trial in 1999 charged with 67 counts, including murder, attempted murder, embezzlement, fraud, drug trafficking and drug dealing. However, in the 1999 trial Basson had been acquitted of all the criminal charges against him. The verdict sparked outrage among anti-apartheid activists, who accused the presiding judge, Willie Hartzenberg, of gross bias.

Court records of both trials reveal that the police supplied various drugs (dagga, heroin, LSD and 200 000 mandrax tablets) to the SADF's Special Forces. After a meeting between Basson, Adriaan Vlok, who was minister of law and order at the time, and the then police commissioner, Johan Coetzee, the police forensic-science laboratory supplied 9 tonnes of dagga and about half a million mandrax tablets to Delta G, one of two front companies in the apartheid state's chemical and biological warfare programme. This programme was called Project Coast and was headed by Basson.[8] The drugs were to be used for 'research' – a euphemism for experiments that would lead to the use of mandrax, in particular, as one of the military's principal weapons of mass destruction (and distraction). The nefarious objective was to find an effective chemical agent or drug that would incapacitate angry crowds, suppress dissent among individual anti-apartheid activists and sedate SADF prisoners. It was also rumoured that conscientious objectors were used as chemical guinea pigs.

Basson's mandrax experiments were so successful that Delta G was ordered to produce an extra 1 000 kilograms of methaqualone for the large-scale manufacture of the drug. Basson was not only adept at manufacturing the real deal and flooding disenfranchised communities with this highly addictive drug. He also oversaw the production of more than 100 000 lookalike mandrax tablets in 1985 to distribute among the units of the ANC's armed wing, Umkhonto we Sizwe (MK), who were suspected of partaking of the lucrative trade to raise funds. The plan was to flog the fake tablets to MK drug traffickers to locate and disrupt their smuggling routes. No one seems to know what became of the knock-off tablets.

There was nothing particularly well organised about these crimes, as has been confirmed by both military experts and avid readers of *Captain Devil Saboteur* photo comics of the 1970s. But what they lacked in strategic planning or originality, the perpetrators made up for in enthusiasm.

In addition to Mandrax, Basson also spearheaded the manufacture of Ecstasy in copious quantities. In 1991 Basson asked the then surgeon general, Neils Knobel, for $2.4 million to import 500 kg of Ecstasy into South Africa from Croatia, which was approved. However, between 1992 and 1993 he dabbled in his own home lab and produced more than 900 kg of a crystalline form of Ecstasy. The aim of this evil alchemy was two-fold: to temporarily subdue rioting stone-throwing mobs into 'stoned' crowds and for it to be gradually distributed among the black townships. This was planned neither to lift the spirits of the oppressed, nor to dispel the states-of-emergency blues, but rather to promote drug dependency and turn anti-apartheid activists into submissive dope heads. The rationale behind this strategy was possibly that for revolutionary rabble rousers hooked on drugs, the future fruits of liberation would assume secondary significance next to a daily supply of ludes and white pipes.

Inducing drug dependency would not happen overnight, of course. Tolerance towards and dependency on psychoactive substances occur over time, depending on dosage and DNA. And the drugs couldn't simply be handed out like leaflets. They would be distributed through a diffuse network of street gangs, corrupt nightclub security firms and merchants operating from inner-city alleyways and street corners.

There are so many accounts of Basson's experiments that used anti-apartheid activists and guerrilla fighters as lab rats, from supplying riot police with drug-laced teargas, to forcing SWAPO prisoners to skydive without parachutes, that truth and lore sometimes conflate. But the overwhelming memory left with Basson's victims and their families is of someone whose acumen in drug manufacturing was matched only by his ability to disseminate disinformation. For example, according to records from the Truth and Reconciliation Commission, in 1987 Jeremiah Mtuli left his home in the Pretoria township of Mamelodi to join MK. He was accompanied by nine youths, who mistakenly believed that they were going for military training. Instead, they were ambushed by the SAPS, injected with an unknown substance that was manufactured by Basson's unit and blown up in a kombi to make it look like an accident.

Some of the targets of Project Coast's chemical-and-biological-warfare efforts backfired. In January 1992, for example, Mozambican government forces were purportedly attacked by a deadly substance that was believed to have been sprayed on them by an SADF plane carrying chemical and biological weapons. After causing several fatalities among the Mozambican troops, the substance was identified it as a nerve agent known by its code name, BZ.[9]

Under pressure from the UN, US and the UK, who were

increasingly concerned about Project Coast, the then president, FW de Klerk, ordered the gradual dissolution of the chemical and biological warfare programme. In January 1993, following a high-level government investigation into South Africa's secret pro-grammes, Project Coast was wound down and Basson was given early retirement from his position as head of the programme. De Klerk authorised the destruction of all chemical-and-biological-warfare research. Years later, however, it is still suspected that Basson's drug supplies were simply relocated, as hundreds of kilograms of chemical agents remained unaccounted for when an inventory was taken during a government investigation.

The wholesale distribution of mandrax in South Africa was not restricted to the slums of Cape Town. One of the channels of traf-ficking was allegedly a criminal network within the ANC-in-exile involved in smuggling diamonds and mandrax between Zambia and South Africa.[10] Cars would be stolen from South Africa and driven over the Zambia–South Africa border with the hollowed-out door panels filled with cash. On the other side, the money would be exchanged for mandrax, ivory, diamonds and forged currency, perpetuating a culture of graft, entitlement and self-enrichment that still afflicts clusters within the ANC Government today. Their business partners sometimes included crime bosses whose ideological leanings were often antithetical to those of the liberation struggle but who were bonded by a common denomi-nator: the irresistible lure of cash.

The networks stretched throughout the country, but one of the fulcrums was Hillbrow, then a cosmopolitan inner-city suburb largely inhabited, until the mid-1980s, by Greek, Italian, Portuguese, Lebanese and Israeli immigrants. The 'Brow' was then the epicentre of Joburg's nightlife. One of the godfathers of the club and drug scene was a man I have dubbed (for my own personal saftey) 'Johnny the Porra' (South African slang for a person of Portuguese descent) or Big John. Having first arrived in South Africa in 1966, he soon established himself as something of a tycoon on the streets of the Brow. This was the era of disco, strobe lights, big hair and white three-piece suits. New York's Studio 54 was the global template and Big John succeeded in building impressive, albeit more parochial, replicas thereof with his clubs. These places were renowned not only for their music and glamorous underage waitresses and patrons, but also for their libertine approach to sex and drugs. However, the jet-set clubs weren't Big John's sole source of bread and butter.

The Portuguese businessman was allegedly linked to prostitution, extortion and murder. In the 1980s he also oversaw one of the most successful mandrax runs from Zambia to South Africa, often under the guise of a second-hand clothing business. He was apparently mates with the late Joe Modise, the commander-in-exile of MK. Modise was based in Lusaka, Zambia, in the early 1980s and subsequently became South Africa's first minister of defence under the new Constitution. During his years in exile, he was linked to a criminal network within the Lusaka-based ANC's security department allegedly engaged, inter alia, in smuggling gems and mandrax into South Africa.[11]

Johnny the Porra had left South Africa for Zambia in 1984, only to return in 1986, after having been deported during Zambian President Kenneth Kaunda's drive to stop the mandrax trade. His cop comrades back in South Africa allegedly included apartheid policeman Panganathan 'Timmy' Marimuthu, who was subsequently convicted of mandrax dealing but, despite being sentenced to three years, did not spend an hour behind bars.

Everyone who was anyone in club land knew of his extramural money-making schemes. Yet 'The Untouchable', as he soon became known, managed to evade the evidently malleable arm of the law. His legendary escapes include an unexplained quashing of a deportation order. In 1988 National Party Minister of Law and Order Adriaan Vlok had attempted to expel him from South Africa as an undesirable person. Vlok conveyed his conviction that Big John was not an asset to the country to the then minister of Home Affairs, Stoffel Botha. But Botha declined to act, citing the fact that the businessman had had permanent residence and vested interests in South Africa since 1966. Botha decided, therefore, that, in the public interest, deportation was not justified.

If that didn't indicate that he had friends in high places, then his acquittal on fraud charges and the withdrawal of two charges of murder and four of attempted murder suggest the scales of justice were obscenely tipped in his favour. And he certainly wasn't averse to playing on both sides of the fence, so to speak. He also hobnobbed with members of South Africa's exiled communities and politicians in Lusaka, and even opened a nightclub with Kaunda's son, Panji.

As the excessive eighties evolved into the naughty nineties, the Portuguese tycoon's choice of merchandise also allegedly switched from the poor man's drug, mandrax, to the nasal lubricant of the filthy rich, famous and foolish, cocaine, and its cheaper, crystallised derivative, crack. He, however, was not the one who introduced crack to a society seeking harder, higher experiences. That dubious honour, in the Western Cape anyway, belongs to Colin Stanfield, leader of The Firm – a conglomerate of Cape Town's most feared drug barons. What made Johnny the Porra's contribution to crack addiction particularly sinister, however, was his choice of allies and accomplices: Nigerian syndicates, which were rapidly establishing roots in the inner-city areas of Bertrams, Berea and Hillbrow, and apartheid's most evil henchmen, members of the Civil Cooperation Bureau (CCB).

Inaugurated in 1986 with the approval of the SADF's General Magnus Malan, by 1988 the CCB had become fully operational. Many of its minions would subsequently be drafted into the notorious Directorate of Covert Collections, a military-intelligence wing of the SADF that conducted dirty tricks aimed at destabilising the country as it entered the negotiations period. These included the violent involvement by the infamous Third Force in train massacres and hostel killings, as well as in the arming and training of Renamo, Ciskei Security Forces and Inkatha.[12]

Provided with lethal chemicals by Dr Death to be used against prominent anti-apartheid activists, the CCB, under the leadership of Eugene de Kock, comprised elements from the SADF, SAPS and paramilitary Border War unit Koevoet – entities that were intent on sabotaging South Africa's nascent democracy. Johnny the Porra's sidekicks and minions included a former regional boss of the CCB, who was a manager at one of Big John's hotels, a cesspit of sin in Hillbrow, where forged identity documents and passports were churned out with the efficiency of an assembly line. He was also a suspect in the assassination of human-rights lawyer and SWAPO member Anton Lubowski.

The other right-wing thugs who were tight with Big John included Ferdi Barnard, who was subsequently convicted of assassinating academic and anti-apartheid activist David Webster, and who fell prey to the vampire's vapour, as addiction to crack cocaine was dubbed on the streets; Corrie Goosen, who lived large and died young, like many of his mafia heroes; and Eugene Riley.

Riley had trained with Koevoet to fight against SWAPO in Namibia and had worked with Barnard in the Brixton Murder and Robbery Squad. Like his patriotic partners, Riley had notched up quite a few 'extracurricular' crimes, including donning a balaclava cap, blackening his face, boarding township commuter trains and throwing black passengers off the carriages. Under his tutelage were several opportunistic, arguably psychopathic, peddlers of information and arms enthusiasts, who followed their leader's instructions with alacrity. Their murderous acts formed part of a Third Force strategy: to sow further conflict between the ANC and the Inkatha Freedom Party, and to fuel black-on-black violence. This, Riley had often explained to me, was part of the political strategy of the protectors of apartheid. Riley also admitted responsibility for thefts of firearms, ammunition and explosives from Jeppe Street Police Station, apparently on the instructions of Joe Verster, who occupied a senior position in the CCB. These weapons were to be provided to the Inkatha Freedom Party as a means of disrupting a peaceful build-up to the 1994 democratic elections by fomenting civil war.[13]

Wielding a baseball bat, Riley had also smashed in the skull of a former accomplice who had ratted on him over a botched diamond-smuggling deal in Botswana. He also dealt in drugs, supposedly in exchange for information, but ultimately for the profits they yielded.

In a thesaurus on morality, Riley would have been listed as a synonym for 'monster'. Yet he was an enigma: capable of horrendous, racist brutality, yet generous and gentle towards those he deemed to be exploited and vulnerable, like children, the elderly and animals. Yet when it came to black-skinned South Africans, his eyes would glaze over as though a switch had been tripped in his brain. He had been programmed to believe they were sub-human. He felt justified in the violence he inflicted.

His rationale for participating in Johnny the Porra's smuggling activities, be they diamonds or drugs, was simpler: it was merely about the money. Together with Barnard, his 'broer in arms', with whom he was at one stage inseparable, he would hang out at the Quirinale Hotel, another of Big John's dens in Hillbrow. It served as a quasi-headquarters for the CCB and Big John-inspired plots, while the members liberally availed themselves of all the hotel services: unlimited liquor, drugs and prostitutes of varying ages and assets.

* * *

I was introduced to Riley at a Hillbrow coffee shop in 1993, shortly before the assassination of Chris Hani. He knew I was a journalist and had expressed the need to offload some of the horrifying baggage he had been carrying since the 1980s. I don't know whether it was guilt and remorse, or just plain fear that there would some day be a terrible retribution exacted against him for his part in murdering, mutilating and muzzling anti-apartheid activists – or whether he was finally coming to realise that he had backed the wrong side of history. He regaled me with repugnant, yet fascinating, terrifying and not always credible, tales about his assignments both on behalf of Johnny the Porra and the CCB.

Like the minions he trained, Riley was a master of disinformation. Deconstructing his narratives about drug trafficking, kidnapping, assassinations, Third Force violence and general larceny had propelled me headlong into a sordid, paranoid world of double agents, spooks and conspiracy theories. Riley would provide me with information that I would then pass on for verification to trusted media colleagues, like Ivor Powell, who was then a journalist with the *Mail & Guardian*, and far better connected than me and much more streetwise. Yet, surprisingly, most of what Riley told me was the truth – about Big John's drug trafficking, the SADF origins of the CCB, plans to destabilise the new South Africa by inciting violence through the Third Force and the plot to assassinate Chris Hani, which Riley ominously told me about a couple of days before it happened. Initially I dismissed his prediction, even after he had revealed Military Intelligence documents warning of the impending assassination and raising the sinister possibility of a wider plot between factions within the ANC and apartheid Military Intelligence to kill the popular South African Communist Party leader before the 1994 elections. The key informant was an ANC/Military Intelligence double agent codenamed 'Ramon', described in Riley's documents as the source of the information on the impending assassination. It was only after Hani had been killed and Riley had introduced me to Amin Laher, aka Ramon, that the full impact of his information sank in.

A dapper man of dubious repute, with expensive tastes and an unquenchable thirst for unworldly young Afrikaner women, Laher was the former son-in-law of another notorious drug trafficking kingpin, Shariff Khan. That was apparently how he and Riley had met. When he was a cop at Brixton Murder and Robbery, Riley had been sniffing Khan's spoor. Laher adopted an assortment of *noms de guerre*, including Joseph Brunner, the name by which I was first introduced to him.

Riley praised Laher as one of his most reliable sources, a

respected MK soldier and intelligence source with the ANC's Department of Intelligence Services, who had earned the grudging respect of the CCB. In turn, Laher had claimed former Department of Intelligence Services member Ricky Nkondo (now a National Intelligence Agency divisional head in Deputy Intelligence Minister Joe Nhlanhla's office) was 'associated' with Riley before Hani's death.[14] According to Riley's girlfriend, Julie Wilken, so too was Mo Shaik.[15] Wilken even volunteered to take a polygraph test and passed, although her allegations were neither confirmed nor denied by Department of Intelligence Services officials.

Laher offered to give me additional documentation that would confirm that the assassination had been planned by factions hostile to Hani within the ANC, but insisted that I should not investigate their veracity. Terrified of becoming a pawn in their perverse game of destabilisation and power mongering, I refused.

I terminated my association with Riley in December 1993. Early in January 1994, he called me, crying uncontrollably. 'I have seen the light and I am haunted. I got in too deep with the diamonds, the violence and now the drugs. I couldn't get out. I'm going to spill the beans on everyone and hopefully I will be forgiven for the harm I have done to my country.'

Three weeks later, Riley was dead – officially by his own gun, but probably at the hands of his partners in crime who knew he was about to pimp them.

Three years later, together with Stefaans Brümmer, my colleague at the *Mail & Guardian*, I exposed aspects of the hitherto unknown details behind the alleged conspiracy to assassinate Chris Hani.[16] By then I was also in possession of sheaves of incriminating evidence, plied on me by one of Riley's few surviving friends, against political figures both on the Right and Left who were embroiled in racketeering and drug trafficking. I had this confidential, documented information in my possession. But after a break-in at my apartment (during which only my computer and some floppy-disk backups were taken), after faeces were dumped at my front door and after receiving several anonymous death threats, I handed some of the incriminating documents, particularly those pertaining to Hani's assassination, to the Truth and Reconciliation Commission. I entrusted the names of prominent drug-trafficking connections to the care of a close friend and streetwise private investigator by the name of Gary Lazarus. He, too, subsequently died and I was never able to retrieve the documents he had stashed for me with over-eager ingenuity.

That was in 1999. By then, intent on distancing myself forever from the politico-criminal cesspool in which I had inadvertently become immersed, I had quit my job at the *Mail & Guardian* in Johannesburg and relocated to Cape Town. Exploring and exploding myths entails ducking the shrapnel and minimising the afterburn. At the time, I still fervently believed the sullying of the Rainbow Nation by apartheid's illicit armies to be the final suppurating spurts of a dissipated regime.

Little did I realise the extent to which the infection had seeped into the post-apartheid anatomy, or the challenges that lay ahead in preventing its spread.

14

SULTANS OF SIN

Even on a day unmarred by the prevailing Cape Doctor wind, as one travels towards the sea along Cape Town's N2 highway between the bookends of the mountains, the wind accelerates almost imperceptibly, the dust begins to dance in spiral swirls, and the attractive contours of the city mutate into the rough-edged topography of the Cape Flats. The Cape Doctor is the local nickname for the howling southeaster, which turns roof tiles into decapitating missiles, clears pollution and heralds the onset of the fairest Cape weather. The wind seems to gust harder here, though, whistling through the informal settlements spread across the landscape like misshapen patchwork quilts, through the interminable rows of RDP houses framed by backyard hokkies and among the cramped apartment blocks that characterise the Cape Flats. Located on the fringes of the urban-planning maps, these ghetto-like suburbs are surrounded by crescent-shaped streets forming impenetrable peripheries around them. Today these grid-like blocks are some of the most painful monuments to apartheid social engineering.

It is here, predominantly in the 'Coloured' suburbs, that the consequences of drug addiction are most evident, where the post-apartheid pot of gold remains tragically elusive as the children of the Rainbow Nation turn sickly shades of grey. This is courtesy of the vapours they suck from light bulbs and bottles fashioned into crude pipes, stuffed with rocks (crack) or 'lollies' loaded with tik.

Every drug has its own genealogy, insofar as sourcing and distribution are concerned. When it comes to crack cocaine in the Western Cape, the accountability for flooding the Cape Flats with this drug lies with the late Colin Stanfield. Although he lived lavishly in a plush home in middle-class Rondebosch, Stanfield hailed from the poverty-stricken slums of Valhalla Park. Violence was so endemic in this suburb that it was rumoured that even members of People Against Gangsterism and Drugs (PAGAD), a militant movement that brazenly took on (and out) the gang bosses from the mid-1990s until 2002, were reluctant to go there.

In 1991 Stanfield established and assumed leadership of the cartel known as The Firm, an amalgamation of individuals comprising prison-gang chiefs and their street counterparts. Bolstered by its status as the most powerful drug syndicate on the Flats, The Firm soon secured control of the mandrax trade. With the country in the throes of transitional instability and the globalisation of the narcotics industry, it made good business sense, however, to jump onto the crack wagon. But there was rivalry between Stanfield and the Staggie twins, Rashied and Rashaad, in the competition for hegemony of the crack market, the latter through their own gang, the Hard Livings, which was the dominant gang in Manenberg.

The Americans gang was the arch enemy of the Hard Livings and, until the early 1990s, these two were the most powerful gangs on the Cape Flats, embroiled in brutal turf wars with each other. Stanfield persuaded both that it was in their best business interests to keep the peace by working together under the umbrella of a cartel and to adapt their structures so they could cooperate and compete with foreign syndicates.[1]

By 1995 The Firm had cornered the market and fixed prices for the drugs, enabling Stanfield to amass millions of rands in profits. The Staggie twins also prospered handsomely from their 'coup de crack', deploying their loyal lieutenants, such as Desmond Holland, Hard Livings' hit man and gunrunner, to secure distribution across the city via taxi drivers, prostitutes, drug-den owners and nightclub bouncers, as well as on their home turf, Manenberg.

The Staggies were known to drive through the potholed streets of Manenberg, dishing out fistfuls of R100 notes to the cash-strapped community. They also established a debt-relief office at Die Hok, their gang headquarters, where they would help desperate residents with cash gifts to settle their bills or put a decent meal on the table. The Staggies' largesse was not conditional on financial repayment. Instead, the settlement demanded was eternal subjugation to the wishes of the gang.

The origins of gangs along the Cape Flats can be traced to over a century ago, to the sexually violent prison 'Numbers' gangs established by Mzuzephi 'Nongoloza' Mathebula, a 19th-century bandit. In environments of containment, fear and alienation are easily transferred to an alternative authoritative vessel. Prison serves therefore as a training ground for initiation into the ritualised Numbers hierarchy. It is a brotherhood sealed in blood – both a flag of identity and a gateway through which one may enter after passing specific rites and rituals, but from which one is rarely permitted to leave. In the last two decades, the influence of the Numbers gangs has grown beyond prison walls and their power surpasses even that of their street counterparts. They are now drug lords and their alliances extend to international crime cartels. Today, 'the number' takes precedence over all other allegiances. Their generals call the shots, even from behind bars. Their brothers on the outside do their bidding via lieutenants and juvenile runners, some of them as young as nine or ten.

To the dispossessed youths of the Cape Flats, in particular, gangs have become their ghetto families, giving them a sense of identity, belonging and respect – a defence against personal pain. In order to reduce the lure of the drug gangs, viable alternatives – positive rituals and role models – have to be provided.

Yet, to date, despite political rhetoric about youth empowerment and socio-economic upliftment, this has not happened on the scale required to transform the lives of those still oppressed by poverty, crime and despair.[2]

Today, tik-fuelled youths continue to sell drugs and kill each other so they can graduate up the ranks. In 2013 alone, the body count from inter-gang conflict exceeded the number of casualties in a conventional combat zone, with hundreds of innocents caught in their crossfire.

And therein lies the central, paradoxical power exerted by the gangs over the communities that are both beneficiaries of their largesse and victims of their collateral damage. They are not malevolent outsiders wreaking mayhem on traumatised communities. They are the enemy within, having grown up on the very streets they have learnt to terrorise. They are sinners and saviours, the cause of violence, yet the symptom of a collective sense of dispossession that grew with the forced removals of Coloured communities from Cape Town's District Six. The pain inflicted by their crimes is mitigated by the financial blanket they offer to those whom the system has left out in the cold. It was understandable, therefore, that in 2000, when Stanfield was convicted for tax fraud, he was hailed as a hero by a loyal contingent of thousands of supporters from the very neighbourhoods that were being destroyed by the consequences of substance abuse: gang warfare and violent crime. Community support for Rashied Staggie was also widespread when he was sentenced for arranging the gang rape of Chantal Knight, a teenage police informant, and for the theft of weapons from a police depot.

The lynching of Rashaad Staggie by PAGAD on 4 August 1996 unleashed a war of attrition between the gangs, and brought the existence of urban terrorism in the Western Cape to the attention of South Africa and the wider world. Between 1996 and 2002, several prominent gang bosses, previously regarded as untouchable, were assassinated by members of PAGAD's paramilitary forces. Their modus operandi included drive-by shootings and bomb attacks targeting gangs, and, later, the security forces and the general public.

Hits were put out on PAGAD dissidents, police investigating the organisation as well as a magistrate presiding over trials of PAGAD members. But in this violent chaos, it wasn't always clear who was responsible for what: vigilantes from within PAGAD, National Intelligence officers planted within the organisation or gangsters trying to emulate the methods of their foes. Shortly after Staggie's death, gang leaders across the province had formed CORE (Community Outreach), a reformed gangsters' union of sorts, which pledged to help empower the ravaged communities. Instead, however, they metamorphosed from street gangs into the operational fronts for organised-crime syndicates.

During the negotiation phases for a democratic South Africa, both the government at the time and the ANC were discussing amnesty and indemnity from prosecution for crimes committed during apartheid. Gang bosses argued that they too should benefit from these negotiations, as they were also victims of oppression.[3] With one eye firmly focused on redressing apartheid's ignominies and the other on consolidating its place in the global arena, South Africa's fledgling democracy was therefore unprepared to deal with the escalating scourges of drugs, violence and organised crime that subsequently engulfed the Cape Flats. Well, that's the official narrative, anyway. The truth is more convoluted.

* * *

The fact that gang bosses like Staggie and Stanfield were sentenced not for drug trafficking, murder or organising prostitution, but for rape and tax evasion points to a disturbing scenario that was well established before the advent of democracy. It has been documented that, during apartheid, street gangs were recruited by apartheid's security police and their agents to act as informants and 'informal' assassins in their mission to suppress anti-apartheid activists. For example, the late Jackie Lonte, founder and leader of the 10 000-strong Americans gang, was closely connected to the CCB and was paid by the death squad to eliminate United Democratic Front supporters.[4]

As 1994 approached and scoring votes in the most contested province in the country became more ruthless, the Hard Livings aligned themselves with the ANC, while the avowedly right-wing Americans backed the National Party. Gang leaders paid for buses to transport prospective voters to political rallies held by both parties. Gangs ensured that political parties could campaign on their turf. What would they receive in return? Well, that was never made clear. What is known is that these favours and allegiances were significant factors in why the authorities failed to crack down on gangsterism and the illicit economy.[5]

The blurring of the boundaries between criminal activity and crime intelligence spawned the rise to power of Cape Town's most feared underworld boss, Cyril Beeka.

Like Eugene Riley, Ferdi Barnard, the Staggie twins – and millions of other South African men of his generation – Beeka was the unwitting progeny of apartheid. But he became one of the apartheid system's most ferocious agents, and was programmed to be a 'man that evil does'. He was also an equal-opportunities rogue – living proof to the gang bosses who ruled the Cape Flats that previous ideological affiliation was no hindrance to success in the business of crime. Having previously acted as an agent for apartheid's military- and national-intelligence authorities, once the ANC assumed the political helm in 1994, Beeka seamlessly switched sides, providing his services to the new democracy's National Intelligence Agency. After he was gunned down by a volley of bullets in 2011, an ANC flag was draped over his coffin as a testament to his unswerving allegiance to his new masters.

Cyril William Beeka was born in 1961, one of the six children of a Cape Town reformatory principal. A physically imposing and fearsomely strong man, he was a karate expert, who trained youngsters in the martial arts, and an expert dog breeder. Aptly, he was nicknamed the 'Rottweiler of Kuilsriver'.[6] Through his security companies, Red Security and Pro Access Security (the former was co-owned by his brother Edward), he also controlled Cape Town's club scene. His reign of the city's underworld helped consolidate the growth of prison and street gangs into sophisticated organised-crime empires working in cooperation with their global counterparts, including the Moroccan, Italian, Middle Eastern and Russian mafias, as well as the Japanese Yakuza and Chinese Triads.

During the 1990s, Beeka exerted nothing short of a reign of terror over the city in his efforts to monopolise the distribution of drugs throughout his domain. To this end, he was assisted by a group of Moroccan henchmen, under the leadership of Houssain Ait Taleb, a feared figure in Cape Town's bouncer industry. Wearing militia-style apparel, the Moroccans would apply methods of persuasion that were legendary and sometimes lethal. If a club owner refused Beeka's offer of protection, which included him receiving a sizeable per centage of takings and drug-distribution rights, his baton-wielding brotherhood would beat patrons to a pulp and even torch their premises. To this day, suspicion rests on Beeka and his cohorts for the 1999 Planet Hollywood bomb blast at Cape Town's V&A Waterfront, which claimed two lives. The finger of blame, however, was pointed at PAGAD, which had already notched up a reputation for vigilante-style terror. By 1999 the NPA and National Intelligence Agency had between them 400 dockets of assaults – bombings and drive-by shootings – across the Cape Peninsula, crimes that they hadn't been able to solve.[7] By 2002 most of PAGAD's leadership were behind bars, but no one was ever convicted for the bombings at the Waterfront, the Blah Bar in Green Point or St Elmo's in Camps Bay.

Throughout this period, PAGAD insisted it had been framed, and pointed to a conspiracy between crooked law-enforcement officers, gangs and bouncer companies to secure the lucrative two-way flow of narcotics into and beyond the borders of the Mother City by 'creating a distraction and a scapegoat'.[8] In 2011, while

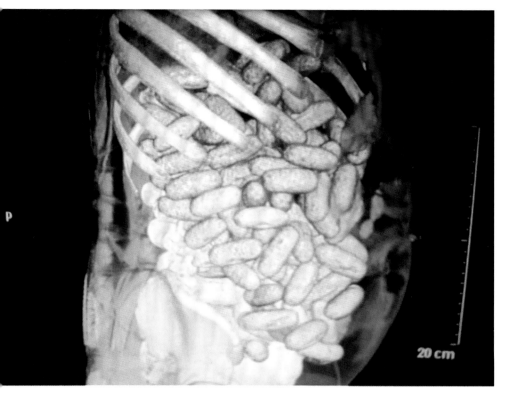

acking it in: An X-ray image shows the stomach-churning lengths drug mules are repared to go to in order to smuggle their illicit cargo.

ree at last: Released in April 2012, after 8 years in a Bangkok prison, drug mule hani Krebs is embraced by his mother at R Tambo International Airport.

Sisterly love: Joan Sacks worked tirelessly to secure the release of her brother, Shani Krebs.

Top: Former South African beauty queen Vanessa Goosen was arrested in Thailand for drug smuggling in 1994 and released in 2011. She insists she was set up as a decoy.

Right: In 2008, 23-year-old Thando Pendu was sentenced to 25 years in Klong Prem Prison, Bangkok, for drug smuggling.

Top: A mother's anguish: Prison photographs are painful reminders for Nozukile Pendu of her daughter Thando's tragic fate.

Left: The Pendu family at home in Thabong township (Welkom): From left, Sipho (Thando's sister), Wandile (her nephew), Nozukile, Jabulani Khubone (Thando's uncle); front: Andisiwe (Thando's youngest sister).

Top: An unlikely heroine: Since the 2005 arrest of her son, Johann, in Mauritius for drug smuggling, Patricia Gerber has become a crusader for the rights of South Africans incarcerated abroad.

Middle: Human-rights lawyer Sabelo Sibanda is lobbying for the establishment of a prisoner transfer treaty that would enable South Africans incarcerated abroad to serve a portion of their sentences at home, close to their loved ones.

Bottom: From Interpol to underworld: It took six years for Jackie Selebi, disgraced former police commissioner and head of Interpol, to fall from top cop to corrupt crook.

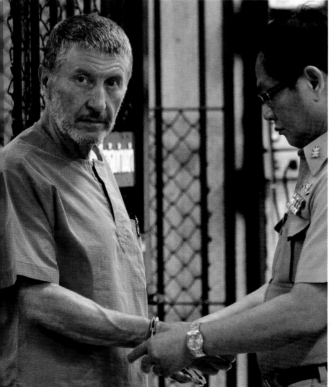

Top left: Disorganised crime: It was Selebi's former pal, drug lord Glen Agliotti, who hung him out to dry.

Top right: Death and dishonour: Dubbed Dr Death, Wouter Basson is a South African cardiologist and former head of the country's covert chemical and biological warfare project during the apartheid era.

Left: The pizza connection: Vito Roberto Palazzolo, also known as Robert von Palace Kolbatschenko, is allegedly an Italian mafia kingpin. He has hobnobbed with South Africa's political elite both during and after apartheid. In 2012 Palazzolo was arrested by Interpol in Bangkok.

South African – Brazil – Nigerian – Thai Connection: Nicolene's case

From the information provided by Nicolene; the picture below shows what I know so far regarding the relations between the 'gang' and 'victims'.

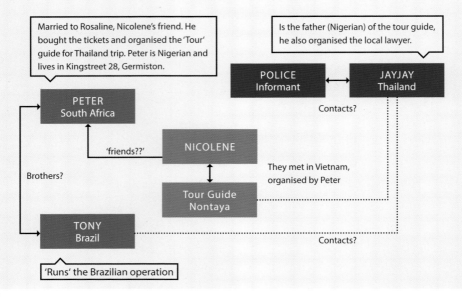

The usual suspects: Syndicate members in South Africa, Brazil and Bangkok recruited Nicolene Kruger to smuggle drugs into Thailand. She and Babsie may have had the same handlers.

South African – Brazil – Nigerian – Thai Connection: Babsie's case

From the information provided by Babsie; the picture below shows what I know so far regarding the relations between the 'gang' and 'victims'.

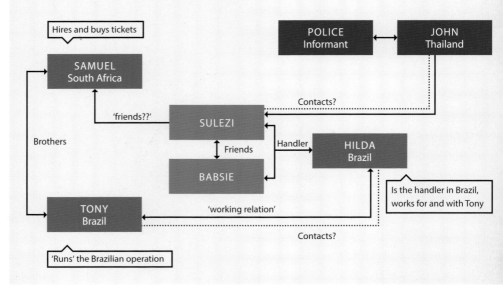

The South Africa–Brazil–Bangkok connection: A meticulously constructed organogram details the syndicate connections who, Babsie insists, forced her to smuggle drugs.

olubabalo 'Babsie' Nobanda became the unwitting poster child for South
frican drug mules when she was arrested and convicted for attempting
o smuggle cocaine into Thailand hidden in her dreadlocks.

embers of a Nigerian–Bangkok syndicate traced by 'Al' from evidence
ven by convicted drug mules and through Facebook.

Top: Fridah Tembo: Zambian sales executive by day; recruiter of drug mules for a Nigerian syndicate by night. The photo on the left was taken with my secret spycam.

Left: Janice Linden was sentenced to death in April 2010 for smuggling drugs into China. In December 2011 she was executed by lethal injection – the first South African to be executed in China.

I was conducting research for a *Special Assignment* investigation into the demise and resurgence of PAGAD, a senior prosecutor in the NPA conceded, off the record, that they had not ruled out the possibility of a broader conspiracy to shift the focus away from the burgeoning drug trade, and the gangs who distributed narcotics, onto the gangsters' enemy, PAGAD, instead. However, my attempts to obtain on-the-record comments from the NPA, the National Intelligence Agency and the SAPS on the bombings and PAGAD's allegations came to naught on the grounds of 'national security'.[9]

Some consideration was given to a probe of this broader conspiracy. Confidential documents penned by the NPA, however, admitted that the investigators had little experience of such investigations, and therefore no evidence of such a conspiracy was found. Yet the dominant rumour doing the rounds at the time was that, shortly before the deadly blast, Planet Hollywood had refused Beeka's offer of protection.

Beeka's other partners in crime included Yuri 'the Russian' Ulianitski, with whom he carved Cape Town club land into their personal fiefdoms.

Vito Palazzolo was also a close ally, as was the sophisticated, fresh-faced but unnerving Mark Lifman, a wealthy and politically connected Sea Point property tycoon, fashion mogul, poker champion and strip-club owner. Repeatedly, Lifman has been accused, but never convicted, of committing sinister crimes, ranging from extortion and fraud to sexual offences. For example, in 2005 he was arrested on nine charges – seven of sexually assaulting young working-class boys aged between 12 and 19, one of the attempted murder of his alleged pimp and one of defeating the ends of justice. Although he was ultimately acquitted in 2009, Lifman is allegedly regarded with fear and suspicion, even by some of the most brutish members of Cape Town's underworld.

In 2012 Lifman was again arrested and charged, this time alongside a former bouncer, his business partner, the fearsome Andre Naude, on 300 counts of fraud and contravening the Private Security Industry Regulatory Authority Act, for allegedly operating an unregistered security company called Strategic Protection Services. Despite extensive media coverage of the trial, since their last appearance in February 2014, the case against them, or reports thereof, seems to have fizzled out.[10] Apparently, the security tactics employed by Strategic Protection Services were brutally reminiscent of the methods used by Beeka in the late 1990s to maintain his grip on Cape Town's club scene.

Local gang leaders Rashied Staggie and Jerome 'Donkey' Booysen, leader of the Sexy Boys, also enjoyed a constructive working relationship with Beeka. After Beeka's assassination, Lifman and Booysen attempted to assume the mantle of Cape Town's bouncer bosses, amassing vast fortunes from property, clubs and car dealerships.[11] During Lifman's sex trial, Booysen became a familiar figure, displaying theatrical shows of support for his good mate by glaring menacingly at the media, loudly threatening children's-rights activists, who were baying for Lifman's blood, and almost punching several young protesters who pelted Lifman's luxury car with rotten fruit each time the suave accused drove into or out of the Atlantis court, where the trial was held. He also hurled wads of cash at onlookers converging on the scenes of bedlam, who variously cheered or jeered at his flamboyance. It should also be noted that Booysen was allegedly the last person Beeka visited before he was taken out.[12]

His former apartheid affiliations did not prevent Beeka from forging allegiances with certain revolutionary militants, such as the man behind the bombing of Durban's Magoo's Bar, ANC operative Robert McBride (later Ekurhuleni police chief and, since February 2014, the new head of the Independent Police Investigative Directorate). It should be recalled that McBride was the Foreign Affairs director for South East Asia, during Selebi's stint at Foreign Affairs in the late 1990s, when Joan Sacks had tried unsuccessfully to lobby for the establishment of a prisoner transfer treaty with Thailand. In 1998, together with Beeka, McBride was charged with the vicious assault of a woman in a brothel, although the charges were subsequently dropped.[13]

McBride and Beeka also partied with former members of right-wing death squads, such as the late Dirk Coetzee, during the former's tenure with Foreign Affairs.

But the man to whom Cyril Beeka appeared to be most closely connected shortly before his assassination was former head of South Africa's intelligence services, Mo Shaik, whom he accompanied to the 2007 ANC Polokwane conference, which unseated Thabo Mbeki.[14] Beeka, it was reported, was in charge of protecting voting security at the venue and was acting as Shaik's personal bodyguard, further reinforcing the sinister interface between criminal, intelligence and political networks.

Beeka also consorted with dodgy private-investigation and security entities, whose management enjoyed close affiliations with the 'usual suspects', particularly Palazzolo, Agliotti, Kebble and Selebi. Beeka would facilitate the awarding of strategic port-access contracts to a particular company, thereby giving it control over the entry and departure of cargo containers and, by extension, his own lucrative import/export dealings. He had a finger in every narcotics pie in Cape Town and heaven help anyone who dared to challenge his authority or double-cross him. Like Riley, in an instant his veneer of charm, generosity and lightheartedness would flip into a violent temper from which neither men nor women were spared.

His partner, Ulianitski, was no different, except that he would commission his underlings to beat up those who dared interfere with his domain of drugs, gambling and prostitution. I once found myself on the receiving end of, not his deadly wrath, but his 'persuasive' warning system. I had been investigating allegations that Ulianitski and his associates were intimidating, assaulting and extorting money from Cape Town horse-racing jockeys. I tried to interview one of their alleged victims. Clearly terrified, he refused to speak on the record, but referred me to a club owner who apparently possessed incriminating footage of Ulianitski threatening him unless he let them distribute cocaine and Ecstasy on his premises. The footage revealed Ulianitski rattling off the names of politicians and sports personalities who were his and Beeka's insurance policies. These people would protect them from the repercussions of their crimes.

In an article published in the *Cape Argus*, I made no mention of the footage, but covered at length Ulianitski's influence on Cape Town's clubs and drug underworld, and seeming ability to commit crimes with impunity. A week later, in the early hours of a Sunday morning, outside a bar in Sea Point, my former partner and I were accosted by Ulianitski and his scrawny Bulgarian sidekick, 'Mario'. The latter sported a ponytail that bore no coincidental resemblance to a rat's tail. Ulianitski viciously assaulted my partner, punching him to the ground and repeatedly kicking him in the ribs. Mario lunged for me, probably intent on doing much the same, but somehow I managed to elude his puny grasp and sought refuge among the throngs of revellers outside the nearby restaurants.

The horror of the attack was augmented by people's reluctance to help. Despite my desperate pleas for them to contact the police, otherwise reputable Sea Point restaurant managers slammed their doors in my face. This was Yuri the Russian, after all, and their fears of reprisals far outweighed the moral imperative of assisting a vulnerable, patently terrified woman. Ulianitski left my partner groaning and bleeding on the pavement, and the rodent-like Mario slipped back into the gutter from which he had initially emerged.

We reported the attack to the police, laid a charge of assault with intent to do grievous bodily harm, as well as attempted murder (Mario had cocked his gun in my partner's face). The next day, we were visited by a member of the Scorpions, who entreated me not to publicise the assault lest I compromise existing cases against Ulianitski. Reluctantly, I agreed but insisted on being accompanied by the police to an illegal Sea Point casino from where I had learnt Ulianitski's accomplice, my inept attacker, operated. There, I positively identified him and was given the assurance by the police that they would return later to arrest both of them. They never did.

As he was a good mate of the owners of the private-investigation company where I was moonlighting at the time, Beeka later invited me for a 'commiserative' lunch. Compassion oozing like sweat from every pore of his burly body, he clucked and cooed and shook his head when I described in vivid detail my narrow escape from the Bulgarian rat.

Beeka pinched my cheek. 'But, my darling, that should serve as a warning not to poke your perky little titties in places they don't belong,' he said, his voice simultaneously assuming the texture of honey mixed with arsenic. 'I hope you have learned your lesson. It could have been so much, much worse for both of you.'

Demurely, I nodded. Shortly after imparting this sagacious advice, Beeka performed effective, but, in his world, relatively benign, revenge on a journalist far too immersed in her own sense of missionary zeal. He provided me with what I believed at the time to be a great lead for a print story on the hazards of club drugs. Beeka resented all drugs, unless, that is, he was their sole procurer, supplier and profiteer. He told me about a club that was distributing impure Ecstasy tablets, from which a 15-year-old had died as a result of an overdose. He put me touch with the victim's distraught mother. I took the bait, forgetting in my journalistic fervour, to request proof of a death certificate. As it turned out, the story was a hoax. Afterwards, I learnt that the bogus parent had been summarily dispatched to KwaZulu-Natal to escape the journalistic frenzy that ensued.

By then, I had been accused of 'manufacturing' the story, tarred and feathered by my colleagues and shunned into a journalistic exile in which I languished for several years. As a freelance journalist, I was only as good as my last story. My professional integrity had been discredited and, consequently, no reputable newspaper would hire me. Having already pissed off apartheid spooks and hit men in Johannesburg, I was loath to further irk Cape Town's most fearsome thugs, like the Kuilsriver Rottweiler, the Russian Terrier and the Bulgarian Rat. So I alternated between navel gazing, wound licking and panic attacks, see-sawing between the relief of having had my life spared and the despair of what seemed to be the termination of my career.

The fact that both Ulianitski and Beeka were subsequently terminated almost converted me from an atheist into a believer in karmic justice. It enraged me that Beeka's coffin was draped in ANC colours and he was eulogised in epithets usually reserved for saints. Several years before his death, he had relocated to Johannesburg. There, he mixed with the likes of Lolly Jackson, the flamboyant owner of Teazers strip clubs, before Jackson, too, was murdered.

One of Beeka's other brothers in arms was Sam Hamade, a Lebanese bogus prince and army officer with a penchant for Ferraris, military apparel and fake SANDF accreditation, and a habit of flashing his firearm in public places. Apparently, Hamade had access to an arsenal substantial enough to destabilise the Middle East. He also had a beef with Beeka over a luxury car that the latter had purchased from him but didn't pay for.[15]

Beeka was also associated with Czech national Radovan Krejcir, another alleged organised-crime kingpin, who entered South Africa in 2007 from the Seychelles on a false passport. He was a fugitive from his home country and was wanted on various charges, including fraud and kidnapping. In his ongoing efforts to attain asylum in South Africa, he has claimed that he will be murdered by his political enemies if he is deported.

Jackson was allegedly shot in May 2010 by Greek Cypriot George Louca, who subsequently fled to his motherland. In February 2014 Louca was successfully extradited to South Africa but, at the time of writing, had yet to stand trial. According to independent investigator Paul O'Sullivan, who has also placed Krejcir at the top of his sin list, Louca met Krejcir in prison during 2007. Allegedly embroiled in gold smuggling, drug trafficking and money-laundering schemes, Krejcir was introduced to Jackson by the Cypriot.[16]

Since 2009, the official body count of individuals associated with Krejcir has reached ten (and still counting), all of them involved, allegedly, in drug trafficking, according to intelligence sources. The most recent fatalities were Czech Jan Charvát and Jason 'Ronnie' Domingo, who in December 2013 were killed in a bomb blast at Krejcir's business premises in Bedfordview. Several weeks earlier, Lebanese national Sam Issa, otherwise dubbed 'Cripple Sam', was assassinated. Issa, who was a known associate of Krejcir, had previously been implicated in drug trafficking. In April 2014, *The Star* reported that Krejcir was likely to be charged with the murders of Issa and German supercar specialist Uwe Gemballa.[17] He has also been accused of conspiring to kill crime-intelligence cop Colonel Nkosana 'Killer' Ximba and O'Sullivan.

At the time of writing this book, Krejcir was standing trial alongside Hawks members Samuel 'Saddam' Maropeng, George Nthoroane and Jan Mafokeng for attempted murder and kidnapping after a drug shipment to Australia allegedly went missing. Krejcir has already been charged with the murder of alleged Zimbabwean debt collector Phumlani Ncube.

Beeka's name was allegedly found on a hit list during a police raid on Krejcir's Bedfordview home shortly after the bouncer king's assassination. According to media reports, the pair had made plans to go into 'business' together, but apparently mistrust had developed between them shortly before Beeka was murdered.

So, who was behind the hit on Beeka and why? The list of suspects with motives would make for a brilliant spin-off of the murder-mystery game Cluedo. After his death in March 2011, rumours abounded that Beeka had fallen out with his comrades in crime, that he was in the process of 'spilling the beans' and had even agreed to turn state witness against Krejcir.[18] With Beeka's demise, the pendulum of power swung to his former lieutenants, Lifman and Booysen, who assumed control over the Cape Town club scene.

My disquieting suspicion as to the identity of both Beeka's and Ulianitski's killers without any arrests having being made persuaded me that I should not poke any part of myself into the drains controlled by thugs and drug lords.

* * *

As it turns out, I haven't needed to sniff out new sewers in search of South Africa's sultans of sin. The drains of old still overflow openly with criminal cartels, whose trade in contraband, including drugs and human lives, allegedly extends to trade in government decisions as well. Bar the abovementioned assassination and several impressive convictions of certain kingpins under the Prevention of Organised Crime Act of 1999, for too many of the usual suspects it's still business as usual.[19] Some continue to camouflage their crimes under legitimate enterprises. Others swaggeringly stake their turf claims based on arguments about entitlement or more prosaic needs.

Granted, the history of organised crime in South Africa has been shaped by oppression. Acknowledging this legacy should lead to a greater understanding of its present grip on South African society. Redressing past inequities will inevitably reduce the allure of gangs. Effective law enforcement will most certainly serve as a future deterrent to crime cartels. And adequately addressing the consequences of organised crime depends on the ability and will of all the gatekeepers of our democracy to protect the constitutional rights of our citizens, whether free in South Africa or incarcerated overseas.

But there seemed to me to be neither the ability nor the will on the part of government to even acknowledge that fundamental human-rights violations are being perpetrated against naive South Africans like Thando Pendu. She would spend much of her adult life behind bars for a crime she insisted she didn't willingly commit, isolated from her family, ignorant of the expedient union between crime and politics, and of her constitutional rights. It would be left to the determination of a few unlikely heroes to fight for her and hundreds of other South Africans locked up abroad.

186

15

BABSIE

I was further motivated to continue with my investigations into transnational drug smuggling, and its links to human trafficking, by a series of events that began unfolding towards the end of 2011. In December of that year, most of the South Africans who had been incarcerated in Thailand from 1994 were preparing themselves for early release. This was due to various amnesties that had been granted. Dawn van Niekerk was the first to return, followed by Gladys Naidoo and Shani Krebs, almost exactly 18 years after the day of his arrest. Vanessa Goosen had been granted an amnesty in October 2010. Unlike Vanessa and Shani, who were extensively interviewed and subsequently embarked on high-profile careers as motivational speakers and authors, Dawn and Gladys, as well as Nila Duginov and Octavia Malevu, opted to avoid the media spotlight and set upon quietly repairing the remnants of their shattered lives.

In less than six months after the announcement of the amnesty by the Thai authorities, however, three new South African 'recruits' had been caught and ended up replacing those who had just been released. One of them became the unwitting poster girl for drug mules worldwide when press photographs and television footage of her cocaine-filled dreadlocks made global headlines.

Twenty-three-year-old Nolubabalo Nobanda, otherwise known as Babsie, was apprehended on 3 December 2011 at Bangkok's Suvarnabhumi Airport. She was picked out by the immigration police and led to a room where cameras were installed. During the press conference, a Thai police officer remarked that an immigration official had noticed 'some white powder' in her hair and that had led the authorities to take her in for questioning and to unravel, literally, her elaborate Rastafarian camouflage. Only, the photographs and footage confirm the absence of any visible white powder in Babsie's hair. The reality is that Thai customs officials had been tipped off and had alerted the press long before she landed. When cross-examined during her trial, the police officer altered his story and claimed an informant had been the source of the intelligence about the cocaine in her dreadlocks.

What subsequently emerged from Babsie's sworn statement echoed the tragedy of Thando's fate, almost three years before. Born in Grahamstown, Babsie was studying law in Johannesburg and occasionally worked at the court as a translator. One day, in November 2011, her old friend, Sulezo Rwanqa, offered Babsie what she thought was the opportunity of a lifetime. Sulezo had a Nigerian friend in Port Elizabeth called Samuel Uchengo, who ran a small amenities shop in Upper Hill Street called New Age. He had a brother living in Brazil, Tony Uchengo, who owned a business in hair chemicals, she said. Sulezo then claimed that Tony had employed her to sell the hair chemicals in South Africa and invited Babsie to join her in Brazil to meet him.

This and the following are extracts taken from Babsie's sworn statement: 'We went to see Samuel who told us not to worry; he would organise the ticket, even pocket money! We were to fly from Cape Town to Argentina and from there to São Paulo, Brazil.'

But Samuel had booked them on different flights: Babsie was to leave a day after Sulezo because 'the flights were full'.

When Babsie arrived in São Paulo, Sulezo and a man came to

escort her to the Hotel Topiza. Babsie and Sulezo were told to go to a bus stop the next day, where a woman would be waiting for them. Her name was Hilda, an elderly South African. She told the girls that she was working for Tony and that her job was to take care of the girls who came to work for him. She mentioned the job would be hard and dangerous. That is when Babsie realised that the job supposedly selling hair chemicals entailed smuggling drugs for the Nigerians: 'She said Samuel was recruiting South African women for Tony and other Nigerians selling drugs … I told Hilda I was not prepared to be a smuggler … She said it was too late. The Nigerians would kill me … or attack my family in South Africa if they thought I was a threat … I thought Sulezo had been misled by Samuel and Tony but she did not look shocked at all. We were to swallow the drugs wrapped in condoms. I cried. I was vomiting but was forced to try. I cursed myself for having been so stupid. They then suggested that the drugs be wrapped up in my hair. I agreed, seeing it as a way out of Brazil.'

Babsie only learnt that she was going to fly to Thailand when she got to the airport on the day of departure and her ticket was given to her. 'There I was going to meet Sulezo and [someone called] John … The Nigerians told me that Sulezo had taken 15 kilograms of drugs to Thailand. In Thailand, it seemed the immigration officers knew that I was coming. They went straight for me and took me to a separate room. The cameras had already been set up. I told the police that I was coming to Sulezo and John. They phoned the two but their phones were off. I told the police to let me go but follow me until I meet Sulezo and John. They refused. I deeply regret the hurt this has caused to my family. I also apologise to South Africa as a whole. To this court, I express my heart-felt apology. By the time I came to Brazil there was no way of turning the clock back. Although Sulezo was in Thailand, she was never arrested. Since she returned to South Africa, she has not visited my family.'

* * *

In the interim, Janice Linden, a 36-year-old South African woman convicted of drug smuggling in China, had been executed in December 2011, despite desperate efforts by her family in South Africa to get her sentence commuted to life. In 2008 she had been arrested at the Baiyun International Airport after 3 kilograms of tik had been found in her luggage. Throughout, she had protested her innocence, but several court appeals against her execution had proven futile.

'You must come and see me soon.' Those were the tearful words of Linden to her two sisters, Nomalizwi Mhlophe and Priscilla Mthalane, during a 45-minute visit to Guandong Prison, the day before she was executed by lethal injection.

According to media reports, Linden was not aware that she was going to die the following day, and one of the conditions of the visit was that her sisters from Durban were not allowed to tell her. They were also prevented from disclosing that their mother and uncle had died earlier that year.

When they saw their sister for the last time, she was chained to what looked like a wheelchair, with her hands and feet bound. Separated by a thick glass panel and surrounded by Chinese warders, they were unable to even embrace their distraught sibling for a final farewell.

Devout Roman Catholics, the sisters requested permission to sprinkle holy water on Linden, but the authorities refused. Their plea to take one last photograph with her was also declined.

After Linden's death, her devastated family echoed the accusation made by Sabelo Sibanda that the South African Government had sacrificed the rights and dignity of its citizens at the altar of relations with its Asian trading partners.

In an interview with journalist Mpume Madlala in December 2011, Linden's nephew, Ntando Mthalane, bluntly articulated his family's dismay and disgust: 'My opinion of the government is that they could have done more, but they didn't. But I am sure that if it was voting time they would have done more and she would still be alive. If we trade with China, I am sure that they could have done something, but they let her die,' he said.[1]

*   *   *

In December 2011, media reports also detailed the 'escape' of 'Nono', a young woman who, apparently, had been duped into taking a job overseas, forced to swallow over a kilogram of drugs on four different continents, and deprived of both food and finance for 'disobeying the syndicate's orders'. Fortunately, she had escaped from Istanbul, Turkey, where she was booked on a flight to Bangladesh, together with two other South Africans, and was now in witness protection.

At the airport the women had been interrogated by customs about their impending trip to Bangladesh. 'We told them that we were going there to meet our sister who was going to buy us tickets to South Africa, and they offered to convert our tickets. That is how we managed to escape from the drug lords,' 'Nono' said.

In an interview with South African journalist, Gcwalisile Khanyile, the 30-year-old woman said she had responded to an advert in the classified section of newspaper *Isolezwe* in October 2011.

'I phoned the number and I was interviewed at the Teacher's Centre in Durban for what seemed like a legitimate job at a shoe factory, where I would be in charge of transporting shoes from Nepal to South Africa,' she said. During the interview, she said, there were two Nigerian men and one Zulu-speaking woman.

When she landed in Nepal, she was informed of the real purpose behind her recruitment: 'We were a group of nine when we left the country. When we got to Nepal, the Nigerian guy told us that we have got to be kidding to think that we can be brought all the way from Africa to Asia just for shoes. That's when we were told that we will be transporting drugs from one country to another.'

After being subjected to a period of 'training', during which she was force-fed baby carrots to rehearse for ingesting the real drugs, she was made to swallow 102 pieces of cocaine – just over a kilogram: 'I took the cocaine from Nepal to Bangladesh. From there I went to Bolivia to collect more drugs which were to be taken to Bangladesh. Nigerian drug lords rule the world. They have their people in each and every airport around the world. They have pictures of all their drug mules. I suspect they thought we ran away with the drugs, whereas we made a U-turn to South Africa prior to collecting them.'

'Nono' added that her handler was also adept at manufacturing fake passports.

Once again, her account is eerily similar to Thando's – and, more recently, Babsie's. In fact, she also reported having seen Babsie in Brazil, but Babsie was part of another group.

She added that none of the women were permitted to leave the hotel where they were being 'trained' without being accompanied by an enforcer. They were also forbidden to phone home. If they couldn't consume their allotted quota of drugs (in narco-speak, 'pieces'), they would be punished by being deprived of food.

Former Hawks spokesman McIntosh Polela had confirmed that the women had allegedly escaped from a Nigerian syndicate, but declined to comment further 'for fear of jeopardising investigations and revealing the identities of the women'.

Without connecting the dots between the local recruiters and their transnational accomplices, the cops would come up with squat. In the case of Thando, when they had been provided with concrete leads, they had failed to even bring in Thembi for questioning.

I found it nauseating to think of the scenario of these young women holed up in sordid hotels in foreign countries, coerced into becoming body packers. However, without a trustworthy intermediary who was close to these South Africans, who could interview the women about their recruiters, handlers and enforcers, and cross-compare their information in search of recurring names and recognisable identities, I felt any further investigations that I undertook would be little more than examples of passive, armchair reportage.

Babsie's statement seemed to me like a grim facsimile of the circumstances surrounding Thando's entrapment. What if Janice Linden had also been a victim of human trafficking?

My first impulse was to fly to Thailand to interview Babsie, but I wasn't prepared to become a self-appointed victim of Thailand's lese-majesty laws. A preferable option was to connect with a trustworthy source in Bangkok – someone with neither a political, personal nor criminal agenda, who would have some access to her and the remaining South African women incarcerated in Lard Yao Prison. But my options were limited. Alex, the Liberian who had provided me with an invaluable introductory course to the drugs network in Bangkok, had returned to his homeland. Another contact, Anke van Niekerk, who, through a Christian group had been my initial contact in Bangkok during 2009, had also left. And I suspected that Elizabeth Kramer Grimm, Shani's altruistic girlfriend, would be expending more than enough emotional energy, courtesy of Shani's imminent release and departure, to be able to serve as a useful intermediary. As for the South African Embassy, based on its flaccid reaction to my information pertaining to Thando's case, that was a no-hoper.

Then, it happened. It was one of those serendipitous events of circumstance, timing and whatever else one chooses to ascribe to fate. In March 2012 I had written an article for the *Mail & Guardian* on Shani's release, attempting to convey through written wordcraft what the often profoundly shallow medium of television can't achieve. Although the piece was penned to convey both the plight of the South African prisoners overseas and their families at home, the subtext was more complex: that the supply-and-demand chain in the narcotics industry forms a symbiotic relationship, that one cannot address one component without addressing the other and that there is no prospect of successful resolution of the so-called war on drugs unless the problem is tackled on the dual fronts of supply and demand.

The piece elicited an ebullient response: several of Shani's worldwide network of friends posted messages on Facebook expressing support. One of them, Louise Roth Fisher, a South African expatriate living in Australia, mentioned that she had been in regular contact with some of the South African women incarcerated in Bangkok, particularly Dawn van Niekerk, who had spent 18 years behind bars. Like Vanessa Goosen, Dawn had also given birth to her daughter in prison and sent her back to South Africa when she was eight months old.

Louise gave me the name of a remarkable man living in Bangkok. He was not South African, but over the years had become a friend and mentor to the South African women in Lard Yao. He visited them on a weekly basis, sent regular reports on their welfare to their loved ones in South Africa, made representations on their behalf to the South African Embassy in Bangkok and helped them financially. In short, a guardian angel. Since Babsie's arrest, he had started visiting her as well. I had not met him during my trip to Thailand in 2009 but had heard of him. Apparently he was brilliant, sometimes brash and definitely not a man to be messed with. Louise kindly provided me with his email address and I composed what I hoped would be a persuasive plea for assistance. His response was prompt and welcoming:

Hi Hazel, thanks for your mail.

It will be my pleasure to help you in whatever way you feel I can contribute to your work. I have been visiting (and still do every week) men as well as women inmates in Thailand over the last four years, mostly South Africans. When I saw your report, I did realise that some of them are actually not drug mules but victims of human trafficking. For sure, in Thando and Babsie's case, they both refused to carry drugs! ... I felt something ought to be done to avoid more victims, but also to help those still in the hearing phase of their trial (it is too late for Babsie) and make the Thai justice system aware that these people are victims of human trafficking rather than mules; they were forced (misled, threatened) to do it. The only way to achieve this, I came to realise (thanks to your report), was to give it as much media attention as possible. In Babsie's case, for example, we argued with her lawyer that she should inform the judge that Babsie did what she did under duress. The reply was, 'Well, can you prove it? What does the SA police say?' etc ... Obviously we couldn't and the argument was thrown out ... I got them all to write down their statements and I have their permission to hopefully trigger some investigations in SA whereupon that could be used here in their trials ...

I can share with you the difficulties and frustrations that we are encountering when it comes to helping the inmates, to get necessities to them, the games the guards play, the red tape we have to go through, just to get them one pair of underwear for example ... The difficulties to get the families to visit them longer than normal, overseas families do not come every week, the non-committal help from the embassy in this matter etc ...

I can give you insight into the difference between the men and the women's conditions (I regularly visited Shani and Willem, and still visit one male inmate in Bangkwang); compared to the women, the men live in a five-star hotel ...

So, Hazel, to cut a long story short, I would be delighted to help you out. Just let me know how you would like to proceed, I am open for your suggestions; emails, Skype calls, just call or whatever you feel is appropriate.

With that email, the smoke swirling about in my wilderness of mirrors, which had been clogging my nostrils and blurring my sight, suddenly began to clear.

16

THE ALCHEMIST

Most fiction writers comply with a formula that I like to call the 'holy trinity' of characterisation: they categorise the villains, victims and heroes who drive the plot. In life, however, the boundaries between good and evil, innocent and guilty are not always so easily drawn. Sometimes fact confounds even the most adventurous imaginations, adding credence to Mark Twain's dictum that truth is stranger than fiction, because fiction is limited by possibilities. In other words, in order to be believable, fiction has to make sense. Truth isn't hampered by such prescription. That four-letter 'F word', 'fact', stamps any narrative, however strangely contorted or implausibly attenuated, with a seal of legitimacy that appears incontestable.

As journalism teaches one, however, every story is dependent on its angle of vision. Just as the cameraman uses point of view to sharpen the contours around certain subjects, thereby augmenting their significance at the expense of others, likewise journalists shift the frame and focus to heighten selected shapes of truth over others. This creates the effect of a meticulous representation: a partial re-structuring, re-creation and re-presentation of a reality that ultimately defies neat categorisation.

Moreover, in our sometimes circuitous search for the truth, we might paradoxically resort to traversing the darkest recesses of the imagination, while acknowledging that accurately piecing together empirical evidence, facts that defy the most depraved of fantasies, constitutes a greater challenge.

And, truth be told, fiction would be hard-pressed to convincingly conceptualise two more unlikely heroes than Patricia Gerber and a Bangkok-based stranger who had become the guardian angel to numerous South African woman incarcerated in Bangkok's Klong Prem Prison. It is not merely due to an over-saturated diet of detective novels and photo comics during my youth that I dare not publish his name. Emissaries of organised crime infiltrate places of incarceration, whether as corrupt warders, planted inmates or drug-trafficking syndicates who visit the mules to secure their silence through threats and bribes. And, as I was to discover through my long-distance support of Thando, individuals operating under the guise of religious ministries sometimes serve as proxies for the gangs, defrauding the inmates of desperately needed money by persuading their families to transfer the funds into their own personal bank accounts, under the pretext that the money will reach its beneficiaries more rapidly than via the inmate's embassy.

If any of these individuals were to latch on to the role my Bangkok connection has played in assisting the South African prisoners, especially women, I have no doubt he would be targeted for elimination.

Consequently, the alias I have chosen for him is Al – short for 'the alchemist'. A name with transformative associations, it alludes to his brilliant investigative prowess and ability to navigate the transnational maze of narcotics networks stretching from South America and Asia to South Africa. However, his alchemical potions have not been those most typical to the covert trade, like surveillance cameras, encryption software and forensic techniques. Al's arsenal has comprised the more pedestrian, informal instruments of information technology, namely social media.

Our introductory exchanges began via email and progressed

to Skype, BBM and Facebook. Through Facebook we were able, with essential pointers from Patricia, to uncover certain people, and deconstruct hierarchies of drug lords, enforcers, handlers, recruiters, mules and decoys.

Al regularly visited the South African women incarcerated in Klong Prem, motivated both by a genuine desire to assist them and a growing outrage at what he perceived to be the failure of the South African Embassy to fulfil even the most rudimentary of diplomatic services, such as attending the trials of arrested South Africans, informing their families of their convictions or facilitating their access to educational material. These services fall under the Vienna Convention on Diplomatic Relations (1961) and Consular Relations (1963), respectively. The South African Government slavishly adheres to these treaties when it comes to non-interference in the judicial processes of sovereign states, but chooses to ignore them when it comes to providing basic support to its citizens incarcerated overseas. For example, under Article 36 of the Vienna Convention on Consular Relations, which is the accepted standard for all 167 member countries, citizens imprisoned outside their own country must have access to their consular representatives. Consuls are empowered to arrange for their nationals' legal representation, and to provide a wide range of humanitarian and other assistance. Local laws and regulations must also give 'full effect' to the rights enshrined in Article 36.[1]

Unfortunately, when it comes to South Africans imprisoned abroad, our embassies vary widely in their interpretations of 'access' and 'rights'.

To those who felt abandoned by the government and harshly judged by society, Al offered succour. He became their intermediary to a world from which they had been locked out and unable to access through the conventional channels. They were dependent on letters from home, censored and often irregular, to maintain their increasingly tenuous link to life beyond the prison walls. Al was their conduit and confidant, offering both practical advice and a compassionate, non-judgemental ear to those who admitted having knowingly attempted to smuggle drugs, due to desperation or greed, and were facing consequences that many felt were not commensurate with their crimes.

He also listened with horror to the narratives of women who insisted they had been tricked or coerced into drug trafficking and had no choice but to obey the syndicates or face being murdered by them. These accounts propelled him beyond the role of support system into becoming a tenacious investigator by the realisation that several of these so-called convicted mules did not deserve to be there in the first place. 'This is human trafficking,' he said. 'Coercing naive, but innocent people to do things they don't want to do is trafficking! I know it, you know it, your government knows it ... yet nothing is done!'

So struck was he by this realisation that he compiled a dossier called 'Three Little Piggies – A Dark Tale of Nigerian Deceit'. The title is a composite of the allegory about the three little pigs who leave home and are threatened by their dangerous external environment, and the nursery rhyme 'This Little Piggy Went to Market', which exemplified the struggle among the working classes of 18th-century England in the face of the imminent mechanisation of society.

Al's little piggies were three particular convicted South African drug mules incarcerated in Klong Prem, but they were emblematic of all the South African women who had been lured or ensnared into the dense network of transnational drug trafficking. The 'dark deceit' part of the narrative referred to and identified several Nigerian vendors in the 'market'. These were individual syndicate members based not only in Bangkok, but also Cambodia and Mexico, who, although living physically apart, were inextricably connected to the women in prison, to one another and, disturbingly, to a vast coterie of South African professional drug mules.

Al sent this dossier, with its meticulous analysis illustrated by means of organograms identifying drug networks and their links to the mules, as well as photographs of certain syndicate members, to Patricia and me. He gave us permission to use the information in whatever way we chose. I believed it would be of enormous assistance in furthering my investigations into Thando's handler in Bangkok, and Patricia was determined to pass it on to those in government who had the capacity to act on Al's intelligence.

'Looking back at all the events that led me to write up this tale of deceit,' Al wrote, 'I am wondering why I do all this, as there will be nothing I can do to stop all this muling and decoying; the fight to stop all this needs to be fought in South Africa. However if my nosy exercises can contribute to that fight in South Africa, I would be happy.'

His case studies included Babsie, the most high-profile of the South African mules since the release of Vanessa Goosen and Shani Krebs, Nicolene Kruger, arrested in Thailand in November 2011 for being in possession of cocaine, and Adelina Lephutha Ononiwu, who was caught in April 2012 with 2 kilograms of crystal methamphetamine.

In January 2012, Al had been contacted by Babsie's mother, Honjiswa, and uncle, Lutsiki, who learnt that he was regularly visiting the South African inmates. 'They asked if I could help them out in liaising between them and Babsie,' he explained.

On 19 March 2012, Babsie was due to appear in court to make a statement relating to the coercion she had faced leading up to her arrest, hopefully in mitigation of her sentence. Al was present to assist with translating and, as he was savvy in Thai law, to provide guidance: 'While we were talking to Babsie, a tall, blonde white woman, another South African inmate awaiting her hearing, asked if she could give me a message to send to her family in South Africa,' he wrote in his dossier.

Her name was Nicolene Kruger and she had apparently been unlawfully arrested by police in Bangkok and driven to Pattaya, where she was forced to remain overnight. The following day she was driven back to Bangkok, formally arrested and charged with cocaine trafficking.

The third little piggy, Adelina Lephutha Ononiwu, was a

self-confessed professional mule. She knew what she was doing and she visited other mules regularly when she lived in South Africa. Unfortunately, when she was arrested, she had been recruited to be the decoy, unbeknown to her. From the way she was caught, it is clear that she had been offered as a trophy to the Thai narcotics police.

Of the three, Babsie's case appeared incontrovertibly to have been one of human trafficking. The other two women presented somewhat patchy, convoluted and contradictory narratives. It was only after many visits that Al began to understand their painful but deliberate trajectories into the criminal economy.

Below, I have paraphrased Nicolene's story, as penned and narrated to me by Al:

A single parent with nine children, Nicolene had been a drug addict, sucked into a symbiotic pit of dependence and duplicity, which included participation in the drug trade to support her habit. She had an uneasy association with the Nigerian syndicate that supplied her with drugs and expected other forms of payback when she couldn't afford them.

Nicolene socialised and worked in the bars of Germiston and Brakpan. She claimed she had been set up by a friend, whose Nigerian husband, 'Peter', had offered her a 'trip' to Brazil to take her mind off her woes. He had even organised a tour guide to accompany her on a visit to Thailand on her way home. On 20 November 2011, Nicolene boarded a plane to São Paulo. Clearly, 'Peter' was extremely well connected – so much so that after she had run out of money and called him in desperation, Nicolene was informed by him that his brother 'Tony' would sort her out. Sure enough, Tony gave her 500 dollars, and the next day she was off to Vietnam.

There she was introduced to Nontaya Kaensen, daughter of a Nigerian father and a Thai mother. It was only much later, after the two women were arrested for drug trafficking, that Nicolene heard Nontaya had prior convictions for drug smuggling.

On 29 November, they arrived in Bangkok together. As they were about to check into a hotel, two men approached them. They were police officers, but did not identify themselves as such. They confiscated Nicolene's phone and passport, before bundling both women into the back seat of a car and shoving their luggage in the boot. They were driven to a house in Pattaya (120 kilometres from Bangkok), where they were forced to remain overnight.

The following morning, the women were driven to a Bangkok police station, where Nicolene's bag was opened, revealing 7 kilograms of cocaine inside.

On 14 March 2013, Nicolene and Nontaya were both found guilty of trafficking. Each was sentenced to 33 years in jail, although Nicolene's term was reduced to 22 years for 'admitting guilt'.

Despite the court records stating her guilty plea – Thailand's court-appointed lawyers will not represent farangs unless they admit guilt – Nicolene had consistently said to Al that she was innocent. But there were obvious contradictions in her account. As with the sex trade, in the world of drugs, there is always a quid pro quo. And, given her history of addiction, it is not far-fetched to presuppose that the 'pro quo' attached to Nicolene's 'quid' entailed smuggling drugs into Bangkok. Whether she did so willingly remains a subject of contention. However, three issues are worth highlighting in relation to this dismal tale so diligently documented by Al.

Firstly, there were obvious procedural irregularities committed by the Thai police who seized and searched Nicolene's luggage and ultimately arrested her. Secondly, Al insisted that the South African Embassy committed a shocking dereliction of duty in its handling of this unfortunate woman's rights and recourse to a fair trial.

In his dossier, Al wrote that Nicolene's lawyer could not speak English, that the guilty plea she was forced to sign was in Thai and that there was no translator present to assist her. This is where the South African Embassy had a duty to intervene. But it did not. An embassy representative did not even attend Nicolene's trial and did not inform her family of her conviction or sentence. Al had to break the news to her children at home, who were still reeling from a family tragedy: one of Nicolene's children had died shortly after her incarceration, supposedly from a drug overdose.

The third issue of significance is Nicolene's mention of 'Tony', Peter's Nigerian 'brother' in São Paulo, who supposedly assisted her with the cash. Al was convinced this was the same Tony who had met Babsie in Brazil, suggesting a link between the syndicates.

It was left to Adelina, the third little piggy in Al's dossier, to join the dots.

According to the account she gave Al over a period of months, Adelina was close to a fellow professional mule, a certain Lucky Herman, whose boyfriend, Bobby Norseman, was a South African pulling the syndicate trafficking strings from Cambodia. In June 2012, Adelina had been en route to Cambodia, via Nigeria, with a stopover in Bangkok. While in Lagos, she had encountered several South African mules but was not allowed to have contact with them, she said.

But she named a list of Nigerian and South African–born syndicate members she had met in Lagos, whose roles within the syndicate included 'cooking' the stuff, as she called it, handling the mules and enforcing their authority over those who might harbour second thoughts about their participation in the trade. According to Adelina, her friend Lucky also joined her in Nigeria before Adelina's flight to Bangkok.

'They were supposed to travel together,' Al said, 'but something came up and Adelina had to go first and alone. She flew via Kenya to Bangkok and was supposed to connect with a flight to Cambodia when she was picked up by the narcotics police at Bangkok Airport on 18 June, 2012.'

Adelina firmly believed she had been set up by her friend,

Lucky. As the vagaries of transnational trafficking would have it, Lucky's own fate would not live up to her name. On 24 August 2012, she too was arrested, at Mumbai Airport, with 18 kilograms of amphetamine in her luggage. She had been apprehended by India's customs-intelligence unit while she was on her way to board a flight to Ethiopia.

Angered by her betrayal at the hands of her 'sister' and possibly spurred by remorse, Adelina had provided Al with some gems of information. She had met Hilda, Babsie's handler, and Peter in Brazil. She also spoke in detail of her journeys across each hemisphere and just about every time zone. And she offered further evidence of the transnational links between drug syndicates using South Africa as a launch pad for their illicit trade and their connections as far afield as Cambodia, where Bobby Norseman operated, and Mexico.

She had also provided Al with the names and numbers of the Nigerian syndicate members, and the places she had frequented with them in Orange Grove, Norwood and several other Johannesburg suburbs. Al passed on this information to me and, indeed, much of it added up. For example, I had established that a certain Ben (senior syndicate members never disclose their surnames to the mules unless they are bogus names) owned several clubs in Orange Grove, including Fashion Society, off Grant Avenue, as well as a dodgy den called Groove Comfort, off Louis Botha Avenue, which was no longer operating as a club but which, Adelina revealed to Al, was used to stash their illicit cargo. Unable to check out all the places myself, I passed on the information to 'Ted', my contact in Organised Crime.

His findings confirmed my suspicions: 'We all know about "Ben". He goes by several names but was working for your friend, Chika Odimara, the one you were investigating in 2001, who was wanted by both Nigeria and the DEA [Drug Enforcement Administration], and who was eventually deported from South Africa.'

Again, the usual suspects. My investigation into Odimara, briefly mentioned earlier in this book, had gone nowhere, even after his deportation. Now I understood why. Odimara was in deep with the Alberton mafia, who were tight with Agliotti and, of course, Selebi. Ted continued: 'After Chika's deportation, Ben became one of the kingpins. In Gauteng, he's got about 17 senior lieutenants underneath him.'

Apparently, Ben's fiefdom extended through all the cardinal points of Gauteng – Randburg, in the north, Glenvista, in the south, Alberton and Benoni, in the east, and Florida, in the west – and beyond.

Adelina had recalled meeting Thembi, Thando's 'recruiter', somewhere in Orange Grove, but couldn't remember the exact location. She also expressed ignorance of anyone called Nonso Okeke, Thando's Nigerian enforcer who had watched her every move during her ill-fated sojourn in Bangkok.

* * *

Of course, Al and I had to treat Adelina's information with a degree of scepticism: after all, she was a pro trained in manipulation and duplicity. Nonetheless, most of the nuggets she provided were of considerable value, as our subsequent research would prove.

Al's principal investigative modus operandi was simple but rigorous. And it yielded spectacular success, notwithstanding the constraints imposed by his brief prison visits, the unsympathetic Thai authorities and an indifferent attitude on the part of the South African Embassy in Bangkok. During his weekly visits, he would interview the women and ask them to write down their accounts, which he would then compare with the sworn statements they had made after their arrests.

His first breakthrough in terms of identifying their handlers emerged from a conversation with Babsie: 'On 31 July 2012, Babsie received a strange visit in jail. A man called John visited her. Initially she was going to refuse the visit (inmates can always refuse a visit), but she thought it might have been me. So she went to the visiting area and the man asked who she was and where she came from.'

Al continued: 'Babsie was smart in replying: "Why do you want to visit me if you don't even know my name and where I am from?" The man then went to another booth to speak to another woman and left Babsie sitting alone. After a while, he returned to Babsie but appeared uncomfortable and wanted to leave.'

It should be recalled that in her sworn statement submitted to the Thailand court, Babsie had mentioned that on her arrival in Thailand she was supposed to meet up with a syndicate member called John.

In the interim, through her website, Locked Up in a Foreign Country, Patricia Gerber had been assembling her own intelligence database. Her informants included professional mules who, under the cloak of anonymity, wanted to expose the syndicates – either out of remorse or revenge. They had directed her to Facebook, where some of the less discreet syndicate members had set up profiles, and downloaded pictures of themselves and a vast network of 'friends'. On Patricia's instructions, Al downloaded five photographs of Nigerians residing in Thailand, whom the mules had identified as drug-syndicate members. On his next visit, he showed them to Babsie. And indeed, she recognised one of the photographs as belonging to John, the man who had mysteriously visited her. His Facebook name was Oge Nwebuisi.

Then, Patricia, Al and I were able to begin making the connections, one Facebook profile at a time. This entailed the onerous and sometimes almost voyeuristic task of perusing Oge's list of friends (he boasted hundreds). We trawled through the web pages, thumbnail photo by thumbnail photo, populated by names provided by the mules who had made contact with Patricia. With the help of Al's meticulous organograms, the process was akin to unravelling an intricate fractal calculation. We would type in a name mentioned by a mule on a friend page.

If it came up positive, it would provide a portal to another list. And another ...

Al's surveillance of the South African–sourced Nigerian narcotics network stretched as far as Mexico, where a certain Kingsley appeared to be the big fish. He posted photos on separate Facebook accounts under two pseudonyms: Jark Kingsley and Kingsley Onyeka. But it was evident from the identical smirks and preening devotees on both pages that the two profiles were one and the same person. His Facebook photo albums were resplendent with nubile young things, principally of African and Mediterranean origin, to whom he referred, paternalistically, as his little fishes. Judging from the dates of certain photographs, Jark had made regular pilgrimages to South Africa, to attend evangelical praise functions, which, from the comments accompanying the images, seemed like a cross between Disneyworld and the second coming. With few exceptions, most of the syndicate members identified by Patricia, Al and myself belonged to a religious ministry or church. There were so many 'hallelujahs' and 'praise the lords' that one felt like a witness to the Rapture.

Based on the information provided by Babsie, Nicolene and Adelina (the latter had given him the password to her Facebook account), Al would download photos and present them to the three women in Klong Prem under the guise of showing them family photographs (to outwit the suspicious prison warders). He would then have to wait until the following week before he received a response. If it was in the affirmative, we would share our excitement as we gained further access into a world of shadowy, evangelical narcissism ... with the various agents unashamedly flaunting the bounty of their illicit trade joined by a chorus of gushy professional mules clearly intoxicated by the risks and the rewards.

*　*　*

However, as we feverishly searched for and uncovered more links in the syndicate's chain of command, there was one name that remained elusive: Nonso Okeke, the Nigerian living in Bangkok who had been Thando's enforcer. I had scoured the Internet in search of articles or reports that might mention his name in a drug bust, to no avail. Every time I typed 'Okeke', it either came up blank or that specific Okeke was not affiliated to any of the syndicate members who had been positively identified by the women in Klong Prem.

Late one night, I logged onto Oge Nwebuisi's page. In the blank line above the friends list, I typed 'Nonso'. A photograph appeared: Joshua Nonso (Bangkok). I clicked onto it and discovered a very brief friends list, some of whom I recognised from the photographs we had already positively identified, either of mules or those occupying links higher up in the chain of command. Unlike Oge, Nonso Okeke obviously chose his friends more prudently. Then I saw it: friends with a Thembi Dlamini.

The photograph was of Thando's recruiter. I struggled to breathe. Then I messaged Al. It was about 8 am in Bangkok: 'I think I have found Thando's enforcer. He isn't named as Nonso Okeke, but rather Joshua Nonso. You need to show his Facebook photo to Thando.'

Al's immediate reply: 'OMG!'

Al was due to visit the prison the following morning, but he didn't want to hand over the photograph directly to Thando. His reason: he was concerned she might innocently mention his visit to a certain woman from a Christian ministry, who regularly visited Thando, ostensibly to assist her – a woman with dodgy drug connections. If the woman knew of his investigations she might alert the syndicates who still maintained a watchful eye over convicted mules and decoys. Al would not risk his and Thando's safety. He mentioned the woman's name: Shamalee. It struck a familiar chord.

Since our first meeting in January 2009, together with Dan, her long-suffering boyfriend in Port Elizabeth, I had been sending Thando money to help her buy soap, toilet paper, sanitary towels – basics that are denied female inmates unless they have the money to pay for them. I had heard reports of the South African Embassy delaying the transfer of funds and had opted instead to deposit the money in the bank account of Anke van Niekerk, the South African in Bangkok who had been my contact when I went there to interview Shani in 2009. Anke had since left Bangkok, but before her departure she had put me in contact with a woman called Shamalee Senaratne, who also visited the South Africans. I had contacted Shamalee and, encouraged by her willingness to assist, had entrusted her with the small amounts of cash Dan and I occasionally sent to Thando. Shamalee would send me intermittent email reports on Thando. She would also update me diligently on her new contact details, which, she explained, changed regularly due to her frenetic global itinerary, performing apostolic work all over the world, particularly in Africa. I had interpreted the updates as proof of her devotion to her spiritual calling and dedication to Thando's welfare.

I informed Al of my connection to Shamalee. His response horrified me: 'Hazel, I know that woman. She is a crook and possibly involved with the Nigerian syndicates. She has defrauded many people out of considerable amounts of money. Worse still, she has been systematically fleecing many foreign prisoners, using her so-called ministry as a front. Charges have been laid against her and there is a warrant out for her arrest.' He added: 'She's in and out of the country all the time and regularly changes addresses to elude the authorities.'

It would therefore be ill-advised for Al to have direct contact with Thando, lest Shamalee or one of her connections caught wind of their exchange. The only way he could get the photograph of Joshua Nonso to Thando was via Babsie, with whom Thando had become close friends.

The period between Al slipping the photograph to Babsie, and her then showing it to Thando, seemed interminable.

A week later, he emailed me: 'We're making progress. Thando

recognised him. Joshua Nonso is indeed Nonso Okeke – the man who kept Thando a virtual prisoner in Bangkok!'

He added: 'As soon as possible we need to send this information, together with the dossier on the Three Little Piggies, to the Drug Enforcement Administration in Bangkok and the South African authorities. Without their effective intervention and prosecution of these crime syndicates, this information is useless.'

I ached to tell him my fear – that taking swift, decisive action would not be able to overcome the wall of indifference I had already come up against. I articulated nothing of my misgivings to Al, though, opting to bury my pessimism beneath the buoyancy of the moment.

17

STELLA

December 2012

'Stella' sauntered into the room and, from her studiously practised gait, I could tell she was not a woman who wore her heart
on her sleeve. She'd rather settle for a designer label or five, on
her sleeve, handbag, red-soled shoes and any other visible parts
of her person. She paraded them with a coquettish sway of her
hips, a toss of her waist-length weave and an unambiguous 'fuck
me or fuck you' pout.

I disliked her on sight, not because of how she had earned her
stripes – journos are not judges – but because of the arrogance
with which she flashed her spoils and, most of all, because she
believed her 'profession', as drug mule, has conferred upon her
a certain celebrity status that demanded the reverence of the
media. Even nailing the interview, despite the fact that it was she
who initially contacted me, entailed tortuous negotiations with
a contact who behaved like her personal media spokesperson.
I now berated myself for every miscreant's existence I had ever
glamorised. This had sometimes been inadvertent, but often
came about from my compulsion to infiltrate deviant minds: not
those motivated by desperation, aspiration, anger or despair,
not the opportunist who smashes the window of a car because
of a laptop left carelessly on the passenger seat. The criminal
minds that are often most persuasively, perversely seductive are

those who narcissistically, nonchalantly regard others' lives as less valuable than their own, as cheap currency to be traded or sacrificed: dead cows for piranhas.

Such people include South Africa's sultans of sin, mentioned in previous chapters, whom I deemed as too big to jail, much like the US government's take on collapsed banking giant Lehman Brothers – 'too big to fail'. Stella certainly did not fit the profile of these high flyers. Nevertheless, she occupied a more solid footing in the narcotics hierarchy than the dispensable decoys. She was a professional mule, she was good at her job and she wore her membership of the illicit economy as a designer badge of honour.

Stella had contacted me shortly after my second *Special Assignment* exposé on Thembi was broadcast in February 2010. She had met Thembi in Johannesburg in 2008, she told me, and remembered a young, waif-like woman hanging on Thembi's arm and off her every word: Thando Pendu.

'*Eish*, Thembi was behaving like a mother to Thando – buying her clothes, taking her to restaurants and clubs,' explained Stella.

I'm not entirely sure why Stella had made contact in the first place. Initially, I thought it was to offer assistance with my investigation and I had been grateful for the additional information she had provided on Thembi. It was all off the record and I was bound not to reveal her as a source. At the time, she had been careful not to reveal the details of syndicate names and places frequented by Thembi and her Nigerian entourage, for reasons that were entirely pragmatic. She wasn't about to pimp one of the sisters, especially not one who was a source of lucrative work for her. But she did reveal that Thembi was not just a recruiter of mules and dead cows. She also made the occasional trip herself to Asia, and not in search of designer knock-offs, as Thembi had tried to persuade me during our confrontation, but to earn extra cash when her reserves could no longer accommodate her voracious appetite for the good life.

Our conversation had become a confessional of sorts, motivated by Stella's desire to 'come clean and rid herself of some baggage', she insisted. But as the shifting timbre of her voice began to match the dramatic content of her delivery, I realised that much of what Stella was telling me was what she thought I wanted to hear. This was not so much a confession as an audition for her TV debut. Of course, she would have been stupid to incriminate herself on camera. But television is inherently a narcissistic medium. It both feeds and fuels people's desires, in varying degrees, to be watched. Particularly for some members of the generation raised on the stodge of MTV and reality shows like *Big Brother* and *The Kardashians*, there is no such thing as too much self-exposure. Their need, like that of the drug addict, is for 'more'. Stella had obviously been caught up in the moment, anticipating the hype her story might generate. And I had been torn between my ongoing desire for scintillating subject matter and my abhorrence of pandering to her red-carpet fantasies.

Energised by the progress yielded through Al's and my intrepid detective work, I was hoping to resuscitate leads that would nail both Thembi and her Bangkok-based Nigerian accomplice, Joshua Nonso. I had emailed Bakar, my affable but mercurial Nigerian connection in Bangkok, to enquire whether he knew of the man in question. The response was an instant 'return to sender' message from my service provider, further heightening my suspicion that, despite his protestations to the contrary, Bakar was also involved in Thailand's narco-trade. Al had also advised caution so as not to accidentally alert Bangkok's double dealers – drug smugglers and merchants who are also Drug Enforcement Administration informants – to our progress. I had notified the NPA's Charmaine Labuschagne in Welkom, but had not yet received a reply. So, reluctantly, I had decided that Stella would have to be my next port of call.

Stella was extremely intelligent, with an expansive vocabulary, courtesy of the many books she had read during her numerous global peregrinations to take her mind off the gurgling cargo in her distended gut. During that initial meeting, she had enlightened me with the graphic detail of an MRI scan, about the intricacies of swallowing and expelling the 'pieces', and had clearly revelled in my undisguised queasiness.

I needed Stella to give me further access to the narcotics underworld and, given the failure of the police to even pull Thembi in for questioning, to follow up my investigation into Thando's alleged recruiter. This was planned for another *Special Assignment* documentary about drug mules to be broadcast in February 2013. Now, for the first time, we were meeting at her house in Florida, Johannesburg. But from the outset, I sensed that meeting Stella on her home turf – let alone at all – was another of my less than ingenious ideas.

'I would love your story to be about me,' Stella said gesticulating dramatically, her artificial nails coated a dayglo green with glitter, resembling neon claws. 'It would make such a great realistic movie, I mean, me coming from the township, what I had to go through in Jozi just to survive. And look at me now. I have travelled the world, I have my own apartment, a car, the most expensive clothes,' she winked, displaying the trademark red underside of her Christian Louboutin platforms.

She continued breathlessly: 'My kid will have a good education; he will want for nothing in his life.' She flicked through a passport that resembled a stamp collection, pages adorned with every country on the planet. From being a mule, she had been promoted to the position of recruiter, which paid her between R5 000 and R7 000 per 'traveller'. Like Thembi, she also undertook the occasional trip herself, but was starting to tire of the pre- and post-travelling rites.

She assured me that she would let me document the process of being trained for a drug run, which involved certain beauty treatments because the syndicates wanted their mules to look presentable and not draw attention to themselves as 'riff raff' when they went through customs. Documenting Stella's pre-trip prep would therefore include filming her getting facials, manis, pedis, a new wardrobe and, of course, swallowing the drug capsules that clog the mules' innards. She would do this as a 'warning' to young women who do this work. She might even allow me to reveal her identity, provided we put her on a plane to a 'safe haven' afterwards. She would do it for 'the greater good of society', she assured me, and possibly for a book-publishing deal. She added: 'You could even write it for me, as long as you promise not to use my story for your own purposes without my permission. I could sue you for that.'

I did not relish the prospect of becoming Stella's ghostwriter. Furthermore, I was not about to sponsor a makeover, for the purpose of witnessing a self-centred hustler perform a deep-throat manoeuvre. There was also the risk of trusting her enough to allow me to infiltrate her syndicate, to learn more about Thembi and Nonso Okeke (Joshua Nonso) without the fear of her blowing my cover in exchange for another pair of designer shoes. But, before I officially declined to pen Stella's autobiography and her offer to star in her version of a *Special Assignment* reality show, I wanted to get her to really open up, to reveal more of the underbelly of her trade.

'Stella, weren't you ever terrified? I mean, the sheer risks of swallowing the bananas, not knowing whether or not they would burst, not knowing if or when you were going to be arrested?'

'In the beginning, *ja*, of course. But I am now actually fearless. And, sweetie, the only ones who don't know if they are gonna be bust or not are the ones who are. The rest of us, we are protected. Sure there are nerves, but there is also the adrenalin rush. And the money is damn fine.'

'Yeah, right, high risk, high reward.'

'That's the thing. The risk for those of us who are carrying the big quantities is minor. I have swallowed the pieces, or sometimes I've carried them in my overnight bag, which I have left on the plane in São Paulo, for example. And a customs official or police officer has been briefed to come onto that plane once I have disembarked and remove the bag and bypass customs. It's that simple, it's that organised. The big fish even carry the load on private jets and boats.'

'So, why the need for the decoys?'

'Because the arrests look good for the authorities. Technology has progressed – I mean you can soak clothing in cocaine or heroin. You can hollow out the platforms of shoes and stash it in there, not only in suitcases, which is so 1990s. You actually don't need to swallow the shit any more.'

She added, 'Really, cocaine in that girl Babsie's dreadlocks. That was so ridiculous! The newspapers wrote that the Thai customs noticed white crumbs on her scalp and got suspicious. But I watched the TV coverage on the news. There was no white stuff on her scalp. It was only when they cut her dreads that they found the shit. They were waiting for her because she was the decoy. From time to time, the decoys are useful for the stats. They are small fry, losers.'

'So what you are telling me is that it is all predetermined. The syndicate chooses someone to be a decoy? Based on what?'

'Hey, listen when I was recruited I was put through the training, the shopping trips, the beauty parlour, so that I looked like a sophisticated traveller. If she looks too nervous, she is a risk. If she looks too common, she is a risk. If she is too stubborn or wants more money, or gets emotionally involved, she's dead meat. If she changes her mind and tells them she doesn't want to do it ... And, yes, if she doesn't know what she is getting into, if she thinks she has landed herself a great job in another country, man she is dead meat.'

She added: 'And if she tries to pull a fast one, well, she is just dead.'

Stella provided a gruesome account of a mule who had heroin pellets stuffed in her vagina. When she tried to retrieve them, she was short of a couple: 'The guys thought she might have stashed them somewhere for herself because she had developed a bit of a habit. So they roughed her up badly. And then, when she was still conscious, they stuck a coat hanger up her pussy just to make sure they weren't lodged inside. They got them out, but there was blood everywhere. Then I think they dumped her body in the ocean.' She added: 'You dare not mess with those guys. That's why they like me. I show them respect.'

She took out her laptop, a MacBook Air elegantly encased in a red leather cover, and logged onto Facebook. There were photographs of a considerably slimmer Stella at Bangkok Airport, captioned with 'Thank you Jesus for delivering me safely' and several comments from fellow mules and syndicate members: 'Well done, sista. G-d is great', from Lucky; 'Welcome to Bangkok', from David; 'You are beoootifal', from someone who goes by the moniker of 'Pastor John'.

'So what is the largest stash you have ever carried on a drug run?'

'*Eish*, that's a tough one. But once, in 2009, I travelled to Buenos Aires from Portugal with 10 000 Ecstasy pills in my luggage. I actually got quite nervous as we were coming into land. But I managed to get through.'

Then Stella launched into a description of a new breed of mule that bore little resemblance to the image of desperate, cash-strapped or naive individuals who get bust with tiny amounts or, if successful, earn a fraction of their cargo's value.

'A lot of the sisters I travel with are educated, middle class and upward. They travel regularly on holidays in Europe, South America, Asia and Africa. They are much harder to locate because they blend in with your average passenger.'

'So what do these middle-class mules call themselves? Narco-tourists?' I asked facetiously.

Stella ignored me. 'They don't fly to airports like Rio de Janeiro or São Paulo any more because the sensor equipment there is quite sophisticated and all the larger airports are now more closely watched. So they will choose, for example in South America, smaller, quieter airports like Belo Horizonte, Salvador and Recife, which have direct flights to many countries. But, these days, all the biggest quantities come in on private yachts, private jets. The 1 or 2 kilograms of stuff found in a false suitcase compartment or in the dreadlocks of a decoy, ha, that's a joke, man.'

'Don't you ever think of quitting?'

'Sometimes, but the money is so good. It has served my purposes, like, you know, getting me the life I always wanted, and visiting countries all over the world. I even learned foreign languages,' she enthused, gushing forth in Spanish. 'And many of the little fishes [she used the term to refer to other mules] became my sisters. We are all friends on Facebook, on our status page we say we are "in a relationship". And although the big fish, the senior syndicate members, don't disclose their friends, we do, as well as post messages of support to each other and photos of ourselves.'

She then showed me pictures of her scattering dollar bills like confetti and posing next to a flashy BMW, corpulent, mouth agape and the veins in her neck bulging like subcutaneous worms, captioned 'me at work'. Adjacent to the pictures were several 'likes' posted by women with African, Spanish or Asian names and several men with Nigerian names. There were also lots of comments like 'praise God', 'thank the Lord Jesus' and 'Hallelujah'.

'Look, obviously I don't know everyone involved. That would be too risky. And also, the sisterhood has its limits. I love them, but in this business you can't trust anyone, for obvious reasons. They would sell out their own mothers, sisters, kids for the right price – and at R30 000 or R40 000 for a single trip, what do you expect?'

She added, 'We do have our handlers, the guys who look after us once we land wherever, be it São Paulo, Bangkok or Hong Kong. And, of course, the ones who recruit us in South Africa. And it's all Nigies involved – with South African, Brazilian, even Mexican, cartels. They are, like, everywhere.'

As Stella explained, the Nigerian drug syndicates often employ several couriers to carry a single consignment of drugs transnationally. If the cargo is cocaine, for example, the mule would be recruited in South Africa, and would obtain the illicit package in Brazil. Then the mule would fly to a transit country, like Thailand, for example. In the transit country, the cocaine would then be handed to another mule. The second mule would then fly to another transit country, before the final destination was reached, and hand over the drugs to a third mule, who would do the last run, smuggling the drugs into the destination country. The US and Europe have very sophisticated detection equipment. Africa and India are definitely the emerging markets for drugs, she explained.

Stella mentioned the names of fishing towns along Mozambique's porous coastline, like Vilanculos and the village of Xai-Xai, which, she said, were the new nodes in the global narcotics networks.

'I've done a few runs there, but mainly the stuff is brought in by the big guys, usually with the local fishermen. The locals will fetch the cocaine in their dhouws, take it back to shore and sell it in the town's streets, bars, backpackers and private residences.' She added: 'Coke is cheap in Mozambique, because it's cut with strychnine, which is used in rat poison. But what do I know? I'm just a mule, as you media like to call us.' She winked.

'And the decoys?'

'Well, like I said, they are good for the stats and the occasional mule that gets too big for her boots.' Stella leaned forward, in her enthusiasm spraying me with spittle. 'Like, in the past they would be bust for a couple of kilos of coke or heroin. Low-grade stuff, because every gram is worth money, so you don't want to be giving the decoy the good Bolivian shit or whatever. Now it's methamphetamine, or tik, the one drug that you don't need to smuggle internationally because it can be manufactured anywhere locally.'

In the course of my investigations into substance abuse, I had witnessed the ubiquity with which tik kitchens had spread throughout South Africa. Despite several high-profile busts, these makeshift labs had continued to sprout like weeds, particularly in Cape Town. All that is required to make meth is a ready supply of over-the-counter medications containing ephedrine or pseudoephedrine and various household products.

Police estimate that there are over 300 000 users of

methamphetamine on the Cape Flats alone, and that's not counting members of well-heeled society who get off on the product. In the Flats, the daily revenue produced by tik runs into tens of millions of rands. The 'cooks' sell it 'wholesale' to the tik dens or street merchants for roughly R10 to R20 a gram, depending on the quality. A tiny bag of tik with enough crystals for two or three hits might sell for R10 to R20 on the streets. A gram of crystal is then sold to consumers for R350. Do the 'meths'.

Stella said, 'I really feel for that poor sister Janice Linden who was executed in China the other day for meth. That was one major set-up!'

'And what part have you played in setting up the decoys, the dead cows?' I asked.

'I have never recruited anyone, never as a decoy, I swear! Even that homeless girl in Khayelitsha, who I told you about, I only knew about what they had planned for her when she couldn't swallow. And I feel bad for them. But, fuck, they are stupid if they think they gonna get the job or opportunity of a lifetime for free. They gotta know there's going to be payback. And once they check in, it's like Hotel California – they can check out anytime they like, but they can never leave.'

'So, then, you are blaming it on their stupidity or naivety. Is that why are you willing to pimp some of your sisters?'

'I'm not pimping anyone. But it's not like it was in the old days, when we were tighter and we could trust each other more. Since about July 2012, when I was last in Bangkok, there have been so many police raids in the Nana area, especially Soi 3 and Soi 3½, and Ramkhamhaeng Road, in the Bang Kapi district. This is where my connections hang out, and in Thonburi, where Thembi has a place.'

'So Thembi is pretty well set up in Thailand.' It was more of a statement than a question.

'Of course, anyone who does the Thailand–China run knows Thembi. She has three or four South African women staying with her at a time. She makes fake passports for the girls who are going to travel and she operates under different surnames. She was married to a Nigerian, so her surname is Nwabude. Then there's Thembe Mfenqe and Thembi Dlamini. And she lives with this guy in Thabong who is a schoolteacher. His name is Albert something. He regularly beats her up, so it's a pretty hectic relationship. And she now runs this tuck shop in Thabong, close to the school. I think that's where she is recruiting.'

'And her sidekicks in Bangkok? What do you know of them?'

'In Bangkok, she hangs out with a couple of heavy dudes.'

'Like Nonso?'

Stella's lips curled into a satellite-dish of a smile. 'You know Nonso?'

I shook my head. 'No, just heard the name.'

Stella sighed. 'Poor Nonso, he got arrested in 2009. But I heard he got out soon after and was even in South Africa some time during 2010. I can check with Thembi. I've still got her cellphone number. I could call her now, if you want. But it's going to cost you, I'm not doing this for free, you know.'

Journalistic instinct, that trusted seventh sense, kicked in. Notwithstanding her value as an informant, I did not trust Stella as far as I could throw her. And although part of me relished the triumph of hurtling her face-first through her monumental LED TV screen, she was bigger than me and I wouldn't have been able to lift her off the floor of her garishly designed lounge. I could envisage the scenario: she might provide invaluable leads as to the whereabouts of Joshua Nonso Okeke and his ilk. She could also possibly facilitate access to Thembi's network by connecting me to one of her syndicate recruiters as a white woman willing to 'travel'. Apparently, these days, the preferred breed of mules is slightly older and white, the former because they are less of a 'flight' risk; the latter because white girls are not treated with as much suspicion by the airport authorities in Asia, Europe and South America.

But I had no strategy to prevent Stella from selling me out to Thembi, Nonso and the syndicate on a whim. Hopefully, I'd learnt something from my Bangkok experience

'You know, Stella, I think this is all a bit hectic for me. I've decided I'm not going to do the story. Sorry I wasted your time and good luck for the future.' I pressed R200 into her palm, before making a hasty exit.

As I made my way back to the SABC offices in Auckland Park, my hopeless sense of direction ensured that anyone trying to follow me would get as lost as I felt.

18

GUGU

January 2013

I had been given her details by one of the *Special Assignment* investigators. He was not a producer or even a journalist, but a street-smart operator with an extrasensory perceptiveness for stories of the scatological kind. He could sniff out shit better than a greenbottle fly. He said he had worked with her on previous stories and that, in addition to being very reliable, she was fearless. She was also a professional drug mule, albeit no longer practising.

After my encounter with Stella, I was not particularly keen to ingratiate myself with any other body packers, lest, at best, I ended up being cast unwittingly in the role of someone's publicist or, at worst, dead.

Nevertheless, I was still curious to meet this woman, especially when my contact assured me she would willingly assist in hooking me up with a Johannesburg-based syndicate keen on recruiting white women as drug mules. I figured that if I could net even a small shark among the predators, my ongoing, but hitherto failed, investigation into Thembi, would be taken more seriously.

I called her several times but was increasingly deterred by the message on her voicemail: 'Hi, this is Gugu. I've made some changes in my life. And if you've called this number, you are probably not part of them.'

Although she had not returned any of my calls, my intrepid investigator had assured me that despite her apparent reluctance to make contact, she was in fact keen to chat.

I was expecting to meet another Stella-style smartass who would flash the accoutrements of her trade in my face with the bravado of the hunter who mounts his trophies on the wall, above the pump-action shotgun, and regales his captive audience with stories about the thrill and skill of the kill.

I was clearly not prepared for Gugu ...

Rain was pelting the car roof in a parking area adjacent to a dank apartment complex in Braamfischerville, on the outskirts of Soweto, where she was squatting in a bricolage of zinc and concrete shacks. I had expected to be ushered into another live-in commercial for giant plasma TVs and Ackermans furniture. But the apartment entrance was dark and smelt of mildew. A clearly embarrassed Gugu blocked my access to the lounge, and asked instead that we talk in the car.

'The flat is leaking and because of the rain I have had to dry all my laundry in the lounge. It's a terrible, smelly mess.'

She slipped into the back seat and offered me her hand. 'Hi, so nice to meet you. Sorry for not calling back. I haven't had airtime.'

Her voice was purring and, thankfully, unlike Stella, her sentences were unpunctuated by the kind of Kim Kardashianisms that seem to have become de rigueur for many young South African women with material dreams: words like 'whatever' and, of course, 'bitch'. She did, however, emulate the vocal lilt of American sitcom actresses with a rising inflection at the end of each sentence. Wearing a fringe and a Medusa-like mane of extensions that were probably once luxuriant, but were now slightly matted and stringy, she resembled a sullied variation on a pretty doll my mother had bought me when I was little, with her huge, slightly slanted eyes, pert nose and Aquafresh smile.

Yet it was neither her allure nor her slightly affected MTV-style accent, but rather the content of her conversation that rendered me silently gobsmacked. The breadth of her knowledge on corruption in places high and low was more than impressive. Gugu could rattle off the names of just about every tier of player in the Gauteng narco-system, from crooked cops at Hillbrow Police Station, and security guards and staff on the take at the Indian Embassy in Johannesburg, to duplicitous travel agents and businesses operating as fronts for global drug-trafficking syndicates. She didn't seem to possess a molecule of fear in her DNA, which was evident when she offered to set up each and every participant in and accomplice to this nefarious trade.

Gugu was a gold mine of intelligence. But could I trust her?

'Why do you want to help bust these syndicates if they are your source of bread and butter?'

'Because I am out of this scene now. I really want to do something positive with my life, where I get recognition for the good I do and not the bad,' she responded, disarmingly unhesitant.

Mind, anyone could have pre-empted that question, I thought, in the way an aspirant employee might prep herself for the self-marketing presentation before a coveted job interview.

Next predictable question: 'So why did you get into this business in the first place?'

Again, the answer was instantaneous. 'I was raised by a very strict, single mom. I went a bit wild when I was younger. I got into all sorts of trouble and she tried to control me. I got pregnant and she threw me out.' I nodded sympathetically. 'No, but see, that wasn't the reason. I could look after myself. I got a job where I wasn't earning that much, but it was okay. And there was another girl there who looked and dressed like da bomb, even though we were earning the same wages. Eventually, she confided that she made extra bucks by doing "trips" and offered to introduce me to "friends" who could help me to travel. That's how it works. One person introduces you to another, then another.'

She added, 'I wanted the whole package, a beautiful house, a motorbike. I thought this was a way to make quick, easy money.'

That was five years ago, when Gugu was 18. Now, at 23, the

same age as Thando and Babsie when they were arrested, she too travelled the world and, to date, had miraculously avoided arrest, or even worse.

'But I knew it couldn't go on forever. The money was good and it helped me to get my diploma in information technology. But it was also, like, easy come, easy go.'

And there were harrowing moments.

'The first time I had to swallow and there were these guys in the room saying: "Come on, sissy, swallow, swallow, it's business, it's business." And I was scared but there was no turning back.'

On one occasion, her instinct kicked in as she was walking towards the check-in at OR Tambo International, about to board a flight to Nepal. 'On this one particular occasion, I didn't have a good feeling about the trip. There are SAA and Emirates employees at the airport who are in on the drug runs, but normally the mules don't know who they are. Maybe I was paranoid or something, but I felt like I was being stared at by the airport staff, in a suspicious way. I had stuff in my luggage. I was about to check it in but something inside warned me: "Don't do it." So, I said I needed first to go to the toilet and I turned around, left the airport and caught a taxi back to town.'

She added, 'The guys were okay with me because I handed the stash back to them and said I was feeling sick. They didn't care as long as I didn't try to double-cross them or make off with the stash.'

Then there was the time when she had returned from a trip with drugs concealed in packets of cereal.

'We were driving back from the airport and, next thing, this cop car stops us. They go through my things and find the drugs. And I think: "This is it. I'm done for!" One cop gets into the car and instructs the driver to go to Hillbrow Police Station. But then I start talking to him in Tswana and he asks me what I'm doing with these Nigerian idiots and whether or not I wanted to do business with him on the side.'

It turned out the cops were in cahoots with some of the

syndicate members. They would pretend to arrest the suspects and confiscate the goods. Soon after, the suspects would be released without appearing in court and would simply report to the senior members that their consignment was now in the hands of the police. The financial spoils of the confiscated contraband, however, would subsequently be divided between the 'suspects' and the arresting officers. The Tswana-speaking cop was proposing a double deal with Gugu that would exclude her accomplices.

She relayed this to me with such nonchalance that I was tempted to dismiss the veracity of her account. It was only when she asked me to drive her to Hillbrow Police Station and provide her with a spycam, and she offered to record her dubious dealing that I realised Gugu's account was probably authentic.

But, then, in a world where loyalties are contingent on the highest bidder, how could I put my trust in a young woman who had learnt at such a young age to dance with the devil and unashamedly pimp those to whom she owed some allegiance? I wasn't about to be hustled by a 23-year-old drug mule, however charming, for the sake of a story.

'Gugu, if you work with me,' I told her, 'there is not going to be a financial reward for you. I can pay you a daily fixer rate for introductions and any other valuable research you provide.' I cleared my throat and paused for effect. 'But we can't be seen to be complicit in any conspiracy to commit a crime. And, although we can protect your identity, we cannot guarantee immunity from prosecution if a sting operation goes awry. So you'd better give this some thought to determine what it is you really want out of this and whether it will be worth your while.'

She cocked her head quizzically. There was something about her expression that slightly unnerved me. And not in a negative way either. Since the start of this three-year foraging into the pathologies of those entangled in the viscous web of narcotics, both on the supply and demand sides, I had prided myself on acquiring certain self-schooled skills in the science of forensic psychology. For example, I could now read the disease of addiction, regardless of the substance of choice or social status of the consumer. Addicts like Doreen are not quite connected to the conversation. They have a sort of absent-in-presence aura that is noticeable through an intangible but discernible gauze or veil. They might acknowledge my words, laughing and nodding or responding engagingly. But they are elsewhere, looking past or through me to the desired space and opportunity for some purchased relief. The Thandos of this world, the decoys or dead cows unwittingly thrust into the jaws of the predators, are nakedly, heartbreakingly authentic in their fear and innocence. They clutch onto syllables, pauses and speech inflections as though to life jackets tossed to them in a raging sea. And the expression in their saucer eyes is, hauntingly, of guilelessness.

On the supply side of the trade, personified by the likes of Thembi and Stella, like the addict, they, too, acknowledge me without really seeing me; they, too, look past me. But there is no desperate veil of 'elsewhere' over their eyes. Unless they perceive that I might be of some use to them, I will be regarded in much the same way they would treat the mousey girlfriend of a guy they are trying to impress – with contempt, camouflaged as gentility.

Gugu's expression though revealed none of the above. She seemed to be genuinely processing my words, weighing them up, without averting her eyes. She said, 'You know, I've carried more drugs in my body than an addict. Yet I have never touched a drug in my life. And I never will, because I'm scared of what they will do to me. I've seen my friends go downhill through oenga [heroin mixed with dagga] and crack. I feel guilty because I am partly responsible for their situation.'

She sighed. 'I've thought it through and I don't want money, except something to cover transport costs. I don't hate the guys I've worked with. But my kid is growing older. I don't know what I would do if he became addicted. I think I would kill the dealer who sold the drugs to him.'

We were parked outside Hillbrow Police Station. As proof of her sincerity, Gugu offered to find the very officer who had invited her to cut a deal with him on the side, and set him up

'Are you off your head?' I said. 'You can't just walk in there and offer your illicit services to a law-enforcement officer as though you're inviting him out to lunch!'

But Gugu was undeterred. She grabbed the spycam and deftly clipped it to her breast pocket, with the lens barely visible. 'I've done this before. I know how to sweet-talk them and these are people who have no shame. Give me 15 minutes.'

But 15 minutes became 30, then 45. Just as I was about to storm the citadels of Hillbrow's notorious cop shop, she emerged from the entrance and gestured to me to drive to Clarendon Circle, a few hundred metres from the station. She was breathless with excitement.

'I walked in and asked for my guy. He wasn't on duty but one of the officers [she provided his name] asked if he could be of assistance. I told him I had information about drug deals. He then invited me into his office and without disclosing anything really, I let him know I had information. He wants to meet me later away from the station by the Auckland Park KFC.' She giggled. 'He asked me for my number and he was coming onto me really strong. Let's play back the footage and you can see for yourself.'

I couldn't contain my infuriation. I had learnt from my dealings with members of the Thabong and Welkom police not to even attempt to cross swords with the flexible arm of the law, at least not without adequate backup.

'You must be insane! There are two scenarios here: either he's going to set you up and charge you with conspiracy to commit a crime, or he is going to sexually assault you far from the station, where you are completely vulnerable and have no recourse to assistance. Under no circumstances will I consent to this.'

Gugu assumed the expression of a bewildered kitten. Despite my obvious anger at her reckless naivety, I couldn't entirely camouflage my admiration for her courage. But instead of taking on arguably one of the most corrupt police units in Gauteng, my strategy was to target an individual member of a syndicate, located somewhere in the middle of the synapse, someone we could expose on TV as complicit in recruiting drug mules and decoys, who would possibly cooperate with the cops in divulging the names of more senior counterparts. Then we would sit back and observe the response from the SAPS – or lack thereof.

Although visibly disappointed by my apparent spinelessness, Gugu reluctantly agreed to this relatively conservative plan of action.

Again, I cautioned her. 'If you get involved, will there not be repercussions for you, once the syndicate members know they have been set up by you?'

'They won't find me. I have covered my tracks. They do not know where I live now and I will change my number so they can't harass me.'

She then added: 'After this, my new life truly begins.'

The visual quality of Gugu's covert footage in Hillbrow Police Station was poor, given the low-light conditions and the spidery presence of her extensions across the lens. But the audio was unmistakably clear: Gugu's purr and the rasping voice of a male conversing in Tswana. I would have to decipher the contents of their interaction, not for broadcast purposes, but simply to confirm the brazen ubiquity of corruption in certain official corridors. And for a 'dry run', my non-practising mule had exceeded all expectations.

19

FRIDAH

27 January 2013

She was three hours late and I had already crossed the border post of Edginess into the land of full-blown Anxiety. We were seated outside Billy the Bums, one of the many eateries in this Fourways mall. Gugu was rambling on nervously, a compulsive string of sentences that seemed to blur into an unintelligible buzz. Bafana Bafana had just drawn with Morocco in the Afcon quarter-finals, prompting various impromptu vuvuzela outbursts, accompanied by exuberant whoops from the crowds in the cafes, bars and takeaways. With sweat seeping through my shirt and feeling wired from the adrenalin shots each time Gugu's phone rang, I massaged my forehead and checked my watch again.

'Call her once more, Gugs. Tell her we have to leave soon.'

Gugu obligingly dialled Fridah's number.

'Uh, Fridah, it's getting late and I'm scared I won't be able to get a taxi home. How long do you think you will be? ... Okay, we will meet you at St Elmo's.'

Gugu turned to me, apologetically. 'Fridah says they have been watching the soccer but that she will be here in 20 minutes.'

I restrained myself from snarling at Gugu in a misdirected fit of frustration. 'If she is not here in 20 minutes, we leave. It is important to meet her but she is playing us and I'm pissed off. Clearly she doesn't need a white girl that badly.'

* * *

We had already trawled parts of Alexandra township during one of those typical Highveld summer days, with the thunder of an impending electric storm threatening, but never quite managing, to alleviate an uncomfortably muggy day. I had felt caught up in that charged second before a storm is about to break, with both the humidity and that ominous celestial growl seeming to externalise my sense of urgency.

We had been in search of a recruiter, one of those syndicate members perched on the middle rung of the narcotics ladder who selects both the drug mules and the decoys, by any means necessary: persuasion, seduction, coercion, trickery and blackmail.

The plan was to expose the recruiter for the third *Special Assignment* follow-up to the investigation I had begun in 2009. Four years after my run-in with Thembi, Thando's recruiter, there was now so much more at stake than just a compelling narrative and favourable viewer ratings. I wanted to send out a further warning of the consequences, not only to South Africans driven by financial desperation or opportunism into becoming drug couriers, but also to the syndicates who recruited them. I hoped Thembi would get wind of the follow-up and realise that I was still on her trail, and that, even if she had managed to avoid being arrested and charged for her crimes thus far, other recruiters would not be so fortunate. But in order to even access the narco-network, I would be wholly dependent on Gugu's resourcefulness and loyalty. After several frustrating dead ends, I was starting to make progress, thanks to Gugu's invaluable assistance, in my attempt to infiltrate a syndicate. The prospect both thrilled and terrified me.

In a shack bordering an informal settlement along the Jukskei River, Gugu had introduced me to a grizzled elderly woman called Patience, who had eyeballed the *mlungu* with unbridled astonishment before giving Gugu an update on breaking news in the narcotics underworld. The contents of her gossip included who had recently been arrested and released.

'Your friend John has just got out of Sun City,' Patience had

232

said, referring to Gauteng's notorious Diepkloof Prison by its nickname. 'He's out on parole but I know why he hasn't been deported. I think he was a member of the Big Fives.' (This was a reference to inmates who are known, in prison-speak as snitches, squealers or pimps.) 'He gives information to the *boere*, so obviously he's got protection both inside and outside.'

While Patience disclosed the inner machinations of the Big Five, with strategically lowered eyelids I had perused the cramped, squalid room inhabited by this woman who possessed encyclopaedic knowledge of the who's who of the drug-trafficking scene, yet who had evidently profited so little from it. While Gugu punched into her phone various names and numbers, including John's, I tried to settle into a tattered couch that felt about as welcoming as a nail-riddled wooden plank and, judging from the sharp nips I was feeling around my exposed calves and ankles, which also served as the abode to a crew of bugs and mites.

'Hola, John, wassup? It's Gugs. Yeah, it has been ages. Are you around? Sharp. I will see you there in an hour.'

Gugu had just resumed contact with John, a Nigerian drug smuggler and one of her former handlers, who, she explained, could lead us to a recruiter. Taking my arm, she had navigated me out of the shack and towards a taxi rank.

Our next port of call had been a restaurant serving traditional African fare, opposite Times Square, in Rockey Street. This was one of the many hangouts of Africa's legitimate émigrés, as well as some hard-core members of the Zimbabwean, Congolese and Nigerian syndicates. It was there, Gugu had informed me while wolfing down tripe and Nigerian okra soup, that major deals were done, involving gold, diamonds, arms and, of course, drugs.

'Hello, pretty lady! Where've you been? I missed you.' A jovial-looking black man built like a candidate for World Wrestling Entertainment had sauntered up to us, grabbed Gugu by the waist and hoisted her like a wayward cat under his gargantuan biceps. He spoke with the lilting accent of a foreigner.

'Busy, busy, but I'm back,' Gugu had replied. 'Hazel, meet John. He helped me get into the travelling business.'

I had smiled coyly. Displaying the deceptively friendly face of the drug trade, John had flashed me a gallant beam before redirecting his attention to Gugu with undisguised lust.

'John, my friend Hazel wants to travel. Can you help?'

Gently kneading Gugu's shoulders, he had cooed, 'I knew you'd be back. You couldn't abandon your family. But, baby, I'm not the one to talk to. I have to be careful because I am out on parole. I am being closely watched. But I can give you Fridah's number. I think she's looking. But since she and Mark got married, she's become very high and mighty, a real black diamond.'

* * *

The word had been out that a Nigerian syndicate was looking for a white woman to travel to Brazil. Gugu had spread the word that one was available. And here I was, either offering myself up as mule or, depending on the compunction of my recruiters, as a dead cow or sacrificial lamb to the slaughter.

Pinning down a meeting, however, with Fridah, the recruiter, had proven exasperating, given her inability to confirm a specific time and place. In anticipation of it, I felt the stomach-knotting fear of my fate at the hands of the syndicate should I fail to convince Fridah of my bona fides.

Gugu's dismal sense of direction, which was even worse than mine, had augmented my anxiety as we crawled along the N1 north, missing the turn-offs that would lead us to the designated meeting spot in Fourways. Like a seasoned taxi driver, I had performed reckless multiple U-turns in my desperate quest to get there on time.

We finally arrived half an hour late for our 5.30 pm appointment. Gugu had provided Fridah with an up-to-the-second report on our progress through rush-hour traffic, only to discover that

Fridah had other plans for the early part of the evening. If we wanted to meet with her, it was going to be on her terms.

I delicately adjusted the spy camera. I was testing out the latest fashion in covert technology: spycam glasses. The fact that they made me resemble a librarian filled me with confidence: if I looked bookish, then I would not be the sort of 'traveller' to attract the attention of anyone, least of all pesky customs officials keen to up the arrest statistics. At least that's what I hoped Fridah would think. But dusk had already descended and I was concerned about the quality of the video in low light. Then there was the problem of the malfunctioning audio. Fortunately, I had become adept at dealing with the glitches of cheap covert technology of Asian origin and had brought a backup, a spycam whose principal function, as had been the case during my prison visit to Thando, was to serve as a tape recorder. I would have to sync the audio and visuals later.

Ten minutes. Gugu's torrential prattle had tapered off into a brittle silence.

With their ultra-wide-angle lenses, which produced a hemispherical visual distortion, the spy glasses imparted a hallucinatory fisheye view of the world. The contours of the surrounding mall were contorted into an elliptical version of all the shopping centres sprouting around Gauteng. Through the lens I saw concrete monoliths, secular cathedrals of banal rituals of consumption. It was like the residue of a bad acid trip.

Gugu stared at me, mouth slightly agape, obviously convinced, and correctly so, that the wait for Fridah was starting to unhinge me.

Fifteen minutes. 'If she is not here within the next five minutes, we are out of here.'

'Here she comes,' Gugu hissed. Tentatively, my left hand reached towards the spy camera, activating the record button.

'Hey, my sister, you look sharp, so beautiful, and so tall,' said Gugu.

Gushing, Gugu embraced Fridah, who offered each of her

cheeks for dainty air kisses before swivelling gracefully on the toes of her leopard-print platforms.

'It's the shoes. Aren't they fine?'

The timbre of Fridah's voice was smooth, low and lyrical. Her accent was certainly not South African but I could not place her country of origin.

'Uh, this is Hazel, the girl I told you about. She's interested in travelling.'

Our eyes met. Fridah was exquisite, with Byzantine features, almond eyes, finely tapering nose and sensual mouth, a body befitting a catwalk model, and exuding the confidence of a woman immersed in her own sense of self-importance.

Testily, she turned to me.

'Hi, Fridah. Thank you for agreeing to meet me.' I proffered my hand. She ignored it, flicking back her braids with a jingle-jangle of her bracelets, clearly agitated.

With my deliberately drab attire, my bookish eyewear, my back slightly hunched in a posture of submission, if not defeat, I definitely did not fit the flamboyant profiles of professional mules like Stella and her Facebook 'sistas'.

Glancing at her cellphone, Fridah gesticulated in the direction of a motor vehicle parked at the steps of the mall.

'I can't stay long. We have to take someone to the airport tonight. She's travelling to Geneva at 11 pm.' She added: 'My husband is waiting in the car, so you better not be wasting our time.'

Earlier, Gugu had informed me that Fridah's husband, Mark, was a senior member of the syndicate.

'So talk to me.'

I recited my cover story: Hazel from Westbrook, KwaZulu-Natal; a shit of a boyfriend with a gorilla on his back (not drugs but gambling); and a gargantuan mountain of debt.

'I'm desperate. I don't travel often, in fact only once before to Thailand, to the island of Koh Phangan for the Full Moon Party. Do you know the island? It is one of ...'

'Do you have kids?' she snapped.

'Uh, yes, she is 20. And a granddaughter. Here.' Frantically, I flicked the touchscreen of my cellphone to produce the photographs I had carefully selected of a young woman with her toddler, solely to add some weight to my otherwise flimsy cover.

But Fridah was in no mood to cluck over family photographs provided by a proud grandmother.

'So, why should I trust you? Give me three reasons.'

'Because I am desperate, because Gugu is my friend and because I would never endanger my family's safety by betraying your trust.'

Fridah menacingly leaned forward. 'My people are very strict. We don't like it when our girls cross the line. Just two weeks ago we nearly beat a girl to death because she was trying to run away.'

I swallowed, recalling Doreen and my reckless effort to infiltrate one of the Nigerian syndicates in Bangkok. Again, I had failed to notify either a colleague at *Special Assignment* or a reliable police contact of my whereabouts. And, this time, it was not only my life on the line, but also that of Gugu, who had truly proven her mettle, whatever her motives.

'Do you have your passport with you?'

'No, but I can go back to KZN to fetch it,' I offered, only too aware that once Fridah possessed my passport, it would be, both literally and metaphorically, tickets for me. Strategically, capriciously and inevitably without my consent, the syndicate would determine my destination as well as my fate: whether I was to travel to São Paulo, Singapore or Nepal, for example, and whether I would be designated drug mule or duped decoy. They would hand me my flight ticket, but retain my passport until we reached the check-in counter. The night preceding the flight, they would book me into a cheap hotel, like a Formula One, or a guesthouse, maintaining a constant vigil over me in shifts until I had swallowed all the pieces. If my throat constricted and I could not accomplish this feat, or if I expressed too many doubts about doing the run, I would be classified, without my knowledge, as the weakest link in the chain of command and an obvious liability to the syndicate. My punishment: death or arrest.

In this world of recruiters, mules and dead cows, there exists only the crude binary of asset or liability. There is nothing between these dualities. In Fridah's hooded eyes I have no individual identity, just like the concrete-and-glass malls of Gauteng. I signify nothing, other than my value as drug mule or dead cow. And Fridah's undisguised contempt for me merely reflected this pervasive attitude on the part of drug syndicates towards the couriers and decoys. The initial stages of grooming or recruiting might be seductive, as opposed to overtly coercive but, ultimately, as the terms 'mule' and 'dead cow' suggest, all drug couriers are dispensable and dehumanised. They are either beasts of burden or bait.

Time, however, or rather the lack thereof, courtesy of the Geneva flight schedule, was on our side. Fridah was far more focused on her mule being on time for the flight to Switzerland that evening than she was on the desperate, drab white woman sitting before her narrating her tale of strife and offering her travelling services. She was looking at me but clearly did not see me.

She asked for my ID or driver's licence. I provided the former. She glanced at it, then handed it back.

'Do you use?'

'No. My boyfriend had a problem in the past but not any more.'

'So how do I know that you won't take a little piece for him?'

'Because drugs got us into this situation in the first place.'

She suddenly seemed to soften. 'Look, I understand your problem and we can help. We don't force anyone to do anything. We are looking for a white girl to travel to the United Kingdom. We must avoid Brazil for now because we have had some problems there.'

I nodded earnestly, forgetting that the spycam glasses would be recording a syncopated image of Fridah. 'When would you need me to travel?' In narco-speak, the word 'drugs' is rarely employed: the expressions used are 'travelling' or 'taking a trip'.

'I will organise for you to meet my people. But do me a favour:

don't tell them about your problems, because otherwise they will think you are a fake.'

I felt Gugu's heel tapping my shin under the table.

Fridah continued: 'You don't make contact with me. I will make contact with you tomorrow through Gugu. If something happens, I'll go to her house. She doesn't know where I stay, but I make it my business to know where she lives.'

The storm had finally broken, with cacophonous thunder claps, followed by unbroken sheets of rain.

Fridah rose, and without even a farewell, exited hastily to the car parked by the stairs below, where her husband was waiting to whisk yet another drug mule, or decoy, to the airport.

11 February 2013

We might not have known where she lived, but, thanks to Facebook and other social networks, which have eclipsed more conventional investigative methods in term of efficacy, we knew where she worked. Twenty-eight-year-old Fridah Tembo was a senior sales executive at a company called African Management Communications (AMC). Based in the plush Johannesburg suburb of Hyde Park, AMC markets itself on its curiously unimaginative website as a 'business research, business information and business training company producing strategic business events and tailored corporate training'.

However, evidence of its bespoke services is disappointingly lacking. There are no biographies or photographs of the core management team; the 'testimonials' attesting to client satisfaction might easily have been tailored from an online dating site – full of hyperbole but lacking in specifics; and there are no recommendations from South African–based participants. This, despite the fact that AMC's advertising banners include conferences on security at OR Tambo International, an ironic coincidence, given Fridah's 'travelling' proclivities.

One of my contacts, a private investigator, did a brief check on AMC but could not find anything amiss. I decided to conduct a more extensive background check on the company, but first I needed to confront one of the employees against whom I had obtained evidence of drug trafficking. Gugu had supplied me with Fridah's mobile number, but I chose to take the courteously professional approach of contacting her at her workplace, in order to give her the right to reply. This approach was chosen not only in the interests of balanced investigative journalism, but also for the opportunity it afforded of catching her unawares: a tactic that invariably makes for titillating television.

Contrary to popular perception, I am not an ardent supporter of sensationalist sting operations and doorstop manoeuvres. In fact, I dread such confrontations. The moment that the meeting of eyes occurs between accuser and accused is a profound leveller, almost like an accident happening in slow motion. It is a collision, a point at which we are both exposed, an inescapable connection before the tables are turned – and there is nowhere for either of us to hide. Even if there is incontrovertible proof of wrongdoing, there is always the margin for error.

However, there was also a far more pragmatic rationale behind choosing not to engage in the doorstop technique: after having ensnared Fridah in the fisheye of my spycam specs, I had driven past AMC's Hyde Park headquarters. The complex was rimmed by security guards, so the chances of a bolshie duo of journalist and cameraman being permitted inside its perimeter were remote. Conversely, a telephonic 'shoot-from-the lip' recorded confrontation might yield more fruitful and equally entertaining results.

Fridah had implicated herself on camera. At the very least, she could be charged with conspiracy to commit a crime, not to mention drug trafficking and, hopefully, human trafficking, once South Africa's sluggish Human Trafficking Bill was finally passed by Parliament's National Council of Provinces, where it had been languishing for over a year.

There was also a rapidly narrowing window of opportunity to

publicly name and, hopefully, shame Fridah as a ruthless recruiter of mules and dead cows. But she would have to be identified before the well-intentioned machinery of our criminal-justice system could kick into gear. That was a process which, depending on postponements and other machinations of a wily defence team, might prolong court proceedings for months, even years. By then, Fridah could easily have absconded.

But I was getting way ahead of myself.

The phone at AMC was answered by a brisk, professional voice, requesting how she could be of service.

'I'd like to speak to Fridah Tembo.' My voice sounded irritatingly tremulous. A part of me hoped she would be unavailable or travelling somewhere, anywhere, to relieve me of the inevitable acrimony that would follow when she realised she had been set up and bust.

'Who is calling and in what connection would you like to speak to Fridah?'

My timidity faded. 'My name is Hazel Friedman. I am a journalist with *Special Assignment*, SABC3, and I am in possession of evidence that incriminates Ms Tembo in a conspiracy to commit a crime.'

There was an audible gasp. 'What? Oh my word! Hold on please.'

The piped music seemed to blare in harmony with my resurgent fear. 'This is Fridah. What is going on?'

But the low, almost lyrical tone of her voice assuaged any residue of self-doubt. Fridah Tembo: respected sales executive by day, drug mule and decoy recruiter by night.

Initially she expressed shock and indignation. 'Who are you and how did you get my number? Do you know who you are dealing with, who I am? I will sue you for such lies!'

Then cynicism: 'Are you pranking me? This is a joke, right?'

'This is no joke. You have been filmed committing an extremely serious crime and I can't help wondering why a woman with a respectable profession would moonlight as a recruiter of drug mules. Surely you don't need to supplement your income?'

I could not resist the barb – a small payback for having been kept waiting and for being treated with such haughty contempt.

Then incredulity. 'This is impossible. You have the wrong person.'

'Are you Fridah Tembo?'

'Yes.'

'You are 28 years old, from Lusaka, Zambia.'

'Yes I am, but ...'

'Are you a senior sales executive at AMC?'

'Yes, I do sponsorships.'

'Did you escort a woman to OR Tambo International Airport on the 27th of January to put her on a flight to Geneva?'

'Absolutely not! I swear on the life of my child and on Holy God that I didn't!'

'Did you try to recruit a white woman to fly to the UK for the purpose of smuggling drugs?'

'Never, I would never do such a thing. Never! Oh my God, what is going on?'

I invited her to view the incriminating spy-camera footage, to which she immediately agreed.

'I will be there in an hour! Where is the SABC?'

I was surprised that a senior sales executive who supposedly organised sponsorships for high-profile international confer-ences did not know the location of South Africa's broadcasting parastatal. I gave her the directions. As I replaced the receiver, I turned triumphantly to my team, who had been listening intently to our telephonic exchange. They did not share my ebullience.

'She sounds like she's telling the truth. Either she is innocent or a brilliant actress,' they argued.

I began to panic, anticipating an enraged Fridah, with an entou-rage of Nigerian thugs in tow, intent on exacting terrible revenge on the entire *Special Assignment* team.

One of my colleagues alerted security and, together with the executive producer, Busisiwe Ntuli, I rushed to our line manager, Sefako Nyaka, for advice.

After watching the spycam footage, he was sanguine. 'Let her come. I will have an SAPS connection on standby to make an arrest, if necessary.' He then turned to me: 'Hazel, are you sure you have the right woman?'

I nodded vigorously. 'Even if the spycam had let us down and we couldn't get visuals, the voice is unmistakable.'

'Then let her bring it on. In addition to the *Special Assignment* broadcast this week, we will include an insert of your exposé on the 7 pm news.'

Thirty minutes later, I called Fridah again, this time on her mobile.

A more composed voice answered, but softly hissing, poised for attack: 'I am not going to come there. You are pranking me and I have spoken to my lawyer. I will sue the SABC for everything it's got.'

She slammed down the phone to a chorus of whoops and high fives in the *Special Assignment* office.

Later, as I made my way through the SABC's deserted parking area, my eyes were everywhere. Exposing a member of a powerful drug-trafficking syndicate would surely unleash the wrath of a lethal foe. That night I barely slept.

The following morning, I went online. Predictably, both Fridah and her husband had removed their profiles from Facebook, but, fortunately, days before, I had accessed several photographs of the couple, arms entwined. I had also downloaded a beautiful portrait of Fridah, from her now defunct Facebook page. Opening the photo on my laptop, I compared it to the woman I had met and secretly filmed, the recruiter who had arrogantly disclosed to me the brutal fate of a vulnerable woman who had dared to harbour second thoughts about 'travelling'.

The resemblance between the menacing mule recruiter captured in grainy, covert footage and the glamorous woman in the high-res photograph was unmistakable: they were one and the same – Fridah.

20

THE AFTERMATH

April 2013

Apart from a couple of tepid calls, nothing: that had been the response of the police to the *Special Assignment* exposé on Fridah Tembo, sales executive by day and drug-mule recruiter by night. The programme had been aired on 14 February 2013 and feedback from our viewers had been gratifying. I was inundated with leads from the public on drug syndicates operating in their neighbourhoods, as well as repeated requests for a follow-up on the exposé, not to mention an update on Fridah's 'imminent' arrest.

Ultimately, however, the police reaction was an abominable silence.

Another risky assignment successfully executed, and consigned to the investigative crapheap. The fact that she had been exposed on both SABC *Prime Time News* and *Special Assignment* attempting to recruit a white women to smuggle drugs into the UK, and giving details of the type of brutal punishment meted out to those mules who change their minds, made no difference.

Having erased her Facebook profile, Fridah had probably packed her designer wardrobe and fled to Zambia. Or it is possible that she continued her dual career as before. Predictably, she had changed her mobile number, and AMC employees refused to comment on her status at the company after she had been exposed.

The day after the programme was aired, I passed the information on Fridah and her Nigerian husband to the Hawks, plus several extra snippets that, for logistical reasons, couldn't be broadcast, but which I was convinced would facilitate the investigation, prosecution and conviction of several senior members belonging to Fridah's syndicate. It is probable that the syndicate to which Fridah belonged was linked to Ben, the Nigerian drug kingpin whom Adelina had named in Klong Prem.

A Hawks spokesperson, Captain William Baloyi, called me several days after the broadcast. I had invited him to view the unedited footage of my meeting with Fridah. 'Do you think if we arrest her she will cooperate?' he asked.

'Absolutely. If you act quickly, I'm sure she'll talk.'

'Would you testify in court if required?' was the question asked of me by Ebrahim Kadwa, then the Gauteng acting head of Organised Crime for the Hawks, shortly after I had interviewed him for the exposé on Fridah. I had nodded.

Kadwa acknowledged the growing problem of South Africans being tricked into becoming drug mules. He was affable on camera, but deftly deflected my questions as to whether or not the authorities allowed South Africans they knew to be carrying drugs to pass through ports of exit without apprehending them.

'Since the beginning of January 2012, there have been 281 arrests of couriers at OR Tambo International, including South African and other nationalities.'

Kadwa continued: 'We have a very good relationship with all law-enforcement bodies overseas and we are well respected for the progress we have made in investigating and apprehending massive consignments of drugs and powerful traffickers intent on bringing them into South Africa.'

By way of example, Kadwa quoted figures from one of South Africa's biggest drug busts, the seizure in 2010 of a whopping 1 716 kilograms of cocaine with a street value of R380 million. Police had conducted a sting operation on a luxury apartment in Knysna. Five suspects had been immediately arrested and a fishing vessel moored at the Waterfront, with the contraband stuffed into every nook, cranny and crevice, had been confiscated. The boat's registered owner, Port Elizabeth resident Shaun Packareysammy, was arrested two months later after being deported from Mozambique. The trial, which lasted until June 2012, resulted in the conviction of Packareysammy and his accomplices, two Chinese nationals, Xing Cuo Chen and Yuwei Yau. Packareysammy was sentenced to 15 years and the other two to 20 years each. It emerged during the trial that Cuo Chen had owned a car dealership in Bedfordview, one of Gauteng's burgeoning hubs of organised crime, and had previously been convicted for ID fraud and mandrax production.

Kadwa admitted that, had it not been for a tip-off, the Knysna syndicate might have got away with it. He acknowledged that one of the strongest components of an investigation was the quality of the intelligence provided by covert operatives and informants. He also insisted that leads 'from the public' were diligently followed up, and encouraged individuals to contact the police with information, should they be approached, coerced or threatened by drug syndicates.

'So, if I show you evidence of a conspiracy to commit the crime of drug trafficking and name the perpetrator, will the Hawks follow this up?' I asked him.

'Show us what you have and we will take it from there,' he assured me. Kadwa might well have taken the evidence. What became of it, however, is open to conjecture. All I know is that it did not result in any arrests. According to 'Ted', my trusted undercover contact, no one was even brought in for questioning. The only person who received any flak after the *Special Assignment* exposé was Gugu. She had bumped into John, the Nigerian drug dealer, who had provided her with Fridah's contact details, at a party in Soweto. He had heard about the programme from his underworld connections and lambasted her for betraying her 'family'. Feigning ignorance, Gugu assured him that she, too, had been duped by the media. She subsequently changed her contact number again but called to let me know she was thrilled with the story and would love to do some more undercover work with *Special Assignment*. As much as I had valued her contribution, I resolved never again to subject either of us to this degree of danger. It really wasn't worth it.

In the chalk-dust divisions between investigative journalist, undercover police operative and informant, the lines can sometimes be crossed. As the former, I was bound by that most sacrosanct code of journalism: never reveal your sources. The murky roles of covert operatives and informants raised a multitude of ethical questions, not only about pimping sources, but also about becoming complicit in committing a crime in order to expose it. For journalists, the commandments are straightforward: thou shalt not! But between the 'shalts' and the 'nots' lie a plethora of possibilities – like using spycams to invade the privacy of suspects, paying bribes to elicit information and even occasionally dipping one's toe into the illicit economy to expose it. Where journalists are definitely on terra *un*firma is in their relationship with law enforcement. If plans for an undercover or sting operation have the support of the strong arm of the law, then one can navigate the tricky fault lines of legality with confidence. Unfortunately, however, within the treacherous domain of transnational drug syndicates the demarcation lines between law enforcement and crime are particularly blurred, given the extensively documented complicity between certain cops and the criminal underworld. I had no real assurance that, should I successfully infiltrate another drug syndicate, the police would cover my back. And the longer it took to make an arrest, the greater the opportunity for Fridah to abscond, removing a huge chunk of the prosecutorial armoury that I believed I was helping to build against the syndicate.

* * *

Days became weeks and then months, but I was determined not to become subsumed by the sense of impotence that had prevented me from pursuing the investigation more vigorously into Thembi two years before. And there was more at stake than the sense of triumph that accompanies getting the story and successfully completing an assignment. As Patricia, Al and I had agreed, this was not only about advocating for the establishment of a prisoner transfer treaty, it was also about nailing the recruiters and drug lords who, despite substantial leads from the three of us, still continued to evade accountability. It was about exposing complicity in the police force and even higher up the political ladder. And it was about, hopefully, motivating the South African Government to persuade their Thai counterparts – and, for that matter, every country in which South Africans are incarcerated – to review the convictions of citizens who might not be perpetrators of drug trafficking, but victims of human trafficking.

This last component of the wish list was certainly the most ambitious, if not downright utopian. I believed it could have global repercussions, especially in light of the fact that the overseas media had been reporting on similar cases for many years: usually young women lured by 'friends' and drug cartels into either becoming drug mules, or decoys to enable professional drug mules to evade arrest.

Still vivid in my memory was a call I had received in July 2012 from a Vietnamese contact of Alex, my connection in Bangkok, who had been my first tutor on the Nigerian drug syndicates.

Her name was Suki, and she was the sister of a young woman called Tina, an accountant working in Bangkok. Through an internet dating site, Tina had connected with a Nigerian man also living in Bangkok. They became lovers and decided to take a trip to Cambodia, and then on to China. According to Suki, the Nigerian, whose name was Jerry John, had wanted to introduce Tina to his friend from South Africa, a certain Bobby 'Horseman', who was residing in Cambodia. On hearing the mispronounced surname of Bobby Norseman, Adelina's Asian 'handler', I gasped.

Apparently, Bobby had been a wonderful host, showering Tina and Jerry with food and gifts, for which he refused any payment. He asked just a small favour: before flying from Cambodia to China, Bobby asked Jerry to carry a small bag for him. Jerry was already overloaded with bounty from Bobby, so Tina offered to carry the bag. It was the least she could do to repay his hospitality.

Tina was apprehended by Chinese immigration police as she went through customs when it was found that the bag contained heroin. After a quick trial, she was sentenced to death. In February 2011 she was executed by lethal injection. She was 18.

Alex had given Suki my details in the hope that, although it was clearly too late for her sister, the South African Government might be able to extradite Bobby 'Horseman' and prevent other impressionable young women from being tricked into becoming decoys, like her sister. A name Suki mentioned next turned my already asthmatic breathing into a hoarse rasp: Janice Linden. Tina had written to say that she was incarcerated with the South African, who had also been sentenced to death for smuggling methamphetamine. As mentioned previously, Linden had repeatedly protested her innocence, but to no avail. She too had been executed in 2011.

I had tried to explain to Suki that, apart from the fact that South Africa has no prisoner transfer treaty, the sheer numbers of our citizens landing up in foreign jails for drug smuggling prevented any humanitarian gesture being extended to our government. Clearly dismayed at my apparent apathy, she had slammed down the phone.

In fact, since December 2011 there had been scores of South Africans arrested abroad for this crime. And these were not stats released by DIRCO, but published on Patricia Gerber's website, Locked Up in a Foreign Country.

Patricia had said in December 2012 that the situation was getting out of control: 'Sometimes the South African embassies aren't contacted and the media is none the wiser unless alerted to the fact.'

During another informative on-camera interview for the 2013 *Special Assignment* documentary, she had provided me with an update on African countries that, in addition to South Africa, had joined Nigeria in becoming major departure and transit points for the narcotics trade. In recent years, just as Stella, the mule, had insisted, Mozambique had joined the pantheon, as had Tanzania. Both these countries had become the source of hundreds of mules entering Hong Kong, carrying drugs from Pakistan and Afghanistan. Hong Kong prisons now housed over 200 inmates from Tanzania alone.

'Yet in these countries, as in South Africa, the authorities are not doing enough to arrest the drug cartels responsible,' Patricia told me. 'For every South African drug mule and decoy arrested in a foreign country, there is a recruiter and drug lord walking free in our country.'

Patricia emphasised that the most effective way of apprehending the drug lords is through evidence provided by those arrested. She also refocused my attention on her failed court application in 2009 against the South African Government for refusing to enter into a prisoner exchange agreement with the Government of Mauritius.

In an affidavit, Dayanand Naidoo, then director of consular affairs at the former Department of Foreign Affairs, had stated that neither Patricia nor her son, Johann, had ever provided information to the police about the syndicates who had recruited South African mules and decoys.

Patricia differs on that: 'Since 2006 we have supplied the police and Interpol with relevant information about drug cartels, including their cellphone numbers. There had been no follow-up.'

In response to one of her many letters sent to SAPS and DIRCO over the years, Patricia had received a response from Hawks head Anwar Dramat. He had politely denied her accusations that essential information pertaining to South African recruiters of drug decoys had not been adequately followed up, if at all, and that the police knowingly allowed decoys who they knew to be smuggling drugs out of South Africa to be arrested overseas. Patricia's riposte had been scathing:

> In the past year the Locked Up organisation has seen a dramatic increase of family members contacting us. Six South Africans have been arrested in Indonesia alone. The modus operandi is identical and the drugs methamphetamine (tik) placed in a hidden compartment of the suitcase. None of these citizens packed their cases themselves. They then walked through the security at OR Tambo to board their flights to Indonesia via Singapore. In one of the cases the SAPS were informed and all the information given to them. It was in their power to stop and arrest the suspects at OR Tambo International before their departure but they did nothing. If the first priority of the police were combating and prevention of crime, surely we would have seen a decrease and not an increase in people being recruited as decoys. Our organisation has made a very clear distinction between drug decoys (the victims) and drug mules (the willing participants). We have clearly stated that drug mules continue to carry drugs in and out of our airports and are protected by some corrupt airport officials and SAPS officers.

Patricia possessed court papers from the trials of alleged drug mules, which provided documented evidence of police officers who had been forewarned of the identities of individuals carrying drugs through South African ports of exit, but had failed to detain them before their departure. Instead, the officers would simply alert their overseas counterparts to make the arrest. Patricia had also raised the case of her son, whose alleged South African recruiter had neither been arrested nor charged, despite the evidence against her.

Patricia's frustration mirrored mine in the limp aftermath of the *Special Assignment* exposé in February 2013 of Fridah Tembo, but, unexpectedly, one person had been genuinely affected by the story: Mbulelo Bungane, DIRCO's director of consular affairs. Since the arrest of her son in 2005, Patricia had been doggedly nipping at DIRCO's heels, asking for meetings with its consular representatives. But apart from the occasional platitude barked back in response, everyone in the department had seemed equally dogged in their refusal to engage with her on any meaningful level.

Everyone, that is, except for Bungane. Patricia had remarked to me that, from their brief exchanges, Bungane had seemed genuinely interested in what Patricia had to say. I had also interviewed Bungane for the February story and was impressed by his sincerity and straightforwardness in acknowledging the shortcomings of some of our consular services towards South Africans incarcerated abroad. He also seemed more willing than his predecessors to address some of the iniquities being perpetrated against them. Immediately after the broadcast, he called Patricia and asked to meet with her. That was the first time anyone from the department had taken the initiative to make contact with her.

The exposé had also included an interview with the Department of Correctional Services, which had announced in 2012 that a prisoner transfer treaty was on the cards. This might read as a radical backtrack on the part of a government that, a few years ago, had been frustratingly obdurate in its refusal to consider the possibility of such a treaty. Apparently, the Department of Correctional Services had been in behind-the-scenes talks with SADC countries to implement such an agreement, principally for practical reasons. Currently there are more than 8 000 foreigners from more than 80 countries incarcerated in South African prisons, costing the South African taxpayer R264 a day, or R96 000 a year each. But, cautioned Correctional Services Deputy Director James Smallburger, although low-level talks had begun ten years ago, the process was akin to running a very long race. They were nearing the end, but there was still, crucially, quite a distance to go, including reaching consensus with the government departments involved, such as SAPS, Home Affairs and DIRCO, as well as the countries taking part in the discussions. The legislation would also have to change and, based on the sluggish pace at which a key piece of legislation combating human trafficking was proceeding, this could take well over a decade.

At the time of my February exposé, anti-trafficking laws in South Africa were still fragmented into legislation dealing separately with sexual offences, while the Children's Act addressed only the trafficking of children. The more opaque domain of human trafficking for the purposes of drug smuggling had not been adequately confronted by legislation. South Africa was a signatory to the UN Convention against Transnational Organized Crime and the Protocols Thereto. Signed in December 2000 and entered into force on 29 September 2003, this convention contains three protocols, which target specific areas of organised crime. Of particular significance for those who are prosecuted as perpetrators of crimes, instead of protected as victims, are the first two protocols: to Prevent, Suppress and Punish Trafficking in Persons, Especially Women and Children, and the Protocol against the Smuggling of Migrants by Land, Sea and Air. These protocols represented a major step forward in the fight against transnational organised crime, because they acknowledge the complexity of cases involving human trafficking, and the need to foster and enhance close international cooperation in order to tackle those problems.

States that ratify these protocols commit themselves to taking a series of measures against transnational organised crime, including the creation of domestic criminal offences (participation in organised criminal cartels, money laundering, corruption and obstruction of justice); the adoption of new and sweeping frameworks for extradition, mutual legal assistance and law-enforcement cooperation; and the promotion of training and technical assistance for building or upgrading the necessary capacity of national authorities.

However, certain UN member states who have signed these protocols, such as South Africa, are not legally bound to comply with their recommendations. And, as the inconvenient truth of my toothless investigations had confirmed, without hard-hitting legislation in South Africa specifically targeting the crime of human trafficking, the likelihood of recruiters such as Thembi and Fridah being punished was minimal.

* * *

But I was not prepared to be deterred and, in March 2013, about two months after the *Special Assignment* exposé, I was primed for a follow-up to the Fridah sting and my ongoing investigation into Thembi, Thando's recruiter/trafficker. I was determined not only to track down the latter again, but also to pressure her into making admissions about trafficking Thando and other South African women, forging passports and conducting the occasional drug run herself. I still had all her personal details, which I had passed on to the South African Embassy in Bangkok, Interpol and Organised Crime in Bloemfontein, including her telephone contact details. When Colonel Gerber had collected the information on her in Cape Town, two years before, he had advised me not to attempt any further contact with her lest I inadvertently alert her to the investigation they were about to conduct. In good faith, I had obeyed, waiting so patiently for due process to take its course that Job himself would have been impressed.

Half-heartedly, I dialled Thembi's mobile number. Of course, she would have changed it, if not after my altercation with her in February 2010, then surely after subsequent *Special Assignment* broadcasts, during which she had been named and, at the very least, shamed into assuming a lower profile.

The voice that answered was unmistakably Thembi's.

I tried to speak but my vocal cords, already raspy from regular debriefings with Johnnie Walker and Peter Stuyvesant, were clogged, as though with gravel. I literally had no voice. And even if I had succeeded in croaking a retort, what could I possibly say to a woman of such arrogance that she hadn't even bothered to change her number? I slammed down the receiver, my initial shock replaced by fury.

I then contacted Charmaine Labuschagne. 'It has been almost three years since I handed in the information to the authorities,' I said, 'and nothing has been done to even bring Thembi in for questioning. Either the cops or someone higher up the political ladder is protecting her.'

It took all my efforts at self-control not to launch into a string of expletives.

'Hazel, there's a lot we need to discuss because there is something very wrong here. But definitely not on the phone.'

'I'll be returning to Welkom. I want answers. And this time, on the record.'

My plan was first to fly to Grahamstown to meet Babsie Nobanda's family, who, since her incarceration, had been in regular contact with Al in Bangkok. In fact, several months previously, Babsie's mother, Honjiswa, had managed to visit her daughter in Klong Prem and, as usual, Al's support had been overwhelming, particularly when Babsie's grandmother passed away and Honjiswa did not have the heart to break the tragic news to her already traumatised daughter. It was left to Al to tell her after her mother's departure. Babsie's uncle, Ntsiki Sandi, a Grahamstown-based advocate, had also kept close tabs on her case through her Bangkok-based legal counsel and, of course, Al.

Sentenced to 15 years, Babsie had narrowly escaped serving 30 years behind bars after the presiding judge read her statement and believed there were extenuating circumstances. Although dire, Babsie's situation was much better than that of Thando, who, without the advantages of an educated and influential network of friends and family, had all but been abandoned. She had also fallen prey to the machinations of syndicates, who had stolen the money I had sent her.

Even worse, Shamalee Senaratne, the bogus do-gooder, had almost persuaded Thando to marry a Nigerian inmate in Bombat Prison, in Bangkok so that she would 'benefit' from the prisoner transfer treaty between Nigeria and Thailand. That was in 2010. About that time, I had started receiving late-night calls from 'Marc', a Nigerian inmate in Bombat, which houses petty drug dealers and users, all of whom, although on the lower rungs of the syndicate ladder, are kitted out with cellphones. Thando had given him my number. She was going through a terrible time and he believed her best, her only, option was for them to get hitched, as he was going to be released and repatriated in the near future. Shamalee was their go-between, performing the role of love courier as she facilitated correspondence between the two prison church services. At that time, I was totally ignorant of Shamalee's duplicity. I interpreted her role as clumsy and naive, albeit noble in intent. But the thought of Thando, already sacrificed as dead meat, only to be ensnared yet again ... Although cordial, my voice couldn't quite conceal my horror.

'Under no circumstances should you and Thando marry. We are making excellent progress with a prisoner transfer treaty in South Africa and any attempt on Thando's part to avoid serving her sentence would compromise her case.'

Of course, that was a fib. But no matter how dire Thando's situation, she was much safer behind bars than in the hands of a drug syndicate in Nigeria. Again, Doreen's fragile face and perilous fate resurfaced in my mind. Try as I might, I couldn't expunge her from my psyche. Thankfully, the marital plot never materialised and after a few more calls, Marc was released and repatriated, alone. But Thando still remained vulnerable.

Isolated in Thabong, Thando's mother, Nozukile, was unaware of the growing support base for South African drug mules and decoys through websites such as Locked Up in a Foreign Country and regular media reports. Meanwhile, Thando and Babsie had become close friends in prison. So it seemed appropriate that their mothers should meet.

I contacted Honjiswa and offered her a paid-for return flight and accommodation in Welkom, courtesy of *Special Assignment*. The plan was for her to spend a few hours with Nozukile while *Special*

Assignment filmed their interaction. Honjiswa seemed thrilled at the prospect of meeting another mother who was enduring the kind of agony few could possibly begin to comprehend.

However, Honjiswa requested that I email her the details of the itinerary so that she could confer with her family and legal advisors. They wanted her to maintain a low profile in the wake of certain developments in her daughter's case. In the aftermath of Babsie's conviction, two alleged Nigerian dealers, David 'Lucky' Bosco and Athnetius 'Willie' Njoku, had been arrested in Port Elizabeth in connection with a multimillion-rand international drug-smuggling ring, to which Samuel Uchengo and his brother, Tony – Babsie's 'handlers' – might also belong.

A heavily guarded Port Elizabeth property, which had been identified as a regular meeting place for scores of Nigerians and South African women, was apparently a notorious drug den, and the Port Elizabeth cops were familiar it – not all of them for the right reasons.

Babsie had accused her lifelong friend, Sulezo, and Samuel of recruiting her at a house in Upper Hill Street, the same street where the two other Nigerians had been bust. She had also named the travel agency, Greenacres, where Samuel had purchased airline tickets for the two to fly to Brazil where they were to meet Tony.

Honjiswa explained to me that the investigation was at a very sensitive stage. I figured this was because the police were trying to establish the Brazilian connection. 'But I would love to meet with Nozukile just to let her know she is not alone,' she said.

Shortly after our conversation that day, I received a call from the Nobanda family lawyer, Matthew Mpahlwa, who curtly questioned me on the 'angle' I would be taking in my interview. I was slightly bemused by the question. After all, anyone who has ever followed the various stories I have done on drug mules would be aware of their recurring investigative refrains: firstly, not all of the South Africans arrested as drug mules are perpetrators of drug trafficking, but, as in Babsie and Thando's cases, are in reality victims of human trafficking. Secondly, not enough is being done to bring those responsible for recruiting the mules and decoys to book. Thirdly, a prisoner transfer treaty makes sound economic sense, given that South Africa currently feeds, clothes and provides shelter for 8 000 convicted foreign nationals from the rest of Africa. And, finally, a prisoner transfer treaty would not only provide police with invaluable intelligence on the workings and identities of the syndicates, but would also constitute a humanitarian gesture to the families of those imprisoned abroad.

Mpahlwa seemed satisfied with my response. I asked him whether he'd consent to being interviewed when I arrived in Grahamstown the following day. He agreed.

At 6 am, three hours before I was due to fly to Grahamstown, I received a bizarre call from Honjiswa.

'Hazel, I'm sorry, but after consulting with the family and our legal advisors, I have decided to cancel the interview and the meeting with Nozukile. We don't want to attract any further media attention to Babsie's case.'

I fought the urge to scream.

'But why, Honjiswa? Since Babsie's arrest, you and your family have been quoted extensively in the media – television, radio, newspapers. I spoke to your lawyer yesterday and he was in agreement with my methodology and angle. So what has changed since then?'

Her tone was brittle. 'I'm sorry. I cannot discuss this with you.'

My own voice was becoming tremulous. 'Nozukile will be devastated. You are the one person who understands what she is going through.'

'I'm sorry, I truly am, but it has been decided.'

Once again, I had broken a promise to Nozukile, as I had when I told her that I would lobby for Thando's case to be reviewed, an objective I had not been able to achieve.

* * *

As we dodged the crater-like potholes leading to Nozukile's house, I was filled with a sense of dread. She was waiting outside for me, waving, together with Thando's uncle. Inside her living room, the table was buckling under the weight of lovingly laid cakes, snacks and cooldrinks. Recently retrenched from his job on the gold mines, Thando's uncle, Jabulani, had donned a frayed but immaculately pressed suit. Nozukile, still as refreshingly pretty as ever, was adorned in a vibrantly hued traditional skirt, her hair swept up in fetching ringlets.

I avoided her expectant gaze. Instead I turned my eyes to the thin walls, where between the photographs of Thando, were the faith-filled slogans, neatly framed: 'Do unto others ...'; 'Two wrongs don't make a right'; 'In God we trust'.

Of course, two wrongs can never make a right because two wrongs cannot equal each other. For the truly wronged, right can only be achieved through absolute forgiveness, moral vindication, restitution or revenge. Nozukile simply sought justice.

Her expression clouded when she realised Honjiswa was not with us and I truly didn't have the balls to tell her the truth. 'Unfortunately, Honjiswa's mother, Babsie's gogo, died and Honjiswa has had to make funeral preparations. She sends sincere apologies and promises that she will visit you as soon as possible. But we are going to get answers from the NPA and find Thembi.'

Nozukile silently nodded, her eyes still exuding hope and trust, while Jabulani provided me with a brief update on the 'Thembi Watch': 'We haven't seen her in Thabong lately but apparently she is still around, still going by the surname of Dlamini or Mfenqe. We can take you to people who will take us to her.'

'Great!' I enthused. 'But first I have a phone call to make.'

Inside a slightly dank hotel room in Welkom, cameraman Sibusiso (Sbu) Mncedane and I temporarily reversed roles, with me behind the lens and him assuming the mantle of undercover operative.

'Hello, is that Thembi,' he asked in Xhosa.

'Yes, this is Thembi.'

'Thembi Vilikazi?'

'No, Thembi Dlamini.'

'Oh sorry, siesie, I was told this is the number for Thembi Vilikazi in Thabong.'

'Yes, I am in Thabong, but my name isn't Vilikazi.'

'Oh, sorry, sies. There must be some confusion.'

He replaced the receiver, while I gave him the thumbs-up. After the disappointment of Honjiswa's refusal to accompany us, I was beginning to feel re-energised. We knew she was in Thabong, and Jabulani and Nozukile would take us to her.

Several hours later, my ballooning optimism had deflated like a slow puncture. We had driven to the tuck shop she still operated opposite the high school, only to find it boarded up. We had then trekked through Thabong to Thembi's former friends turned foes, who, although apparently eager to point the way, did not have the vaguest idea of the direction in which we should head. Four equally confused contacts, one chronically dysfunctional spy camera and two pee-stops later, and I was ready to immerse my head in one of the numerous rain-swollen potholes we had had to traverse. Pit or pothole, it didn't really matter, as long as the end was quick and relatively painless. Anything, rather than the knuckle-cracking, jaw-grinding, nail-gnawing frustration of knowing Thembi was so near and yet so far. Poor Nozukile was also starting to wilt, unable to suppress a succession of compulsive ear-to-ear yawns. Or were they silent screams? Probably both, given my dismal track record on service delivery.

I was about to contemplate a new career in government, when I experienced a half-hearted epiphany. If we couldn't find Thembi, we'd have to bring her to us. She had been involved in the clothing business, and used it as the hook to bait mules and decoys into the drug-trafficking trade. If Sbu called her again, pretending to be a hawker, we might succeed in reeling her in.

After dropping off a dejected-looking Nozukile and an equally disappointed Jabulani, who nevertheless agreed to accompany us to meet Labuschagne the following day, Sbu made another call to Thembi. He explained that he had mixed up her surname with someone else's, and that she was the Thembi he had been told to contact to purchase knock-offs. But the bitch wouldn't bite. Or perhaps she was telling the truth when she said she wasn't involved in the clothing business any more and therefore could not be of assistance.

My reaction would have been the same had she said she was now involved in an intergalactic mission tracking electronic magnetic pulses in a firmament far, far away.

Unlike Nozukile's, though, my scream wasn't silent.

* * *

The following morning, my mood had improved to a more sanguine acceptance of the Kafkaesque absurdity that seemed to dog this investigation. If I could survive Sbu's dubious swerving around the muddy, potholed roads leading to Nozukile's home, I could survive anything – even the NPA's flaccid slings and sluggish arrows.

At her Welkom office, Labuschagne revealed her astute insight into human trafficking. She could no longer contain her own genuine frustration with the pace of investigations, not only into Thembi but several currently being conducted by Organised Crime in the Free State. But she had to be careful how she phrased her concerns.

'Thembi's case was transferred to Bloemfontein in 2010 and, after his meeting with you, Colonel Gerber followed up on all your information, putting the suspect under surveillance and monitoring the house and cellphone number you gave us. He did this for a month but found nothing.'

I gritted my teeth. Of course he would have found nothing. Thembi might have done her recruiting in Thabong, but her syndicate operated from Johannesburg. She probably possessed multiple mobile phones and SIM cards, just as she possessed numerous fake passports and identities.

'He then sent all the evidence to Interpol for them to intervene and interact with the Thai police in order to get a statement from Thando, because without that, he could not proceed.'

Glancing at Nozukile, she added: 'I understand the frustration of Thando's family, of course. But can you also imagine how the investigating officer must have felt, especially since the Thai police have not gotten back to him about arranging to get that statement from Thando.'

The gritting of teeth became an audible grind. The South African Embassy in Bangkok has an in-house law-enforcement officer by the name of Gregory Gaillard, who is mandated to take statements from South African prisoners. But, then again, Gaillard had been unresponsive to Al's requests for assistance on behalf of South Africans, such as Nicolene Kruger, even before trial. Why would he perform even the most perfunctory of services for a young woman already convicted of drug trafficking and serving her 25-year sentence? Outta sight, outta mind was obviously still the unofficial policy for a department that will not conduct even basic relations with its own citizens incarcerated abroad.

Labuschagne explained that while the much-awaited legislation provided by the Prevention and Combating of Trafficking in Persons Bill was waiting for President Zuma's signature, it was still possible to arrest suspects under a variety of laws, such as conspiracy to commit a crime, abduction, etc. 'But until our Anti-Trafficking Bill is signed, there remain too many loopholes through which these criminals can slip,' she said.

Seven years after it had first been drafted, the bill, an extensive document aiming to provide a holistic and comprehensive framework for tackling human trafficking, had yet to be signed into law.

While the Children's Act 38 of 2005 served to prohibit all forms of trafficking in children, no provision had been made for trafficked adults. Although the Criminal Law (Sexual Offences and

Related Matters) Amendment Act 32 of 2007 applied to both child and adult victims of trafficking, it criminalised human trafficking for purposes of sexual exploitation only.

Besides making trafficking in persons an offence, the long-awaited legislation would create offences such as debt bondage, possessing, destroying or tampering with travel documents, and using the services of victims of trafficking, all of which contributed to innocent individuals becoming victims of this modern-day form of slavery. If convicted, perpetrators could face a maximum penalty of R100 million, life imprisonment or both.

But, equally significant, the law also focused on the plight of the victims, offering them protection and assistance to overcome their traumatic experiences. It provided for 'compensation for care, accommodation, transportation, return, repatriation and reintegration of the victim of the offence' by the convicted trafficker or carrier via the state's Criminal Assets Recovery Account.

'Until this law is passed, our biggest challenge,' conceded Labuschagne 'is to get law enforcement to recognise the links between human trafficking and drug trafficking, and to not simply dismiss these victims as drug mules by applying a 'one size fits all' approach. Unfortunately, until that is done, women in Thando's situation will fall prey to double victimisation by being punished for a crime they were forced to commit when, in fact, they deserve to be protected and compensated, with the full support of our government.'

* * *

Just how deep was the hole into which Thando's case, and others like hers, had been swallowed? Both Labuschagne and Patricia had some inkling, but the former was still reluctant to articulate specific details.

'There is something very sinister going on with Crime

Intelligence, particularly Organised Crime in Bloemfontein,' said Patricia, during one of our regular telephone chats. 'It has either become a contradiction in terms or is starting to resemble the organised-crime cartels it should be investigating.'

By way of proof, Patricia pointed me in the direction of 'Frank', a senior officer with the unit, who, on condition of anonymity, agreed to talk to me.

The case in which Frank was involved concerned Donya Preston, a 23-year-old woman from Kroonstad, who, together with 20-year-old Riaan Stephens, had been arrested at Sam Ratulangi Airport, Indonesia, in August 2012 with 6 kilograms of tik in her luggage. Indonesia imposes the death penalty on drug traffickers. But Donya, it turned out, was yet another drug mule turned decoy, another victim of human trafficking. The officer had no doubt about this. He said: 'Before Donya and Riaan were put on the flight to Indonesia with the drugs, an informant from the syndicate that recruited her called our unit and warned us she was going to be sacrificed. Together with my commander I arranged a meeting with the informant, who told us Donya's fate had been sealed by a Gauteng-based Nigerian syndicate. The informant provided explicit details about the arrangement to entrap Donya as a dead cow and offered to accompany us to Alberton and Meyerton, where he would identify the loci inhabited and operated by the syndicate. He even provided us with the fake passport for another mule who was supposed to accompany Donya, who apparently had backed out of the trip. Most importantly, he provided us with the names of the syndicate members, headed by a certain Ben, and the role each of them played in the hierarchy, such as recruiters, passport and flight coordinators, 'handlers' of the pre-packaged drugs and "escorts" – the euphemism accorded those members who would accompany Donya to the airport and ensure that she was not "diverted" from her flight. Donya had a feeling she was going to be set up and tried to withdraw. For that, she was severely beaten.'

Frank handed me a newspaper photograph taken of a

frightened-looking Donya with two blue-black orbs under her eyes, the fading aftermath of blows to the face.

'The informant went so far as to put his own life on the line by offering to accompany us to OR Tambo International on the day of Donya's flight and to directly point out the suspects.'

Frank also revealed that another convicted South African drug mule, Katherine Dunne, had been coerced by the same syndicate as Donya, and that one of the recruiters, the father of Donya's child, was in Bloemfontein to oversee the syndicate's regional operations.

However, instead of following up on this vital information, the Organised Crime commander displayed a lack of interest and disbelief in the veracity of the information. No pre-emptive action was taken and Donya caught the flight to Indonesia unprotected. A week later, the international media reported on her arrest.

'Thereafter, Bloemfontein instructed me to again approach the informant in order to identify the syndicate,' said Frank. 'Understandably, the informant was extremely angry that we had not intercepted Donya timeously. Too little, too late, is how he put it. Together with Donya's mother, he threatened to go to the media. Nevertheless, he agreed to accompany us to Gauteng, where he pointed out all the relevant addresses. This is where the investigation ceases.'

Alberton, Ben (again), the infamous names and places associated with drug trafficking. Again, a wall of indifference, even hostility, preventing the successful completion of another investigation.

Frank invited me and Labuschagne to join him in Bloemfontein to discuss the impasse and hopefully follow up several more vital leads to this particular crime syndicate. Initially, Labuschagne agreed, offering also to send one of the NPA's investigators, who was involved in several human-trafficking cases.

Unfortunately, the meeting in Bloemfontein never took place, apparently for 'logistical' reasons. But I was given the contact details of the informant who had alerted Organised Crime to

Ben's syndicate. I happened to be in Johannesburg at the time and had paid another visit to Fashion Society, the lounge bar in Norwood apparently owned by Ben, where Adelina had said all the 'big boys' hang out. Ben was apparently out of town on business, according to the bartender. I was relieved: what would I have said or done had he been there? Covertly filmed him with my librarian-style eyewear/spyware? Offered my services as a mule? Asked him if he perhaps knew Thembi and would put me in touch with her again? It would all amount to yet another Sisyphean attempt to push boulders up the hill, only to watch them roll back down again.

Frank had told me the informant was in town. So, donning the threadbare remains of my investigative cap, I called him, and asked if we could meet to discuss Ben.

'Why the fuck do you think I would put my life on the line again by meeting you?' he shouted. 'My entire future is fucked. The brothers know it was me who pimped them. The cops have done fuck all, and I have to spend each and every day watching my own back.'

I tried to assuage his anger by assuring him that if he showed me the operational headquarters of Ben's syndicate and agreed to an interview, his anonymity would be guaranteed. Putting it all on the record was the final frontier of protection, I gamely offered, wanting to believe this to be the case, but increasingly sceptical of my own efficacy as a shield.

The following day, I redialled the informant's number. Predictably, his pre-recorded voicemail message did not even afford me the indulgence of leaving a message.

21

THROUGH THE
PSYCHOTROPIC FOREST

I don't believe in applying polish to dulled pots of gold at the end of fading rainbows. But I also refuse to subscribe to perennial seasons of discontent. My philosophical default setting is generally configured to the 'carpe the hell out of the diem' command.

However, as I wend my way towards Thabong, yet again, I too feel like a beast of burden, buckling under the weight of a failed investigation, its consequences bearing down against me. Thando's uncle, Jabulani, called me. Apparently, Thembi is up to her old tricks again – offering young women from Thabong jobs in Thailand, only to force them to smuggle drugs. He and Nozukile had learnt of this from the parents of Thembi's latest victim, who were apparently unaware of her duplicity until it was too late. It seems that Thembi and the young woman flew to Port Elizabeth, possibly to hook up with Thembi's network of Nigerian connections, and they were due to fly to Thailand. When Jabulani told me this, I immediately thought of Doreen, the young woman I had met in Bangkok, and her tormented trajectory into drugs and prostitution, which had also begun in Port Elizabeth. My first impulse was to contact the Hawks, Home Affairs and Port Elizabeth Airport, which has regular flights to

Thailand. But, without knowing the specifics of Thembi's flight plan, all efforts to apprehend her would be futile. Even if Thembi were intercepted and arrested, from my disgruntled perspective, would this signify anything more than a minor distraction to the parade of powerful and politically connected drug lords? I conveyed my misgivings to Jabulani but agreed to meet the young woman's parents in Thabong when I visit Nozukile.

I have with me one of the recent letters that Thando wrote to me, a beautifully decorated 'Happy New Year' card. At each intersection, I glance at it, guiltily:

'To a special friend ... hello my sister ... please will you send me a photograph of my family, especially my mother? ... thank you for all you are doing.'

I had begun my reply: 'Dearest Thando ...' But my usually florid penmanship had dried up. I had no more words.

Since our first meeting in 2009, she had written to me often from Klong Prem asking for photographs of her mother and sister, and thanking me for my 'love and support', which only served to augment my sense of shame. In one of her more recent letters she still insisted she was in good spirits, despite a noxious rash that had spread from her face to her scalp, rupturing into itchy, suppurating pustules. Without money, prisoners in Thailand are deprived of even the most rudimentary of medical supplies. Unlike their Canadian counterparts, for example, South Africans cannot rely on their embassy to subsidise their medical expenses. Al was trying to arrange funds for ointment and additional medication. He had organised a sponsor who would not fleece her, as Shamalee had, of the pittance that, for farangs, signifies the difference between survival and despair. The new sponsor, a compassionate and generous South African called Johanna Strauss, now regularly writes to Thando, sends her money and is also trying to raise funds for Nozukile and Jabulani to visit her in prison.

As for Shamalee, she acquired first-hand insight into the perils of Thailand's penal system, as a fellow inmate of the women she had cruelly robbed. Al had sent me a missive with an update on the warrant of arrest the police had issued for her on multiple charges of fraud. She was detained for four months awaiting trial before appearing in court in August 2013. She was found guilty. Her punishment: six years' imprisonment – reduced to three years, as she had admitted guilt – as well as the obligation to repay the entire amount she had bilked from her victims.

In another poignant letter, Thando expressed shock and sympathy for Shamalee's sentence, but there was not a syllable of rancour towards the woman who had betrayed her trust. I fervently hoped that, like Babsie, Thando had transcended the pit of anguish into which she had so mercilessly been hurled. Under the circumstances, Babsie was doing well, excelling at her university studies at Unisa and growing in stature as both an artist and, with her perennially sunny disposition, as an inspiration for her fellow farangs.

Al was a constant source of support, dispatching reports on Facebook about her achievements. Thando and Babsie were apparently closer than ever, and Thando had also expressed the desire to complete her studies by correspondence. But without a matric exemption certificate, there was no possibility of that. In her most recent letter, Thando no longer displayed the Pollyanna-type optimism of her previous correspondence. Her skin condition had worsened and her scalp was completely coated by the mange-like infection. Her head had been shaved but her hair grew back in arid, brittle clusters. She had lost a ridiculous amount of weight and had drawn me a picture of her sparrow-like frame that bore little resemblance to the robust young woman I had first met in 2009. She was so listless that she had barely enough energy to rouse herself off her sleeping mat, let alone perform routine prison tasks. In the letter she expressed the fear that she would never see her family again. In the event of her death, would I promise to take care of them?

Were it not again for Al's intervention, Thando would probably have succumbed to depression and disease. Her weakened immune system could not have withstood the plethora of infections in Lard Yao, ranging from TB to more pedestrian ailments like diarrhoea and flu. With the assistance of Babsie, Al persuaded Thando to inform the South African Embassy and insist on being tested by the prison doctors. Surprisingly, given their history of insensitivity, the embassy staff were responsive. They visited her, and she was promptly diagnosed and placed on a course of prophylactics. Although she remains ill, the prognosis is not bleak. If she responds positively to the prescribed medication, physically she will recover. Her psychological welfare, however, will hinge on less tangible remedies.

Al also shared with me the innard-wrenching news penned to him by another inmate, concerning the suicide of an Austrian in a Thai prison. He had sharpened a toothbrush into a crudely hewn spike, thrust it into his ear and bashed his head against the wall, slicing his brain in half.

But not even this glimpse into the agony of incarceration abroad could prepare me for the letter that Al wrote in August 2013, the anger, sadness and frustration of which remain tattooed on my psyche. It concerned another South African woman, called Esther Madonsela, who had been incarcerated in Klong Prem since 2011, but whose name and circumstances had never reached the media. Esther had become desperately ill. So serious was her condition that she was about to be transferred from the prison hospital with its chronically under-resourced personnel to a medical facility outside the prison. The South African Embassy appeared to be entirely oblivious of, or indifferent to, her suffering. After Al contacted me, I alerted Mbulelo Bungane, DIRCO's director of consular affairs, not as a journalist, I underscored, but as a deeply concerned South African citizen. He promised to notify the embassy, which he duly did. The information he received seemed heartening: Esther's condition was not serious, the embassy had reported. I notified Al, who replied, saying that he would visit her soon to make sure. Days later, I received this email from him:

... tomorrow I will visit Esther, who is in the hospital. Did I tell you that the embassy was not even aware of her being sick let alone that she was moved to the hospital? I had to tell them and then they went to visit her ... When I asked about their visit, they told me she was doing well and could walk on her own ... They 'forgot' to ask her what was wrong with her, did not even bother asking for a medical report.

I did not convey my unease at the South African Embassy's bizarrely upbeat diagnosis of Esther's condition, but waited for Al to contact me after his visit. The anticipated email, dated 23 September 2013, made me feel almost as ashamed to be South African as I had been during apartheid:

... and there she was, Esther ... hooked up to life-supporting equipment, ventilator, heart-monitoring devices, three drips. She was unconscious, her eyes open and staring at the ceiling. The head nurse ... sat me down in an improvised office out-side Esther's room. The moment she started to explain Esther's condition, all the alarms attached to the equipment to which Esther was hooked went off ... I could see that Esther went into a seizure. About four to five nurses attended to her and after ten minutes were able to calm her down. The head nurse came back and explained Esther's condition. She was admitted because she went through a long period of fever and headaches when she was in the clinic of Klong Prem ... Once admitted to the hospi-tal, the doctor there ordered a scan of her kidneys, which was performed in the police hospital. The result came back that she had severe lesions in both kidneys ... I was shocked because the embassy had never told me any of this – on the contrary, 'she was fine, she can walk on her own' ... I explained to the nurse that, indeed, much to everyone's dismay, the embassy would not offer any financial help. At that moment, Esther had another seizure and they all rushed to her bedside. But this time the nurse told me she urgently needed to summon the doctor.

271

It took another 15 minutes to stabilise Esther and when the doctor came, he said they now suspected that an additional infection of the brain had occurred.

And the nurse told me it was time to inform the family ... they had done what they could and would continue providing her with supportive care. The nurse said that the day before she had talked with Esther who then was still conscious but in pain; she said Esther was crying and complaining that the embassy does not care at all for their citizens ...

I did not know what to say, I felt so small ... complete strangers to Esther are doing all they can to help her ... and yet the SA Embassy can't even ask the right questions and sends me to find out what is wrong! More nurses came up to me and wondered why an embassy can be so cruel in not helping a citizen clearly in need of help.

A week later Esther was dead.

I contacted DIRCO about Esther's condition and the alleged attempts on the part of staffers at the South African Embassy to disguise the gravity of her condition. Bungane took immediate action and Al was summoned to the embassy in order to clear up the 'miscommunication'.

In June 2014 I received an anguished letter from Babsie – her first to me – in which she detailed the intolerable living conditions, discrimination and human-rights violations she and the other farang inmates endure on a daily basis. No one does anything to intervene, she wrote, because the abominable reality of prison life is concealed from the prison inspectors, UN representatives and human-rights activists who occasionally visit Klong Prem.

Babsie also related an incident in which drugs had been found in the cell she shares with 250 women. Until the culprit owned up, the rest were placed under virtual lockdown and subjected to severe restrictions in the number of letters they were entitled to write and receive, as well as the number of parcels they could accept.

When they protested, they were rounded up by hundreds of baton-wielding prison officials dispatched from the men's section of the prison. 'Please tell the world what is happening here,' she begged, 'and ask our government to sign a prisoner transfer treaty with Thailand, so we can at least be imprisoned at home.'

Somehow, Babsie's letter had entirely eluded the prison's censorship process. Farang inmates are forced to write sanitised letters about sunshine and flowers. Not that she was disclosing anything new, though. For five years I had been provided with a keyhole view of the suffering experienced by my compatriots. Nothing had changed. Yet, each sentence still hit like a baton blow. After reading the letter, I called Babsie's mother to discuss its contents. I then summarised it and emailed a list of its harshest allegations to DIRCO, in Pretoria, without naming Babsie as the source. Then I stashed the letter in my desk among Thando's cards and letters decorated with smileys, hearts and flowers. A few weeks later, news channel eNCA 'broke' the story online about Thailand's horrific prison conditions, publishing the entire contents of a 'leaked' letter Babsie had written to her mother that pretty much echoed the missive she had sent me weeks before. In the letter she named me as the journalist she had initially contacted. Within hours, the story had gone viral on social media with the letter republished in print media worldwide.

After reading my name in the letter, several colleagues grilled me: 'You were given a scoop on a silver platter. Why didn't you run with it?'

So, why had I chosen to sit on it, instead of reacting with customary glee to a breaking story, as a journalist normally would? A couple of years ago, I would have taken that letter, turned it into the basis of an exclusive exposé and milked it for all it was worth. After all, it's who I am; it's what I do: investigating and reporting and yelling 'j'accuse' at the wrongdoers out there, driven by the imperatives of angles, sources and subject matter. After the baddies have been busted, the credits have rolled and yesterday's headlines have been used as lining for the litter box,

I move on. But this story has challenged me like no other, pitting my programming as a journalist against a growing sense of personal accountability and consequence. My colleagues might think I have gone soft by not 'going for broke' on a breaking story. Perhaps they are correct. Perhaps I have sold out to a cowardly alliance of expediency and self-censorship, both of which are anathema to intrepid journalism. But I would prefer to counter that I have bought in to something internal and the acknowledgement that what ultimately drives each of us is a private, often anomalous, quest.

Of course, I still believe in exposing crime and state-sanctioned corruption, whether it is seeping through the corridors of the ANC's headquarters or trickling through ghetto alleys. But the story must go beyond the quick-fix formula of two-minute-noodle journalism. Publicising Babsie's leaked letter verbatim would have served a short-term purpose. But there are more complex ethical considerations beyond the imperatives that feed into and off media sensationalism. As her letter to me confirmed, Thai prisons run pretty much as laws unto themselves, changing the rules and imposing cruel punishments randomly and on a whim. The repercussions of revealing this could be severe for Babsie, already victimised and vulnerable. She had penned a letter that would piss off both the Thai and South African governments. To date, Babsie's prison record was unblemished. A black mark for disruptive or subversive behaviour would nullify her chances for clemency from the Thai king. Perhaps I erred on the side of caution or cowardice. I still don't know. But I was not prepared to take that chance simply for the sake of another story.

Al had embarked on a mission to petition the Thai monarch for a royal pardon on behalf of Babsie and Thando. This is an onerous process involving numerous letters to the king, the excavation of police reports and court papers, personal pleas for clemency from the inmates themselves, supporting documentation from the embassy and, most importantly, a letter of endorsement from the South African Government. Al had recently helped another farang prisoner attain clemency. He was therefore suitably positioned to handle the intricacies of this procedure.

To qualify as a candidate for a royal pardon in Thailand, inmates must have completed at least three years of their sentence and must have admitted guilt. Exemplary behaviour is also a prerequisite. Initially, Al had been concerned that Thando's chances would be compromised due to an altercation she'd had with a prison warder. That's how flimsy the line is between eligibility and disqualification. Fortunately, Thando's good-behaviour status had been restored. Her illness would also improve her chances, and Al assured both women that their pleas would be positively received by the Thai king, as he had successfully secured a royal pardon for the other prisoner. However, the process would not happen overnight, he cautioned. What he didn't disclose to them was that in order for their requests for a pardon to even be considered, they required 100 per cent buy-in from the South African Government.

'In my past dealings with the Thai authorities, they had asked why they should provide a pardon when the inmate's own government does not support it. How do you counter that argument?' Al asked ruefully.

I recalled the sense of helplessness that Shani Krebs's sister, Joan, had felt during the 1990s, when the Thai authorities had requested a letter from the South African Government endorsing her appeal for a royal pardon on behalf of her brother.

I would not allow myself to envisage the additional torment Thando and Babsie would endure – not to mention their families – should our government refuse to write that letter. In the past year, Nozukile's psyche has shown signs of splintering. She cannot sleep or eat properly and is prone to extreme bouts of depression. I fear she would not be able to handle another disappointment.

Nevertheless, I am returning to Thabong, to offer Nozukile another sliver of hope and to make another promise. After five years of incarceration in a foreign land, deprived of even brushing fingertips with anyone outside prison, Thando is now entitled to her first contact visit with her family. Nozukile's flight and accommodation will be financed and she will not be travelling alone. I shall accompany her, less as a journalist than as a friend whose life is now inextricably entwined with hers. So, it's back to Bangkok, to where this all began, fumbling for the clearing through a psychotropic forest that, with every twisted bough, becomes more bewildering.

* * *

I have slid into my own cesspool of disembodied narratives, so I force myself to think of those who survived incarceration and have been freed: Shani, Vanessa Goosen, Dawn van Niekerk, Gladys Naidoo – some of the farangs of 1994.

Shani and Vanessa seemed to be doing well. Vanessa's biography, *Drug Muled*, has been a sell-out success and demand is growing for her services as a motivational speaker.

In an interview in February 2012, with practised politeness, Vanessa answered my questions, even though they sounded bland to my own pain-attuned ears. We were surrounded by the beauty of the Magaliesberg mountains and Hartbeespoort Dam, an ironically bucolic backdrop for an interview on the horrors of incarceration. Vanessa did not want to divulge too much. Like Shani, she was not about to let anyone appropriate her story. Adding an extra dollop of tragic irony to her narrative was the fact that merely weeks before her release, Vanessa's best friend, who had adopted her daughter, Felicia, had suffered a fatal aneurism. After having being sheltered from the normal responsibilities accompanying motherhood, in the worst possible way, of course, Vanessa was about to be hurtled head first into adulthood, without any assistance from the South African authorities.

Although the rehabilitation and reintegration of offenders is supposedly a high priority in the 2005 White Paper advocating a kinder, gentler Department of Correctional Services, the chasm between policy and praxis is particularly wide when applied to South Africans returning from decades of incarceration abroad. If their families can afford it, they are flown back to South Africa where they are supposed to somehow apply Polyfilla to the fractures of their lives. If families and friends cannot afford the plane fare home, they might languish indefinitely within Bangkok's notorious Immigration Centre. If they have been released on parole from prisons in Brazil, Peru or Venezuela, they are forced to roam the streets destitute or eke out a living in order to pay back hefty fines incurred as part of their prison sentence.

Even with her considerable support base, Vanessa's reintegration into mainstream society was an ongoing rite of anxiety: 'I had to learn how to cook all over again, how to be a mother not only to a daughter I barely knew, but to the children of my best friend. I had to help them cope with their grief while containing my own sense of bewilderment, confusion, disorientation and terror.'

Thrust into a technology-driven, postmodern world and a post-apartheid country she no longer recognised, Vanessa began manifesting all the signs of post-traumatic stress: 'Sometimes I thought I was coping. But then I would start shaking and crying for no apparent reason and lock myself in my room, unable to talk to anyone. The final straw occurred when I was trying to cross a busy street. I froze between the oncoming cars. I couldn't move. A traffic officer had to help me over to the other side. It was then that I realised I couldn't carry on this way. I needed help, to heal, to forgive myself.'

'Forgive yourself for what? Haven't you been punished, in the worst possible way, for a crime you insist you never wilfully committed?'

'For what my imprisonment did to my family, to my daughter, to me. I have never used narcotics in my life; at the time I didn't even know what heroin was. Sure, I knew about cocaine, but heroin! I had never even seen it. Yet here I was, arrested with heroin, branded a drug mule. The shame and the pain of it literally killed members of my family.'

She continued: 'Forgive myself for the fact that possibly my chances of becoming a mother again are decreasing, and that I might never be able to be a proper mother to the child I already have.'

At 40 years old, lissom, poised and softly spoken, Vanessa was as alluring as she was when she had been arrested. But beneath her beauty-queen features, under her flawless complexion, the subcutaneous hairline fissures of her psyche constantly threatened to rupture her immaculate veneer.

Freedom is the surface-tissue oil that only helps the scars to partially fade.

She turned away, seeming to survey the landscape, but I could see she was not looking at the surrounds, but through them – into a Bangkok prison cell full of perspiration and desperation, where hundreds of women sleep on the floor in a tangle of legs and arms, and sometimes in puddles of piss.

'When it rains, I feel so guilty.'

'For what?' I couldn't help whispering.

'For the other girls, the ones who remain behind.'

Shani appeared to be basking in the aftermath of liberation. At least that was what was conveyed through his regular, exuberant postings on Facebook. His book, *Dragons and Butterflies*, had been published, a 250 000-word epic that traversed his childhood in an Arcadia orphanage, his incarceration in Bangkwang and the conflicting experiences of his release into a world for which he was utterly unprepared. I had no doubt that it, too, would be a massive success. He was also exhibiting his paintings and seemed to have adjusted remarkably well to life on the outside. But without disclosing the details, Joan had recently intimated that the trauma of his incarceration still simmered and sometimes surfaced in ways that were terrifying to behold. Without adequate tools for rehabilitation and reintegration, Shani, like the others, would have to deal alone with the ghosts of long-term imprisonment. No psychologist could ever possibly access the latent residual reservoirs of anger, pain and lunacy that lurked, threatening to swell and overflow.

Patricia and I continue to be in regular contact. Her breast cancer has been cured and she is hopeful about some developments that seem to bode well for the future of all South Africans incarcerated abroad. DIRCO's Bungane visited her in George and listened intently as she rattled off the litany of human-rights violations perpetrated against our citizens imprisoned in foreign jails. He promised to motivate for a more compassionate approach by the South African embassies mandated to assist them. Patricia had amassed thousands of signatures petitioning for a prisoner transfer treaty, not only with SADC countries but further afield as well, and was planning to present it to Parliament's National Assembly.

Patricia also received a visit from the Hawks, and was contacted by the Public Protector's office and the Independent Police Investigative Directorate. She provided them all with sheaves of information pertaining to members of the police who had not followed up on vital investigative leads into transnational drug syndicates operating from South Africa. Al's dossier, the 'Three Little Piggies' had been included, as had my evidence on Thembi and Fridah. As the dystopian realities of South African crime would have it, shortly after making contact with me, one of the investigators at the Independent Police Investigative Directorate was gunned down during an attempted hijacking. He survived, but, understandably, his zeal for pursuing criminals had been somewhat dampened.

And after nine years of unrelenting determination to highlight the plight of her son and hundreds of fellow citizens imprisoned overseas, Patricia has been rewarded with one of the greatest gifts a parent can receive: a second chance for her child. In March 2014, her son, Johann, sentenced to nine years' imprisonment in Mauritius for smuggling drugs, was given an amnesty by the Mauritian Government. He returned home in June.

Patricia broke the news to me by telephone, her usually matter-of-fact voice lilting with excitement. 'But just because my boy is about to be freed,' she insisted, 'don't think that I am going to give up on all the other South Africans. I am more determined than ever.'

*　*　*

On 29 July 2013, President Zuma finally signed and enacted the Prevention and Combating of Trafficking in Persons Bill, South Africa's first statute addressing the scourge of human trafficking. Professor John Dugard, a human-rights lawyer and expert on international law, was convinced that the definition of victims of trafficking in persons clearly included many South Africans convicted of drug smuggling. In correspondence with Patricia, Dugard made particular reference to the provisions for repatriation and international cooperation to secure the return of South African citizens coerced into becoming drug mules and decoys. 'It is now difficult to resist an agreement to allow prisoners so trafficked to serve their sentences in South Africa,' he wrote.[1]

The passing of this law encouraged Al to follow the royal-pardon route for Babsie and Thando. If his brilliantly constructed dossier hadn't made a smidgen of a difference in the mind of the South African Government, then surely this law would.

Unfortunately, although the bill has been signed, at the time of writing it has not yet been promulgated. To date, no suspects have been charged under the new law, further frustrating efforts to bring perpetrators of human trafficking to book. In April 2014, I contacted the NPA to ask why there continued to be a hiatus between the law and its effective implementation. I did not get a satisfactory response and I left that meeting feeling more perplexed than ever.

However, there have also been some unexpected alchemies.

I received an encouraging call from Sabelo Sibanda, who had believed so ardently in the imperatives of reclassifying the status of Thando and other South Africans convicted under similar circumstances. His impassioned desire for the South African Government to stop sacrificing its citizens on the altar of diplomatic relations was still evident, even though his focus had been diverted to human-rights iniquities perpetrated against his compatriots in Zimbabwe and beyond.

Sabelo was back in South Africa and we met to brainstorm on new strategies to get Thando's case reviewed. I also referred Sabelo to Al in Bangkok and they are working together on petitioning for the royal pardon. Subsequently, Sabelo met with 'Frank', the disillusioned police officer whose efforts to prevent a Nigerian drug syndicate from sending Donya Preston to Indonesia as a decoy had been thwarted by his commanding officers. Sabelo and Frank have pledged to expose corruption in high places and Sabelo is in the process of establishing an organisation championing the rights of human-trafficking victims. He is currently lobbying for greater awareness and support within South Africa and throughout the region. We will meet again soon.

* * *

But, first, Thando wants those photographic keepsakes of her family. Nozukile is waiting.

As I head around the circle leading to Thabong, an ebony fist of smog begins to descend, its fingers encircling the full moon. Through the remains of a rapidly dissipated lunar glow, I almost collide with what seems to be a scene of unspeakable carnage. A truck en route to the abattoir in Welkom, loaded with cattle from nearby farms, appears to have overturned. It is leaning, lopsidedly, perilously. And from where I am, it seems as though its cargo – cattle selected for slaughter – has been strewn like rubble onto the verge. I screech to a halt just in time, shaking, wanting to puke, and feeling as though I have been hurtled face first into the midst of a poem by Edgar Allan Poe that I had learnt by rote at school:

> *O God! Can I not grasp*
> *Them with a tighter clasp?*
> *O God! Can I not save*
> *One from the pitiless wave?*
> *Is all that we see or seem*
> *But a dream within a dream?*[2]

A 'dream within a dream', another detour along an absurd odyssey, redolent with regret, yet simultaneously pregnant with possibility.

The truck is intact; the cows are alive. Edgar Allan Poe merely collided with Kafka on a bad-head day. I turn on the ignition and slowly edge my way back onto the road to Thabong.

NOTES

Chapter 2

1 William Bosch, *Royal Pardon*, Carpe Diem Media, 2007.

Chapter 3

1 See http://www.akha.org/content/bookreviews/verisimilitude (accessed 26 February 2014).
2 Harry Nicolaides, *Verisimilitude*, self-published, 2005.

Chapter 4

1 See reallifethailand.blogspot.com/2007/10/drugs-in-thailand.html; http://www.siam-legal.com/litigation/criminal-defence-drug-offences-in-thailand.php (accessed 26 February 2014).
2 See (Ramphia Lo) Thailand Foreign Prisoners' Support Service, http://www.usp.com.au/fpss/case-jodyryanaggett02.htm (accessed 26 February 2014).

Chapter 6

1 See http://www.stopthedrugwar.org/taxonomy/term/62 (accessed 24 July 2014).
2 This chapter draws from National Drug Threat Assessment 2009, United States Department of Justice; War On Drugs: Legislation in the 108th Congress and Related Developments, a 2003 report from the Congressional Research Service via the State Department website; Report of the Canadian Government Commission of Inquiry into the Non-Medical Use of Drugs, 1972; Douglas Valentine, *The Strength of the Wolf: The Secret History of America's War on Drugs*, Verso, 2004; Thomas C Rowe, *Federal Narcotics Laws and the War on Drugs: Money Down a Rat Hole*, Routledge, 2006; Eric Schneider, *The Drug War Revisited*, Berfrois, 2011; see also http://www.huffingtonpost.com/tag/garry-mccarthy (accessed 1 March 2014).
3 See http://www.huffingtonpost.com/tony-newman/drug-war-obama-reid-christie_b_4638818 (accessed 1 March 2014).

4 See http://www.theguardian.com/society/drugs (accessed 24 July 2014).

5 See http://www.unodc.org/wdr2014/ (accessed 24 July 2014).

6 See http://www.unodc.org/documents/data-and-analysis/WDR_2012_web_small.pdf (accessed 1 March 2014).

7 See http://www.unodc.org (accessed 24 July 2014).

8 See http://www.huffingtonpost.com/2013/07/18/thailand-fights-drug-gangs-golden-triangle (accessed 24 July 2014).

9 See http://www.hrw.org/reports/2004/thailand0704/4.htm (accessed 24 July 2014).

10 Bertil Lintner, *Merchants of Madness: The Methamphetamine Explosion in the Golden Triangle* (co-authored with Michael Black), Silkworm Books, 2009; see also Bertil Lintner, *Blood Brothers: Crime, Business and Politics in Asia.* Sydney: Allen and Unwin, 2002.

11 See http://entheology.com/preservation/kratom-legal-status (accessed 24 July 2014).

12 Alfred W McCoy, *The Politics of Heroin: CIA Complicity in the Global Drug Trade.* New York: Lawrence Hill Books, 1991.

13 Transcript of Causes and Cures: National Teleconference on the Narcotics Epidemic, 9 November 1991.

14 See http://www.drugabuse.gov/Publications/Topics in Brief; http://www.ibtimes.com/medicating-our-troops-oblivion-prescription-drugs-sai (accessed 24 July).

15 *War on Drugs*, Report of the Global Commission on Drug Policy, 2011, http://www.globalcommissionondrugs.org/wp-content/themes/gcdp_v1/pdf/Global_Commission_Report_English.pdf (accessed 1 March 2014).

Chapter 7

1 Thai Prison Life, 4 May 2012, http://www.thaiprisonlife.com/thai-prison-statistics (accessed 4 March 2014); Michael C Howard, *Transnationalism and Society: An Introduction.* Jefferson, NC: McFarland, 2011.

2 See http://www.druglibrary.org/schaffer/govpubs/amhab/amhabc3.htm (accessed 23 July 2014).

3 See http://unesdoc.unesco.org/images/0014/001478/147844e.pdf (accessed 23 July 2014).

4 Stephen Ellis, 'West Africa's International Drug Trade', *African Affairs*, 108(431): 171–196; N Gilman, J Goldhammer and S Weber, *Deviant Globalization: Black Market Economy in the 21st Century.* New York: Continuum, 2011; Howard, *Transnationalism and Society*; Michael D Lyman and Gary W Potter, 'Foreign Drug-Trafficking Organizations' in *Drugs in Society: Causes, Concepts, and Control.* Burlington, MA: Anderson, 2011.

5 Antonio Maria Costa, 'Drug Trafficking is a Security Threat' (remarks at the opening of the Economic Community of West African States high-level conference on drug trafficking as a security threat, Praia, Cape Verde, 28 October 2008, http://www.unodc.org/unodc/en/about-unodc/

speeches/2008-28-10.html (accessed 4 March 2014).

6 Vivienne Walt, 'Cocaine Country', *Time*, 27 June 2007, http://www.time.com/time/magazine/article/0,9171,1637719,00.html (accessed 4 March 2014).

See also: UNODC, *Cocaine Trafficking in West Africa: The Threat to Stability and Development (With Special Reference to Guinea-Bissau)*, December 2007, http://www.unodc.org/documents/data-and-analysis/West%20Africa%20cocaine%20report_10%2012%2007.pdf; UNODC, *Drug Trafficking as a Security Threat in West Africa*, October 2008, http://www.unodc.org/documents/data-and-analysis/Studies/Drug-Trafficking-WestAfrica-English.pdf; UNODC, *World Drug Report 2009*, June 2009, http://www.unodc.org/documents/wdr/WDR_2009/WDR2009_eng_web.pdf; Michael A Braun, 'The Need for European Assistance to Colombia for the Fight Against Illicit Drugs' (statement before the House Judiciary Crime, Terrorism and Homeland Security Subcommittee and House International Relations Western Hemisphere Subcommittee, 21 September 2006), http://www.justice.gov/dea/pubs/cngrtest/ct092106.html (accessed 4 March 2014).

For a good discussion of who controls the cocaine after it leaves West Africa, see UNODC, *Cocaine Trafficking in West Africa*, 20. See also Ellis, 'West Africa's International Drug Trade'; UNODC, *Transnational Trafficking and the Rule of Law in West Africa: A Threat Assessment*, July 2009, http://www.unodc.org/documents/data-and-analysis/Studies/West_Africa_Report_2009.pdf (accessed 4 March 2014); UNODC, *World Drug Report 2011*, June 2011, http://www.unodc.org/documents/data-and-analysis/WDR2011/World_Drug_Report_2011_ebook.pdf (accessed 4 March 2014); Jean-François Bayart and Béatrice Hibou, *The Criminalization of the State in Africa*, International African Institute, 1999; UN Office for West Africa, *Urbanization and Insecurity in West Africa: Population Movements, Mega Cities and Regional Stability*, UNOWA Issue Papers, October 2007, http://www.humansecuritygateway.com/documents/UNOWA_UrbanizationInsecurityWestAfrica.pdf (accessed 4 March 2014); G8, 'Action Plan Aimed at Strengthening Transatlantic Cooperation in the Fight Against Drug Trafficking', Paris, 10 May 2011, http://www.g20-g8.com/g8-g20/g8/english/the-2011-summit/declarations-and-reports/appendices/action-plan-aimed-at-strengthening-transatlantic.1245.html (accessed 4 March 2014).

7 See http://www.uniogbis.unmissions.org/Default.aspx?ctl=Details&tabid=9915 (accessed 23 July 2014).

8 See http://www.csis.org/publication/so-goes-port-harcourt-political-violence-and-future-niger-delta (accessed 23 July 2014).

9 See http://www.users.polisci.wisc.edu/schatzberg/ps362/ellis2009.pdf (accessed 23 July 2014).

10 See http://www.users.polisci.wisc.edu/schatzberg/ps362/Akyeampong2005.pdf (accessed 23 July 2014).

11 See http://www.countthecosts.org/resource-library/Assessing-Nigeria's-Drug-Control-Policy.pdf (accessed 23 July 2014).

12 See http://www.menso.wordpress.com/tag/drugs/ (accessed 23 July 2014).

13 See http://www.hawaii.edu/hivandaids/Thailand_Country_Brief_Drug_

Situation_Report (accessed 23 July 2014).

14 See http://www.economist.com/node/10263174 (accessed 23 July 2014).

15 See http://www.news.bbc.co.uk/2/hi/778299.stm (accessed 23 July 2014).

16 See http://www.bbc.co.uk/2/hi/africa/8233980.stm (accessed 23 July 2014).

17 Ellis, 'West Africa's International Drug Trade'.

18 Ibid.

19 Ibid. See also 'Fighting Transnational Crime', statement by Robert S Gelbard on 7 December 1995; Gilman, Goldhammer and Weber, *Deviant Globalization*.

20 See https://www.unodc.org/pdf/crime/publications/Pilot_survey.pdf (accessed 23 July 2014); see also Ellis, 'West Africa's International Drug Trade'.

21 The term 'adhocracy' was coined by Alvin Toffler in his best-seller *Future Shock* (New York: Bantam Books, 1972), quoted by Stephen Ellis in https://www.openaccess.leidenuniv.nl/bitstream/handle/1887/13818/ASC-071342346-361-01.pdf (accessed 23 July 2014).

22 Ellis, 'West Africa's International Drug Trade'.

23 Ibid.

Chapter 10

1 JD Mujuzi, 'Prisoner Transfer to South Africa: Some of the Likely Challenges Ahead', *Potchefstroom Electronic Law Journal/Potchefstroom Elektroniese Regstydskrif*: 154–6, ISSN: 1727-3781.

2 Ibid.:152.

Chapter 12

1 See http://152.111.1.87/argief/berigte/citypress/2008/03/03/CP/10/jmpaparas1.html (accessed 24 July 2014).

2 See http://www.nytimes.com/1984/04/10/nyregion/31-charged-by-us-with-running-a-1.65-billion-heroin-operation.html (accessed 24 July 2014).

3 See http://www.mg.co.za/article/2002-01-01-top-sa-spy-linked-to-vito-palazzolo (accessed 24 July 2014).

4 See http://article.wn.com/2012-07-12/Italian_authorities_eager_to_net_big_Mafia_fish_Palazzolo (accessed 24 July 2014).

5 See http://mg.co.za/print/2003-01-31-the-sneaky-side-of-sas-sopranos; see also http://mg.co.za/article/2004-11-08-count-agusta-link-probed-in-palazzolo-hearing (accessed 5 September 2014).

6 P Vale, *Security and Politics in South Africa: The Regional Dimension*. Boulder: Lynne Rienner Publishers, 2003; B Gilder, *Songs and Secrets: South Africa from Liberation to Governance*, Oxford University Press, 2013.

7 See http://www.iol.co.za/news/crime-courts/palazzolo-a-very-big-fish-say-italians-1.1340364 (accessed 24 July 2014).

8 See http://www.m24arg02.naspers.com/argief/berigte/citypress/2001/12/02/1/6.html; http://www.sundayworld.co.za/news/2011/12/18/no-mercy-in-alien-land (accessed 15 April 2014).

9 See http://www.noseweek.co.za/article/1403/Selebi-and-the-crime-lord-its-not-just-cricket (accessed 5 September 2014).

10 See http://www.mg.co.za/article/2007-05-11-saps-chiefs-dodgy-friends (accessed 15 April 2014).

11 See http://www.noseweek.co.za/article/1426/The-plot-thickens (accessed 15 April 2014).

12 See, for example, http://www.news24.com/SouthAfrica/Khoza-plot-thickens-20010902 (accessed 15 April 2014).

13 See http:www.//mg.co.za/article/2013-02-08-00-druglords-release-raises-ghost-of-missing-soweto-dealer (accessed 15 April 2014).

14 See http://mg.co.za/article/2001-08-31-ghosts-come-back-to-haunt-the-iron-duke; http://www.iol.co.za/sport/a-tale-of-drugs-money-and-cars-1.90760 (accessed 15 April 2014).

15 See http://www.iol.co.za/news/south-africa/cocaine-kingpin-booted-out-of-sa; m24arg02.naspers.com/argief/berigte/citypress/2001/01/28/11/5.html (accessed 15 April 2014).

16 See http://www.iol.co.za/news/south-africa/cocaine-kingpin-booted-out-of-sa-1.58475 (accessed 24 July 2013).

17 Liza Grobler, *Crossing the Line: When Cops Become Criminals*, Jacana Media, 2013.

18 'The extent of drug-trafficking in South Africa: Report on the incidence of serious crime during 1995', National Crime Information Management Centre, SANAB, Quarterly Report 1/96, April 1996; see also 'International co-operation against the illicit production, sale, demand, traffic and distribution of narcotics and psychotropic substances and related activities', High Level Segment of ECOSOC, United Nations, May 1996.

19 *World Drug Report 2011*, New York: UNODC, http://www.unodc.org/documents/data-and-analysis/WDR2011/World_Drug_Report_2011_ebook.pdf (accessed 15 April 2014).

20 See http://www.africa.upenn.edu/Urgent_Action/apic_012697.html (accessed 15 April 2014).

Chapter 13

1 Peter Gastrow, 'Organised Crime in South Africa: An Assessment of its Nature and Origins', Institute for Security Studies, monograph no. 28, August 1998; see also Mandy Weiner, *Killing Kebble: An Underworld Exposed*. Johannesburg: Macmillan, 2012; Mark Shaw, 'The Political Economy of Crime and Conflict in Sub-Saharan Africa', *South African Journal of International Affairs* 8(2), 2001: 57–69; Ted Leggett, 'A Den of Iniquity: Inside Hillbrow's Residential Hotels', *South African Crime Quarterly* 2, November 2002: 19–22.

2 Gastrow, 'Organised Crime in South Africa'; Ellis, 'West Africa's International Drug Trade'; C Goredema, Zimbabwe, in P Gastrow (ed.), 'Penetrating State and Business: Organised Crime in Southern Africa', vol. 2, Institute for Security Studies, 2003.

3 See http://www.scribd.com/doc/62130520/Handbook-for-Rebels-and-Outlaws (accessed 17 April 2014).

4 D Potgieter, 'War veteran links SADF to UNITA ivory slaughter', *Sunday Times*, 1989. See also J Pauw, *In the Heart of the Whore: The Story of Apartheid's Death Squads*. Halfway House: Southern Book Publishers, 1991.

5 See http://www.issafrica.org/pubs/books/Angola/16Dietrich.pdf (accessed 17 April 2014).

6 See https://openaccess.leidenuniv.nl/bitstream/handle/1887/9083/asc_1241486_030.pdf?sequence1 (accessed 17 April 2014).

7 See http://www.news24.com/Tags/People/wouterbasson (accessed 17 April 2014).

8 See http://www.issafrica.org/uploads/Wouter_Basson_Trial_Summary.pdf (accessed 17 April 2014).

9 See http://www.nelsonmandela.org/omalley/index.php/site/q/03lv02167/04lv02264/05lv02335/06lv02357/07lv02372/08lv02378.htm; books.google.com/books?isbn=1851094903 (accessed 17 April 2014).

10 See http://www.nelsonmandela.org/omalley/index.php/site/q/03lv00017/04lv00344/05lv00607/06lv00644.htm (accessed 17 April 2014).

11 See http://wikileaks.org/gifiles/attach/167/167391_HIGH%20TREASON.doc (accessed 17 April 2014).

12 See http://www.sahistory.org.za/article/covert-operations (accessed 17 April 2014).

13 See http://www.nelsonmandela.org/omalley/index.php/site/q/03lv02167/04lv02264/05lv02335/06lv02357/07lv02372/08lv02379.htm (accessed 17 April 2014).

14 See http://www.mg.co.za/article/1997-02-07-hani-killing-was-a-double-conspiracy (accessed 5 September 2014).

15 Ibid.

16 See http://www.mg.co.za/article/1997-01-31-i-was-warned (accessed 17 April 2014).

Chapter 14

1 Irvin Kinnes, *From Urban Street Gangs to Criminal Empires: The Changing Face of Gangs in the Western Cape*, Institute for Security Studies, ISS monograph no 48, June 2000; see also Gastrow, *Organised Crime in South Africa*.

2 D Pinnock, *The Brotherhoods: State Control and Gangs in Metropolitan Cape Town*. Johannesburg: David Philip, 1984.

3 Kinnes, *From Urban Street Gangs to Criminal Empires*.

4 See http://www.issafrica.org/pubs/Monographs/No48/Structure.htm (accessed 31 July 2014).

5 Ibid.

6 See http://www.citypress.co.za/news/the-rottweiler-from-kuilsrivier-20110326/ (accessed 31 July 2014).

7 See http://dspace.africaportal.org/jspui/bitstream/123456789/31493/1/ Mono63.pdf? (accessed 31 July 2014).

8 See http://www.news24.com/xArchive/Archive/Pagad-denies-blame-for-blasts-20000830 (accessed 25 April 2014); see also http://www.pagad.co.za/ page/2/ (accessed 25 April 2014).

9 See http://www.sabc.co.za/news/f1/d2ec6b804878861b89b79b12e7ad9fle/ Hit-or-Myth?-20110926 (accessed 25 April 2014).

10 See http://za.gocmenizm.com/news2013/dramatic-arrest-not-called-for_5748.html (accessed 11 September 2014).

11 See http://mg.co.za/article/2012-02-03-battle-for-control-of-the-doors-and-drugs (accessed 11 September 2014).

12 See http://www.iol.co.za/news/south-africa/western-cape/new-mafia-hits-cape-clubs-1.1217387 (accessed 11 September 2014).

13 See http://www.iol.co.za/news/south-africa/mcbride-off-the-hook-in-escort-fracas-1.4723 (accessed 31 July 2014).

14 See http://www.iol.co.za/news/politics/mo-shaik-s-underworld-links-1.383661; see also http://www.mg.co.za/tag/mo-shaik; news.iafrica. com/sa/715991.html (accessed 25 April 2014).

15 See http://152.111.1.87/argief/berigte/citypress/2012/04/02/CP/10/ jpColonel.html (accessed 25 April 2014); see also http://www.rapport.co.za/ Suid-Afrika/Nuus/Valk-wat-skurke-jag-se-vlerke-geknip-20140208 (accessed 5 September 2014).

16 See http://www.mg.co.za/article/2013-10-17-krejcir-a-dangerous-man-to-know (accessed 25 April 2014).

17 See http://www.iol.co.za/news/crime-courts/cards-are-stacking-up-against-krejcir-1.1708379 (accessed 31 July 2014).

18 See http://www.mg.co.za/article/2011-04-12-krejcir-denies-beeka-murder-claim (accessed 25 April 2014).

19 See http://www.sapsjournalonline.gov.za/dynamic (accessed 25 April 2014).

Chapter 15

1 See http://www.iol.co.za/dailynews/news/drug-woman-s-sister-talks-1.1197587 (accessed 16 April 2014).

Chapter 16

1 See http://www.internationaljusticeproject.org/nationalsinstruments.cfm (accessed 25 April 2014).

Chapter 21

1 Correspondence between Professor John Dugard and Patricia Gerber, 22 January 2014.

2 The Project Gutenberg Ebook of *The Works of Edgar Allan Poe*, The Raven Edition, by Edgar Allan Poe.

INDEX

INDEX